POLAND

HUNGARY

UKRAINE

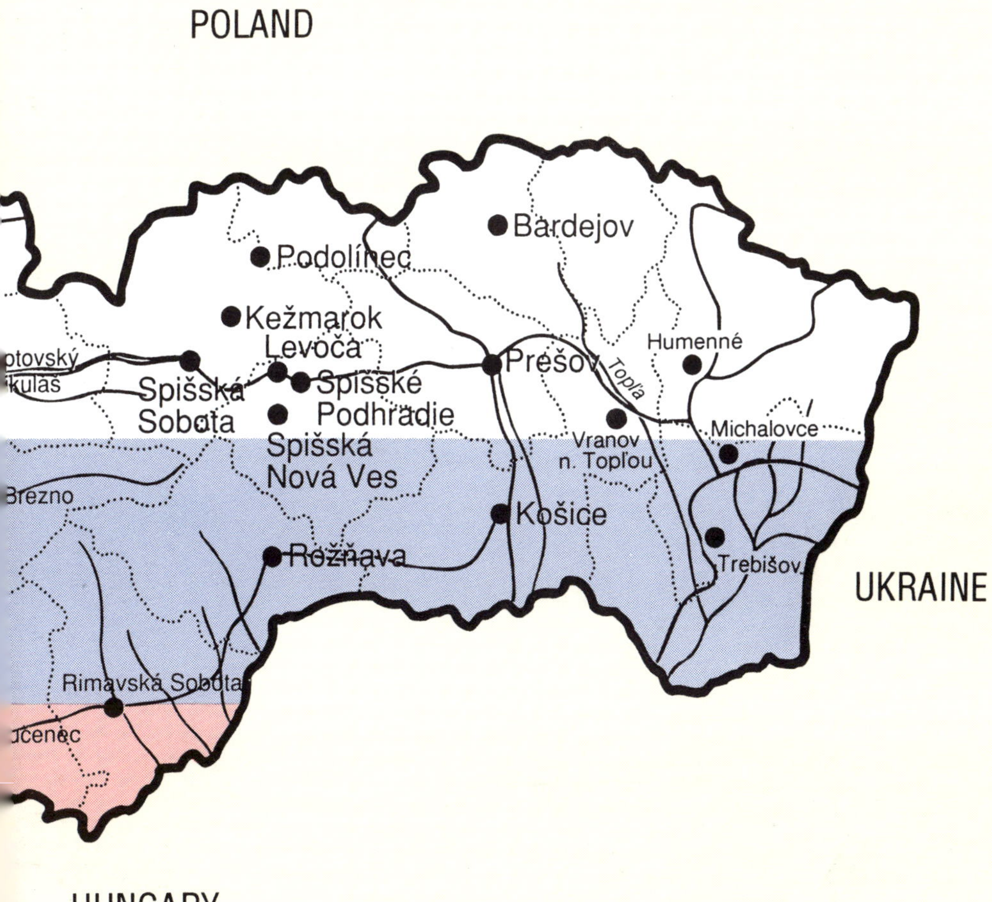

Slovakia

SLOVAK WORLD CONGRESS COOKBOOK

"A Culinary Collection of our Slovak Heritage"

Svetový Kongres Slovákov

Copyright © 1995 SLOVAK WORLD CONGRESS
Authored by Anne Zvara Sarosy
Sandra Sarosy Duve, Co-editor

First Edition
First Printing: 3,000 Copies, June 1997
all rights reserved

Library of Congress Catalog Number: 97-067661
ISBN: 0-917909-00-3

Printed by Krohmaly's Printing Co.
Pittsburgh, PA U.S.A.

TABLE OF CONTENTS

	Page
Dedication	4
Forward	5
Committee	6
Greetings	7
Slovak Culinary Tradition	10
Appetizers - *Predjedlá*	17
Salads - *Šalát*	31
Vegetables - *Zeleniny*	40
Soups - *Polievky*	51
Main Dishes - *Hlavné Jedlá*	82
Breads - *Chleby*	148
Pastas - *Cestovina*	180
Pastries and Desserts - *Pečivo, Zákusky a Dezerty*	239
Holidays	326
Measurements	341
Index	344
Order Form	353

IN DEDICATION TO

. . . the independence of Slovakia as a free and self-governing, democratic nation - January 1, 1993.

. . . a freedom Slovak people share from the tyrannies of foreign supremacy, a freedom of self-expression and a freedom to adhere to the spiritual and cultural values of their ancestors.

. . . the continued efforts of the Slovak World Congress, founded in 1970, whose goals and purposes are:

> To help increase national awareness, spiritual life, socio-economic development, cultural-scientific progress and physical effectiveness of the Slovak nation and all people of Slovak origin;
>
> To represent All Slovaks living abroad;
>
> To promote enthusiasm and interest in Slovak identity in generations, which until now, did not have contact with Slovakia or with Slovak societies in countries in which their ancestors settled; and
>
> To intensify contact and cooperation with the independent Slovak Republic.

. . . Stephen B. Roman, founder and first president of the Slovak World Congress, and those who followed in his footsteps: Joseph R. Kristofik, Marian Šťastny, Leopold Danihels and Paul Rusnak.

. . . to Slovaks throughout the world, in deep solidarity for the preservation of our culture, our heritage, and our ethnic traditions.

Srdečná vďaka!

- The Editors and
Women's Committee

FORWARD

It is the objective of the Women's Committee of the Slovak World Congress to present a cookbook, a culinary collection of treasured tastes and traditions of our Slovak heritage. Tradition is defined as:

. . ."the handing down of information, beliefs and customs by word of mouth or by example from one generation to another without written instruction."

This was often the practice of our mothers and grandmothers with the preparation of our cultural cuisine. As years passed, many of these Old World recipes were refined and revised to adapt to modern methods and trends. In the effort to preserve the authenticity of the traditions that surround our ethnic foods, which was the initial objective of this book, many Slovaks throughout the world have very graciously shared their family recipes. Also included in this collection are many individuals' favorite contemporary cuisine. We sincerely thank all our contributors and hope that in reading this text it will serve as a reminder of your own family traditions.

Often times we do not consider our "everyday ways" as traditions - but the habits, customs and memories we hold as special and dear, truly are. And so, as we immerse ourselves into this Slovak collection of memories, let us ask:

"Bless us, oh Lord, and these Thy gifts,
which we are about to receive from Thy bounty,
through Christ our Lord,
Amen."

Otče náš, všemohúci Pane,	Vďaka Ti, všemohúci vďaka,
Otvor nám Tvoje štedré dlane,	Štedro dáš, čo len duša čaká,
Zveme Ťa ku nášmu stolu	Ďakujeme spolu všetky stvory
Prisadní, budeme jesť spolu.	Ďakujeme, veď Pán Boh je dobrý.

On behalf of the Slovak World Congress - "Dobrú Chuť!"

Anne Zvara Sarosy
Editor

Sandra Sarosy Duve
Co-editor

SLOVAK WORLD CONGRESS COOKBOOK COMMITTEE

PAUL RUSNAK .... Slovak World Congress, President

ANNE ZVARA SAROSY .... Editor
Women's Committee, Chairperson

SANDRA SAROSY DUVE .... Co-editor
Continental Vice President, West
United States of America

NINA HOLY .... Continental Vice President, East
United States of America

MARTHA MISTINA KONA   Heritage and Culture Commission, Chairperson

MARGARET DVORSKY .... Executive Vice President, Canada

ANNA CHULI .... Women's Committee Secretary

****

COMMITTEE MEMBERS

Stephanie Siegel, International Relations, Chairperson
Leopold and Mimi Danihels
George Lupjan
El Nora Rusnak, Esq.

and in memory of
Mary Coleman and Stephen Sroba

President's Message . . .

As President of the Slovak World Congress, I take great pride in sending a warm and heartfelt greeting to all Slovaks around the world. Though many of us do not dwell in our beloved country, no walls or land borders can keep our traditions from us. If we are unable to live within Slovakia, we will let Slovakia live within us. There are no boundaries upon the human heart, nor upon the dreams and wishes of our people.

One way to keep the Slovak culture alive in our hearts is to cherish and follow timeworn and traditional recipes which have been handed down - mother to daughter - through generations. The Slovak World Congress Cookbook contains over 400 recipes and each recipe represents a caring and dedicated Slovak family who desires to keep alive the spirit and traditions of our Homeland. This unique cookbook is an actual testament of the recipes used by our ancestors and one which will be passed along, with loving hands, to future generations. Congratulations to Anne Zvara Sarosy and her cookbook committee who compiled an outstanding selection of mouthwatering recipes in a publication, which I am confident, will find its way into every Slovak kitchen.

Allow me to leave you with a message of Hope and Inspiration as I share with you my dreams for the Slovak World Congress. My vision is to introduce the world to the special heritage, culture and customs of the Slovak People. We are tireless in our efforts to recruit new members to the Slovak World Congress so that we may revive and reunify the two and a half million Slovak residents abroad. We are the only worldwide organization capable of providing representation for all Slovaks around the world.

God bless you and Dobrú Chuť,

PAUL RUSNAK, *President*
SLOVAK WORLD CONGRESS

Ján Sokol
Námestie sv. Mikuláša 3
0805 262 35
arcibiskup trnavský, Metropolita Slovenska

Najchutnejšie sú však Slovenské jedlá - ako bryndzové halušky a zapekané zemiaky. Naše mamy to vedeli najlepšie urobiť.

Ja Vám želám, aby ste tieto jedlá našich starých matier v ďalekom svete nezabudli. Aj svojim deťom odovzdajte zvyky, piesne a iné, čo si Vaši predkovia doniesli do Kanady a Ameriky.

Všetkých srdečne pozdravujem. Modlím sa za Vás a prosím, aby ste si zachovali DEDIČSTVO OTCOV! Aj keď postupne zabudnú reč, nech aspoň toľko vedia, že ich predkovia pochádzajú z krásnej krajiny pod TATRAMI, ktorú volajú SLOVENSKO!

Žehná Vás
v Kristu a Marii

+ Ján Sokol

In Memory of
Stephen J. Sroba
(May 4, 1918 - February 28, 1995)
Slovak American Artist

SLOVAK CULINARY TRADITION

In his **Physiology of Taste,*** Jean Anthelme Brillant-Savarin states that "the fate of a nation depends on the food supply and eating habits." We need food for physical survival as well as for health. We prepare food as a sign of affection, at the same time, food may become a culinary expression of the individual and of the nation through the creation of new dishes and the improvement of old ones. Food and cooking is about heritage, culture, tradition, history and relationships. It is an integral part of a society and a nation.

Unlike other recorded documents, recipes containing family and regional specialties were handed down orally, hence like songs and many stories, they did not survive time. Truly this is a great loss of our culinary "treasures." Nevertheless, some of the ancient Slovak foods are still popular today: bread, roasted meat, kaša and wine. With the help of archaeologists, we acquire a better understanding of everyday life of the Slavic people who settled down in the territory of Slovakia.

In the ninth century during the time of the first Slovak Kingdom, called the Great Moravian Empire, some of the "eatables" were wheat, rye, barley, oats, peas, beans, salted and smoked beef and pork, goat, sheep, game, fat, cheese, butter and eggs. Honey was often used for sweetening. Also, an alcoholic beverage called medovina (mead) was prepared from honey. Vegetables, such as cabbage and cucumbers were eaten fresh and pickled. There were also carrots and turnips. Garlic, onions, parsley and caraway seed were added for flavor in many of the dishes. It is also established that our ancestors planted apple trees, plum trees and later pear trees. As time went on, grape vines were cultivated in southern areas of Slovakia. The other spices as pepper, ginger and cloves from the Far East had been introduced.

Forests had bountiful harvests of berries and mushrooms which became an important ingredient in Slovak cuisine. Rivers were sources of fish. When raised and prepared properly, carp is a tasteful and popular fish.

It is generally believed that the Slovaks and other Slavs learned bread-baking from the Goths, the ancient Germanic people. Long before Christianity, bread played an important role in the Slavic religious rites, consequently the Slovaks treated bread as God's gift. There are many sayings about the importance of bread such as, "Bread is God's gift," "God lives in Bread," or "One never gets tired of eating bread." Often the reverence for bread was shown by marking the dough with the sign of the cross. On the threshold of the home, the guests and newlywed couples were welcomed with bread and salt. This custom is still practiced occasionally today.

Cereals - grains were popular and served in many different ways: in soups, milk, flavored with pork fat, bacon and onions, seasoned with mushrooms, fruits and accompanying various meats. Cooked cereal was an important staple, expressed in a Slovak saying, "Kaša (cooked cereal) - our mother." The cereal consumption decreased after the introduction of potatoes from America. The potato became a significant food addition in the Slovak diet, later followed by pasta and rice.

Because of its strategic geographic location, Slovakia was overrun, invaded and conquered throughout its history by Tartars, Germanic tribes, Husites, Turks and Magyars. It was a part of the Kingdom of Hungary since the tenth century and a part of the Austria-Hungarian Empire since the 17th century until its disintegration in 1918. This diverse assortment of people and foods in the Slovak territory left its indelible mark on Slovak cooking. Consequently, Slovak cooking is influenced by many cuisines especially of the Austria-Hungarian Empire. The cooking influences were intermixed with the nations which were part of the Empire such as Austria, Slovenia, Romania, Hungary, Serbia, Croatia and Slovakia. Since each region influenced the other often it was impossible to state the origin of the dish, as each national group tried to preserve its national identity. Some of the foods were introduced by the Turks during their invasion in the 16th century. They introduced paprika, cherries, tomatoes and phyllo leaves from which strudel evolved. And of course strudel became a favorite pastry in Slovakia and most European countries. Another typically Slovak staple, sauerkraut was invented in Asia and Mongols carried it to Hungary. And the dumplings, well-liked by Slovaks and many Europeans originated in Italy as gnocchi. Czech cooking experience was added after World War I when a new state, Czechoslovakia, was formed.

There are culinary connections and similarities as each nation added and subtracted some ingredients in the same dish. It is interesting to compare, for example goulash, paprikash, stuffed peppers, stuffed cabbage, jam and cheese filled palacinky (crepes) of each nation. There are definite similarities. Slovak cooks, just like other cooks, changed some recipes and a new recipe was created.

Many of the dishes are like those prepared in the last two centuries. They were handed down by tradition, not professional chefs. The dishes were cooked by our mothers, grandmothers, great-grandmothers and others. There was a pinch of this and pinch of that to improve the taste. Some new and modern refinements were made, but we have preserved our national traditions, the Slovak cuisine kept its character, emphasizing hearty, tasty and nourishing food.

Let us mention some of the typical Slovak dishes, such as halušky (drop dumplings) with bryndza (sheep cheese), pirohy, žinčica (special sour milk), jaterničky (mixture of ground pork, rice and spices stuffed in casings and baked), huspenina (jellied pork), soup or gravy from dried mushrooms, chicken, pork, sauerkraut prepared in many different ways. It is true that roasted duck or goose, sviečková (roast tenderloin), veal, lamb cutlets, goose liver from forced-fed geese are regarded as some of the most exquisite dishes.

Slovak cuisine is endowed with innumerable pastry and cake recipes. The housewives enjoy baking homemade sweets and are proud to present their creations of cakes, cookies, pastries, strudels with different fillings, poppyseed and nut rolls, tortes, dessert creams and fruit desserts.

Very special menus are prepared for the holidays of the year. Christmas Eve supper is the most festive and joyous event celebrated in the presence of the whole family. The supper menu varies slightly from one region to another one. Easter is still another culinary holiday.

Eating gives pleasure and creates an atmosphere of relaxation and understanding. A meal shared with family, relatives, and friends provides a feeling of one of life's pleasures comparable to listening to good music, reading a stimulating book or enjoying the fellowship of others. By keeping our culinary inheritance and traditions abroad, we preserve a significant part of Slovak customs. As we have built our heritage upon the foundation of our ancestors, we can determine the foundation for those who will follow us.

>Martha Mistina Kona, *Chairperson*
>Slovak Heritage and Culture Commission
>Slovak World Congress
>
>*Jean Anthelme Brillant-Savarin
> <u>Physiology of Taste,</u>
> Heritage Press, 1949, New York.

ZÁPADNÉ TATRY
Roháče-Ostrý Roháč
(Western) Tatra Mountains

Courtesy of
Mgr. Milan Straka,
šéfredaktor 'Slovensko'
Matica Slovenská, Martin, Slovakia

HRAD BECKOV
Beckov Castle

Courtesy of
Mgr. Milan Straka,
šefredaktor 'Slovensko'
Matica Slovenská, Martin, Slovakia

MODRANSKÁ KERAMIKA SLOVENSKÉHO NÁRODNÉHO MÚZEA
Modra Ceramics
(Slovak National Museum)

Courtesy of
Mgr. Milan Straka,
šéfredaktor 'Slovensko'
Matica Slovenská,
Martin, Slovakia

SLOVENSKÝ KROJ - Slovak Costume
Detva - Spiš Regions

APPETIZERS

Predjedlá

BEEF TONGUE
Jazyk hovädzí

1 beef or calve's tongue
1 cup (¼ L) sliced onion
4 cups (1 L) water
2 bay leaves
2 teaspoons (10 mL) salt
6 peppercorns
6 cloves
3 slices of lemon

Clean tongue carefully by scrubbing well and soak in cold water for 2-3 hours. In a pot, bring water to a boil and add tongue and rest of ingredients. Simmer slowly for about 3-4 hours. When done, let the tongue cool. Peel off skin and slice for serving.

BEST VENISON OR BEEF JERKY
Najlepšia jelenina

3 pounds (1⅓ kg) meat cut with the grain into ⅜ - ½ inch (1-1½ cm) strips
2 tablespoons (30 mL) brown sugar
2 tablespoons (30 mL) salt
½ teaspoon (2.5 mL) pepper
½ teaspoon (2.5 mL) cayenne pepper
1 teaspoon (5 mL) garlic powder

Mix all seasonings, set aside. Remove all fat from meat; cut meat into strips, no more than ½ inch (1½ cm) thick. Put strips into plastic bag, in layers. Sprinkle each layer thoroughly with the seasoning mix. Place in refrigerator for 24 hours. Turn over frequently. Dry on paper towel, hang on wire rack with toothpicks, or place directly on the wire rack, so as the strips will not touch. Dry for 4-6 hours at 150°F-200°F (66°C-95°C). The jerky should be dark and leathery but not brittle. If completely cured, it will keep in a cool place without refrigeration.

Benjamin Gombar,
Saginaw, Michigan U.S.A.

CHEESE BALL
Syrová guľa

2 packages (8 ounces each) (2-225 g) cream cheese
8 ounces (225 g) crushed pineapple, well drained
2 tablespoons (30 mL) onion, chopped fine
¼ cup (½ dL) green pepper, chopped
1 teaspoon (5 mL) seasoned salt
1 cup (¼ L) pecans, chopped

Set aside ½ cup (1 dL) chopped pecans for coating. Mix all other ingredients together. Shape into a ball; roll in chopped pecans. May be refrigerated until serving. Serve at room temperature.

Sister M. Annette,
Vincentian Sisters of Charity
Pittsburgh, Pennsylvania, U.S.A.

CHEESE LOG
Syrová guľa

½ pound (225 g) sharp cheese, grated fine
1 teaspoon (5 mL) onion, minced
3 stuffed olives, chopped
2 teaspoons (10 mL) dill pickles, chopped
1 egg, hard boiled and chopped
½ cup (1 dL) soda crackers, crushed
¼ cup (½ dL) mayonnaise or salad dressing, or more as needed

Mix all ingredients together. Place on waxed paper and shape into log or ball. Wrap in foil. Refrigerate. Roll can also be frozen.

Ethel Mazurek
Allentown, Pennsylvania U.S.A.

COCKTAIL MEATBALLS
Hovädzie fašírky - koktail

2 pounds (900 g) ground beef
1 cup (¼ L) bread crumbs
⅓ cup (¾ dL) dried parsley
2 eggs
2 teaspoons (10 mL) soy sauce
¼ teaspoon (1¼ mL) garlic powder
⅓ cup (¾ dL) tomato sauce
2 tablespoons (30 mL) chopped onion

Sauce:
1 can (16 ounces) (450 g) jellied cranberry sauce
12 ounces (340 g) chili sauce
1 tablespoon (15 mL) lemon juice
2 tablespoons (30 mL) brown sugar

Meatballs: Preheat oven to 350°F (180°C). Mix first eight ingredients, form small meatballs; arrange in a large baking pan, at least 1 inch (2½ cm) or more deep. Bake in oven for 15 minutes.

Sauce: Meanwhile, in a medium saucepan, combine cranberry sauce, chili sauce, lemon juice and brown sugar. Cook over medium heat until mixture is smooth.

Pour sauce over meatballs and continue baking for an additional 15 minutes.

Great for parties!
Makes 60 meatballs.

Josephine Kopachko
Smock, Pennsylvania   U.S.A.

CREAMED CHICKEN LIVERS
Kuracie pečienky

- 1 pound (450 g) chicken livers
- ¼ cup (½ dL) flour
- ½ teaspoon (2.5 mL) salt
- ¼ teaspoon (1.25 mL) pepper
- ¼ teaspoon (1.25 mL) paprika
- 2 tablespoons (30 g) oil
- 2 tablespoons (30 g) butter
- 1 clove garlic, minced
- ½ cup (1 dL) dry white wine
- 2 tablespoons (30 mL) parsley, chopped
- ¾ cup (1¾ dL) sour cream

Cut each liver in half. Dredge with flour seasoned with salt, pepper and paprika. Heat oil and butter in a large skillet until foam from butter begins to subside. Add livers and garlic and cook very quickly, turning so that all the livers become browned and cooked. This should take 2 to 4 minutes. Remove to a heated platter and keep warm. Pour off most of the fat from the skillet. Add wine and parsley and cook, stirring, so that the brown bits are stirred up from bottom of pan. Add sour cream and heat, but do not boil. Taste and add more seasonings, if you like. Return chicken livers to pan and stir well.

Makes 4 servings.

In memory of
Mary Coleman
Guelph, Ontario, Canada

JELLIED PIGS' FEET
Uspenina

4 pigs' feet, split
1 rounded tablespoon (15 mL) mixed whole spice
½ teaspoon (2.5 mL) salt
6-8 peppercorns
2 cloves garlic
1 onion
Paprika

Cook all ingredients together in water (simmer slowly) until meat is tender, 4-5 hours; or in pressure cooker for 30 minutes. Cool, and remove the bones (optional) then strain the liquid into bowls. Add the meat, and set aside, in refrigerator or cold place to jell. Sprinkle with paprika.

This is my husband's favorite!
Emma S. Pella
Land O Lakes, Florida   U.S.A.

JELLIED PIGS' FEET
Kočenina

4 pounds (1¾ kg) pigs' feet
1 teaspoon (5 mL) salt
1 medium onion, sliced with skin
6 whole black peppercorns
1 clove garlic, chopped
Paprika

Wash well in cold water, then in warm water. Put in kettle and cover with water. Bring to a boil and skim. Lower heat and simmer slowly, boiling will make gel cloudy. Add garlic, salt, whole black pepper and sliced onion. Cook until meat falls away from bones, five or six hours. Remove meat and cut into small pieces. Strain liquid. Place meat either in large bowl or pan and pour in strained liquid. Let stand in a cold place until congealed. Sprinkle with paprika, if desired. Rye bread is a must with kočenina.

Caroline Kotula
Syracuse, New York   U.S.A.

LIVER PATÉ
Pečienková natierka

1 pound (450 g) chicken livers
Small onion
1½ teaspoons (7.5 mL) salt
2 teaspoons (10 mL) dry mustard
½ teaspoon (2.5 mL) nutmeg
¼ teaspoon (1.25 mL) cayenne red pepper
1 cup (¼ L) butter
1 tablespoon (15 mL) lemon juice

Cook chicken livers slowly for 20 minutes in unsalted water. Drain well. Grind the livers and onion in a meat grinder. While waiting for livers to cook, mix the following in a cup: salt, dry mustard, nutmeg and cayenne pepper. Add seasoning and butter to the ground up liver. Mix well with a spoon. Add lemon juice, mixing well. Mixture tastes much better when refrigerated over night. Great on garlic toast.

Benjamin Gombar
Saginaw, Michigan U.S.A.

LIVER PATÉ
Pečienková prichutka

1 pound (450 g) chicken livers, chopped, or beef liver, if preferred
1-2 onions
2 eggs, hard boiled, chopped,
Salt, pepper, to taste

Fry chicken or beef livers. Add chopped onions and fry. Mash boiled eggs. Add salt and pepper to taste. Mix all together. Perfect for crackers.

Nina Holy
Slovak World Congress
Vice-President, U.S.A., East West Orange, New Jersey U.S.A.

MARINATED MUSHROOMS
Hríbové predjedlo

4 cups (1 L) water
3 teaspoons (15 mL) salt
½ cup (1 dL) white distilled vinegar
Sugar to create sweet and sour taste
Whole allspice
3-4 bay leaves
Mustard seed
1-2 onions, sliced
2 pounds (900 g) white mushrooms

Place all ingredients together in a pot and cook 20-25 minutes. Do not overcook mushrooms. Cool and drain a little liquid. Make a good season dressing or use bottled oil/vinegar dressing and add to mushrooms. Perfect as appetizers.

Nina Holy
Slovak World Congress
Vice-President, U.S.A., East West Orange, New Jersey
U.S.A.

MEAT BALLS
Fašírky

½ pound (225 g) beef or pork, ground
3 slices toast
2 tablespoons (30 mL) grated parmesan cheese
2 tablespoons (30 mL) parsley flakes
1 clove garlic, minced
1 egg, beaten
1 teaspoon (5 mL) salt
½ teaspoon (2.5 mL) pepper
¼ teaspoon (1.25 mL) basil
Oil, for frying

Soak toasted bread in cold water for 7 minutes and press dry. In a bowl, combine all the other ingredients with the toast and roll into balls of desired size. Brown in oil or shortening until well browned. Place in sauce and simmer until sauce is cooked.

Dolores Paunicka Callahan
Lowell, Indiana U.S.A.

MEAT BALL CREOLE
Gule hovädzie - Kreole

1½ pounds (675 g) chopped beef
¾ cup (1¾ dL) oatmeal
1 teaspoon (5 mL) salt
1 teaspoon (5 mL) garlic salt
1/2 cup (1 dL) tomato sauce
Flour

Creole Sauce:
1 cup (¼ L) tomato sauce
1 cup (¼ L) chili sauce
1 cup (¼ L) water
4 small onions, chopped
1 green pepper, chopped

Meatballs: Mix meat with oats, salt, garlic salt and add ½ cup (1 dL) tomato sauce. Use a teaspoon and roll mixture into small balls. Roll in flour and brown in frying pan.
Sauce: Add all ingredients of sauce and mix well. Add meat balls to sauce and simmer for 30 minutes.

Nina Holy
Slovak World Congress
Vice-President, U.S.A., East
West Orange, New Jersey
U.S.A.

SHEEP CHEESE APPETIZERS
Bryndzovníky

1¾ - 2¼ pounds (800-1000 g) potatoes
Salt
Black pepper
1 cup (130 g hladkej) flour
Oil
½ pound (200 g) sharp cheese (bryndze)

Peel potatoes and grate. Add flour, salt and pepper, mix well. Grease a cookie sheet with oil. With a tablespoon, measure small heaps of potato dough, placing evenly on oiled sheet. Press tops of dough slightly with a tablespoon. Sprinkle tops with cheese. Bake in preheated hot oven 375°F (190°C). Serve bryndzovníky with buttermilk, or, with tea as a snack.

The traditional recipes found in this collection, submitted by Dr. Mintalová, are from the archives of the Slovenské Národné Múzeum in Martin, Slovakia.

PhDr. Zora Mintalová
Slovenské Národné Múzeum
Martin, Slovakia

MUSHROOM PHYLLO TARTS
Hríbové štrudle

3 ounces (85 g) package cream cheese
¼ cup (½ dL) dry bread crumbs
¾ cup (1¾ dL) sour cream
1 tablespoon (15 mL) dill weed
1-2 tablespoons (15-30 mL) lemon juice
½ teaspoon (2.5 mL) salt
4.5 ounces (126 g) jar sliced mushrooms
1 garlic clove, minced
½ cup (1 dL) butter
Frozen phyllo (fillo) pastry sheets, thawed
4.5 ounces (126 g) jar mushrooms

Heat oven to 350°F (180°C). In a small bowl, combine cream cheese, bread crumbs, dill weed, salt, sour cream and lemon juice; blend well. Stir in sliced mushrooms, and set aside. In a small skillet over medium heat, cook garlic in butter. Lightly coat 16 muffin cups with garlic butter, and set aside. Brush large cookie sheet with garlic butter. On work surface, unroll phyllo sheets. Brush one phyllo sheet lightly with garlic butter. Place buttered side up on buttered cookie sheet. Brush second phyllo sheet lightly with garlic butter; place buttered side up on top of first sheet. Repeat with remaining phyllo sheets. With sharp knife, cut through all layers of phyllo sheets to make sixteen 3x4¼ inch (8x11 cm) rectangles. Place one rectangle in each buttered muffin cup. Spoon heaping tablespoons of cream cheese/mushroom mixture into each cup. Top each with a whole mushroom. Drizzle with remaining garlic butter. Bake for 18-20 minutes.

Makes 16 appetizers.

Paul Ďuriš
Channahon, Illinois   U.S.A.

PICKLED FISH
Ryby marinované

4½ - 5 pounds (2-2¼ kg) fish fillet
3 pints (1½ L) cider vinegar
1½ cups (340 g) canning salt
5 cups (1¼ L) white vinegar
1 pound (450 g) sugar
5-6 medium onions, diced
4-5 teaspoons (20-25 mL) crushed red pepper
1 box (100 g) pickling spice

Step #1: Cut fillet into small bite-size pieces and place into glass jar or crockery pot. Mix salt with cider vinegar, stirring thoroughly. Pour over fish. Cover and let stand for 4-6 days at 40°F (5°C) temperature, or in refrigerator.

Step #2: Dice onions, set aside. Mix sugar and white vinegar, stirring until completely dissolved. Rinse fish thoroughly; and into a clean crockery pot or jar, layer fish with onion; sprinkling paprika on each layer. (Use no more than 4-5 teaspoons (20-25 mL) paprika for each gallon of fish). Sprinkle all of the pickling spice across top layer, and pour vinegar mixture over spice and fish. Seal jar, or cover crockery pot, and refrigerate for 7 days.

Step #3: After 7 days, or longer, as the taste gets better the longer it stands, the fish can be eaten. Good with crackers.

The Reverend Michael J. Chonko was ordained to the priesthood in 1943 at St. Andrew's Abbey, Cleveland, Ohio. He is an avid hunter and fisherman. He claims his recipes are proven to be exceptionally good. He has used them all his life. He sends God's blessings, love and prayers to Slovak people throughout the world.

The Reverend Michael J. Chonko
New Castle, Pennsylvania   U.S.A.

SHRIMP MOLD
Morský rak

- 1 can (10³/₄ ounces) (305 g) tomato soup
- 8 ounces (225 g) cream cheese
- 2¹/₂ envelopes unflavored gelatin
- ¹/₂ cup (1 dL) cold water
- ¹/₂ cup (1 dL) onion, minced
- ¹/₂ cup (1 dL) celery, chopped
- ¹/₂ cup (1 dL) green pepper, chopped
- 1 cup (¹/₄ L) mayonnaise
- 11 ounce can (310 g) tiny shrimp

Melt tomato soup and cream cheese in top of double boiler. Dissolve gelatin in cold water and add to soup/cheese mixture. Mix chopped onion, celery and green pepper with mayonnaise and add to mixture. Rinse shrimp in cold water, drain, chop, and mix well with other ingredients.

Spray mold lightly with cooking spray or lightly oil pan for easier removal of gelatin.

Pour mixture into chilled mold. (A fish mold looks especially nice.) Chill at least 24 hours.

To unmold: dip mold bottom in hot water and invert onto serving plate.

Serve with flavored crackers or rye bread rounds.

Makes 5¹/₂-6 cups (1¹/₂ L).

Eleanor Marcuz
Slovak Domovina Dancers
Windsor, Ontario, Canada

WHITE BEAN DIP
Fazuľkové načrenie

Dip:
- 1 large clove garlic
- 2 cans (19 ounce size) (532 g size) cannellini beans, drained, rinsed
- 1 cup (¼ L) fresh basil leaves, lightly packed
- 2 tablespoons (30 mL) fresh lemon juice
- ½ teaspoon (2.5 mL) salt
- ¼ teaspoon (1.25 mL) freshly ground pepper
- Crudities
- Pita chips

Pita Chips:
- 8 mini pita breads (8 ounces) (225 g)
- 1 teaspoon (5 mL) dried Italian herb seasoning, crumbled
- 1 teaspoon (5 mL) paprika
- Nonstick cooking spray

Dip: In food processor, mince garlic. Add beans, purée. Add remaining ingredients; process until basil is finely chopped. Serve at room temperature or chilled with crudities and pita chips.

Makes 2½ cups (6 dL).

Chips: Preheat oven to 350°F (180°C). Split pitas horizontally; cut each half into 6 wedges. Place in single layer on two baking sheets. In a cup, mix seasoning with paprika. Spray pita wedges with nonstick cooking spray; sprinkle with seasoning mixture. Bake 8 minutes or until lightly toasted. Cool.

Makes 96 chips.

Nina Holy
Slovak World Congress
Vice-President, U.S.A., East West Orange, New Jersey
U.S.A.

DAD'S WASSAIL
Sviatočný nápoj - Oteckový

1 gallon (3¾ L) apple cider, unfiltered
1 lemon, sliced
1 tablespoon (15 mL) whole cloves
1 tablespoon (15 mL) whole allspice
1 teaspoon (5 mL) mace
2 sticks cinnamon
1 cup (¼ L) brown sugar, or less if desired
Dark rum (optional)

Place cloves, allspice, mace and cinnamon sticks in a muslin bag. Pour cider into an 8 quart (7½ L) stock pot and add lemon, spice bag and brown sugar. Heat to a boil. Simmer for 15 minutes. Add rum to taste. Serve and enjoy!

Dr. Lindy A. Kona
Chicago, Illinois U.S.A.

HOT WHISKEY
Hriate

1 quart (1 L) whiskey
Honey
Goose lard, fat or butter

In a cast iron pan or heavy pot, heat a small amount of honey. When honey is heated through, add small amount of goose lard, fat or butter. Keep stirring while heating. Add whiskey and mix well. Caramelized sugar can be substituted for honey, giving mixture a golden color.

Hriate was a traditional drink on Christmas Eve, likewise at weddings and christenings. It was also used for medicinal therapy as a cough and cold remedy.

PhDr. Zora Mintalová
Slovenské Narodné Múzeum
Martin, Slovakia

SALADS

Šalát

BEET HORSERADISH
Chren

6 pounds (2³/₄ kg) cooked or 10 cans (9³/₄ oz. each) (2³/₄ L) sliced beets
1¹/₂ cups (3¹/₂ dL) horseradish root, grated (use more or less according to taste)
³/₄ cup (1³/₄ dL) vinegar
¹/₂ cup (100 g) sugar
2 tablespoons (30 mL) salt
1¹/₂ teaspoons (7.5 mL) pepper
1-2 cups (¹/₄ - ¹/₂ L) reserved beet juice (use more or less, as desired)

Drain beets, reserving liquid, and grate. Clean and scrape off outer layer of horseradish root; grate and add to grated beets. Combine remaining ingredients; heat to dissolve sugar. Cool liquid and pour over beets. Mix thoroughly. Pack into glass jars and refrigerate. (Use more or less beet juice, according to taste for a relish-like consistency. Also, use more or less horseradish root, according to taste.)

Chren is particularly eaten during the Easter holidays, and is one of the foods placed in the Easter Basket to be blessed. Chren is a symbolic Easter food and reminds us of the bitterness and suffering of Christ, and the thorns placed upon His head during the crucifixion.

BROCCOLI AND CAULIFLOWER SALAD
Karfiolový a kvetný kapustový šalát

5 cups (1¹/₄ L) broccoli
5 cups (1¹/₄ L) cauliflower
1 cup (¹/₄ L) raisins
¹/₂ cup (1 dL) bacon bits
1 cup (¹/₄ L) sunflower nuts
¹/₂ cup (1 dL) mayonnaise
1 tablespoon (15 mL) vinegar
4 tablespoons (¹/₂ dL) sugar

Combine bite size pieces of cauliflower and broccoli with raisins, bacon bits, and sunflower nuts.
Mix mayonnaise, vinegar and sugar in a separate bowl. Toss salad gently with the dressing and refrigerate. Or chill salad, and add dressing right before serving.

Serves 10.

Karen Parker Komara
Harrisonburg, Virginia U.S.A.

COLE SLAW
Kapustný šalát

1½ pounds (675 g) green cabbage, finely shredded (about 5 cups)
1 medium onion, chopped fine
1 medium green pepper, chopped fine
½ cup (100 g) sugar
½ cup (1 dL) vinegar
½ cup (1 dL) salad oil
½ teaspoon (2.5 mL) black pepper
1 teaspoon (5 mL) salt

In a large bowl, place cabbage, onion and green pepper. In a small saucepan, combine sugar, vinegar and oil; bring to the boiling point. Immediately pour over vegetables. Add salt and pepper. Mix well. Cover and refrigerate for 12 hours or longer.

Anna Sosnicky
Union, New Jersey U.S.A.

CORN SALAD
Kukuricový šalát

1 can salty corn
1 carton plain white yogurt
½ cup (10 dg) cheese
1 tablespoon (15 mL) mayonnaise
½ teaspoon (2.5 mL) salt
½ teaspoon (2.5 mL) ground pepper
1 onion, diced

Drain the corn and place in a bowl. Grate the cheese and add it to the corn. Dice onion and add to mixture. Combine yogurt, mayonnaise dressing, salt and pepper and add to corn mixture. Mix well, cover, and refrigerate for two hours.

Serve as a salad or with crackers, or bread as an appetizer.

Serves 4.

Vargicová Renáta
Zvolen, Slovakia

SOUR CREAMED CUCUMBERS
Uhorky v kyslej smotane

2 fresh cucumbers
2 small onions
1 cup (¼ L) sour cream
2 tablespoons (30 mL) vinegar
½ teaspoon (2.5 mL) minced dill
½ teaspoon (2.5 mL) salt
Paprika

Peel cucumbers and onions. Slice thinly into ice water to which has been added 1-2 teaspoons (5-10 mL) salt. Let stand for 15 minutes. In the meantime, combine sour cream, vinegar, dill, salt and a dash of paprika. Drain cucumbers, lightly squeezing out the water. Pour the sour cream mixture over the drained cucumbers and onions; mix well. Refrigerate 3 to 4 hours before serving.

MIXED ENDIVE SALAD
Miešaný čakankový šalát

¾ -1 pound (300 g-450 g) endive
1 large leek
2 apples
2 carrots
Yogurt (1 small carton, plain)
Juice of one lemon
Salt, sugar, pepper, to taste

Wash endive, drain well, partially dry, and chop to noodle size. Shred apples and carrots; cut leek into thin circles and add to endive. Sprinkle with lemon juice. Add salt and pepper. Sweeten yogurt with sugar and add to salad. Toss lightly. Refrigerate about 1 hour before serving.

Options: Mushrooms or shredded cooked beets may be added for variation. Garnish salad bowl with orange or grapefruit sections. Or, place a few ribbon cut radishes or tomato sections on top.

Anna Škovierová
Očova, Slovakia

OCTOPUS SALAD
*Chobotnicový šalát,
Slovenské jedlá
z Tichomoria*

1 pound (450 g) fresh octopus (canned may be substituted)
1 scallion, sliced
1 teaspoon (5 mL) sesame oil
1 teaspoon (5 mL) soy sauce
Dash of salt
Dash of sugar
Kufui nuts (can substitute with grated walnuts), fried till crisp

Wash octopus in cold water, let soak for 30 minutes. Drain off water. In a pot, bring to boil 2 quarts (2 L) water. Boil octopus for 10 minutes. Drain and discard water. When cooled, slice thin. In a bowl, mix sliced octopus, scallion, salt, sugar, sesame oil and soy sauce. Lastly add the crisp, fried nuts. Refrigerate and chill for one hour. Serve on lettuce leaf.
(Note: if using canned octopus, omit cooking procedure. Continue with remaining method.)

Serves 4.

Eugene V. Oravec
Honolulu, Hawaii U.S.A.

SLOVAK POTATO SALAD
Slovenský zemiakový šalát

8-10 potatoes
1 cup (¼ L) frozen peas
½ cup (1 dL) dill pickle, chopped (use more as desired)
1 small onion, grated or chopped
½ pound (225 g) soft or cooked salami
Mayonnaise
Salt, pepper, paprika, to taste

Cook potatoes in skins. Peel and cut up into small cubes. Cook peas and add to potatoes. Add onion and pickles. Cut salami into small cubes and mix with potatoes. Combine mayonnaise (desired amount) salt, pepper and paprika and add to potatoes.

Millie Heban
Rossford, Ohio U.S.A.

PACIFIC SLOVAK SHRIMP SALAD
Slovenský Pandravový šalát z Tichomoria

- 1 pound (450 g) shrimp (45-60 count, small, fresh or boiled)
- 1 celery stalk, diced
- 1 scallion, chopped
- 1 clove garlic, minced, or garlic powder
- 3 tablespoons (45 mL) mayonnaise
- 1 teaspoon (5 mL) lemon juice
- Dash of black pepper
- Dash of paprika

Boil shrimp (or use canned shrimp). Let cool. Mix shrimp with celery and scallion. Add lemon juice and sprinkle with black pepper and paprika. Add garlic or garlic powder. Stir in mayonnaise and mix well. Cover tightly. Refrigerate for 1 hour. Best served with crusty bread.

Serves 4.

Eugene V. Oravec
Honolulu, Hawaii U.S.A.

SAFFRONED RICE - SIDE DISH
Šofranová ryža

- 1 cup (225 g) rice, uncooked
- 2 tablespoons (30 mL) oil
- 1 onion, minced
- 1/2 teaspoon (2.5 mL) salt
- 1/2 stick cinnamon
- 4 whole cloves
- 1/4 teaspoon (1.25 mL) turmeric and a pinch of saffron
- 1 tablespoon (15 mL) hot water
- 2 cups (1/2 L) hot water

Rinse rice in hot water and drain. Mince onion and sauté in hot oil. Add rice, cinnamon, cloves, turmeric and salt and fry about 3 minutes. Moisten saffron in 1 tablespoon (15 mL) hot water and add to rice mixture. Add hot water, cover and simmer 20 minutes on low heat. Serve as a side dish.

MANDARIN ORANGE, SPINACH SALAD
Mandarinový - pomarančový, špenatový šalát

- 1/3 cup (1/4 dL) vegetable oil
- 1/4 cup (1/2 dL) sugar
- 1/4 cup (1/2 dL) white vinegar
- 1 tablespoon (15 mL) parsley
- 1/2 teaspoon (2.5 mL) salt
- 1/2 teaspoon (2.5 mL) hot pepper sauce
- Dash of pepper
- 4 cups (1 L) torn lettuce (red or green leaf)
- 4 cups (1 L) torn spinach
- 1 cup (1/4 L) sliced celery
- 2 small cans (184 g each) mandarin oranges, drained
- 1/2 cup (1 dL) slivered almonds (toasted)
- 3 tablespoons (45 mL) sugar

To toast almonds: Melt 3 tablespoons (45 mL) sugar over low heat. Add almonds. Stir till evenly coated. Remove from heat. Allow to cool, then break apart. Set aside.

Combine oil, sugar, white vinegar, parsley, salt, hot pepper sauce and pepper in a lidded jar. Shake, and set aside.

In a large salad bowl, place lettuce, spinach and celery. Add mandarin oranges and toasted almonds. Toss. Add salad dressing and toss lightly. Serve immediately.

Serves 4-6.

Dr. Lindy A. Kona
Chicago, Illinois U.S.A.

SAUERKRAUT SIDE DISH
Kyslá kapusta (bočné jedlo)

- 1 small potato
- 1/2 apple
- 1 quart (1 L) sauerkraut
- 2 tablespoons (30 mL) brown sugar
- 1 bay leaf

Peel potato and apple and cut into cubes. Place in pan and add just enough water to cover. Boil until tender; mash. Rinse sauerkraut and add to mashed potato/apple mixture. Add brown sugar and bay leaf. Boil to get hot. Remove bay leaf and serve.

Ethel Mazurek
Allentown, Pennsylvania, U.S.A.

LINDY'S VEGETARIAN SALAD
Vegetariánsky šalát

Salad:
- 2 cups (½ L) cooked couscous
- 15 ounces (425 g) (1 can) garbanzo beans
- 6 green onions, chopped
- 2 medium tomatoes, seeded and chopped
- 1 medium cucumber, seeded and chopped
- 1 cup (¼ L) parsley, chopped
- ½ cup (1 dL) cauliflower, steamed and chopped

Dressing:
- ½ cup (1 dL) olive oil
- ½ cup (1 dL) lemon juice
- ¼ teaspoon (1.25 mL) dry minced garlic
- 1 teaspoon (5 mL) dijon style mustard
- 1 teaspoon (5 mL) salt
- ⅛ teaspoon (.6 mL) freshly ground pepper

Salad: Place cooked couscous in large bowl. Add the chopped green onions, tomatoes, cucumbers, cauliflower and parsley; mix together. Add the garbanzo beans and mix thoroughly. Pour dressing over salad and stir. Refrigerate till ready to serve.

Dressing: In a screw top jar, combine the olive oil, lemon juice, garlic, dijon mustard, salt and pepper. Mix well. Let stand for ½ hour. Shake well and pour over salad.

Serves 4-6.

Dr. Lindy A. Kona
Chicago, Illinois U.S.A.

ESCALLOPED PINEAPPLE
Ananásový nákyp

3 eggs, beaten
1½ cups (300 g) sugar
¾ cup (1¾ dL) margarine, melted
1 can (20 ounces) (567 g) crushed pineapple, drained
4 cups (1 L) fresh bread cubes

Mix eggs and sugar well by hand. Add melted margarine, and mix. Add drained pineapple, blend in well. Pour pineapple mixture over bread cubes. Mix, and put in greased baking dish. Bake in preheated oven at 350°F (180°C), uncovered, for 30 minutes.
Delicious accompaniment with ham or chicken.

Millie Heban
Rossford, Ohio   U.S.A.

HONEY MUSTARD DRESSING
Medový horčicový nálev

¾ cup (1¾ dL) mayonnaise
⅓ cup (¾ dL) vegetable oil
¼ cup (½ dL) honey
¼ cup (½ dL) lemon juice
1 tablespoon (15 mL) minced fresh parsley
1 tablespoon (15 mL) prepared mustard
1 teaspoon (5 mL) pepper
½ teaspoon (2.5 mL) minced onion flakes

Whisk together mayonnaise, oil, honey, lemon juice, parsley, mustard, pepper and onion flakes in small bowl until smooth and creamy. Cover and refrigerate until ready to serve.
This dressing is wonderful on tossed salad greens, spinach or with chicken or seafood salads.

Yields: 2½ cups (6 dL).

Dyane M. Hrifko
Mountainside, New Jersey
U.S.A.

VEGETABLES

Zeleniny

BEST BAKED BEANS
Najlepšia pečená fazuľa

- 1/2 pound (225 g) bacon, diced
- 1/2 pound (225 g) ground meat
- 1 large onion, diced
- 1/3 cup (3/4 dL) brown sugar
- 16 ounces (454 g) (1 can) pork and beans, partially drained
- 16 ounces (454 g) (1 can) kidney beans, drained
- 16 ounces (454 g) (1 can) butter beans, drained
- 1/4 cup (1/2 dL) ketchup
- 2 tablespoons (30 mL) molasses
- 1/2 teaspoon (2.5 mL) dry mustard
- Dash of Worcestershire sauce
- 1 can (16 ounces (454 g) chili beans, not drained (optional)
- 1 package dry onion soup mix (optional)

Brown bacon, ground meat and onion. Add the remaining ingredients, mix well. Bake at 350°F (180°C) for 1 hour.

Benjamin Gombar
Saginaw, Michigan   U.S.A.

GREEN BEANS
Rajčiakové struky

1 pound (450 g) fresh beans, cooked
1 onion, diced
2 cloves garlic, minced
1 tablespoon (15 mL) oil
1 tablespoon (15 mL) parsley
¼ cup (½ dL) butter
8 ounces (227 g) (1 small can) tomato sauce
1 tablespoon (15 mL) tomato paste

Clean, cut and cook green beans. Drain. While beans are cooking, fry onion, garlic in tablespoon (15 mL) oil and butter. Add all other ingredients. Simmer until sauce is thick. Pour over cooked beans and serve.

Sandra Joyce
Slovak Domovina Dancers
Windsor, Ontario, Canada

CAULIFLOWER AND MUSHROOM CASSEROLE
Karfiolový a šampiňónový nákyp

1½ pounds (675 g) cauliflower
½ pound (250 g) rice
2 tablespoons (30 g) butter
2 tablespoons, heaping (40 g) onion, chopped
1½ cups (300 g) mushrooms (champignon)
4 eggs, beaten
½ cup (100 g) cheese, grated
Salt, pepper
Oil or other fat

Cook cauliflower in salted water. When slightly cooled, break into florets, and set aside. Cook rice as directed and set aside. In a skillet, sauté onion in butter. Slice mushrooms and add to onion; sauté until softened; season with salt and pepper. Grease a casserole with oil or other fat. Spread a layer of rice in bottom of casserole, then a layer of mushrooms. Next place a layer of cauliflower florets over mushrooms. Repeat procedure. Beat eggs, add pinch of salt and pour over last layer of cauliflower. Sprinkle with grated cheese. Bake in hot oven 375°F (190°C) for about 30 minutes or until bubbly.

Anna Škovierová
Očova, Slovakia

RED CABBAGE
Červená kapusta

1 medium head of red cabbage, shredded
1 medium onion, sliced thin
2 Granny Smith or Green Pippin apples, peeled, cored and sliced
½ cup (100 g) sugar
1 teaspoon (5 mL) salt
8 peppercorns
3 whole allspice
1 teaspoon (5 mL) caraway seed
2 bay leaves
1½ cups (3½ dL) water
1 tablespoon (15 mL) melted bacon fat
¾ cup (1¾ dL) white vinegar
3 tablespoon (30 g) cornstarch

Combine spices, water and sugar. Add apples, cabbage and onions. Put all in a large Dutch oven and heat to boiling, then reduce heat. Cover and simmer 15-20 minutes until cabbage is tender. Stir up from the bottom 2 or 3 times.
Stir in melted bacon fat. Combine cornstarch and vinegar in a cup stirring until smooth.
Gradually stir into the mixture, cooking and stirring constantly, until thickened.

Serves 8.

Ilonka Martinka-Torres
Castro Valley, California
U.S.A.

MUSHROOM STUFFED CABBAGE
Plnená kapusta s hubami
(Served for Christmas Eve supper)

1 pound (450 g) head of cabbage
1 cup (¼ L) dried mushrooms
¼ cup (50 g) onion, chopped
2 tablespoons (30 mL) fat
2 eggs, hard boiled, chopped
⅔ cup (1.5 dL) sour cream
½ cup (100 g) grated cheese
Salt, pepper, dill

Parboil cabbage to loosen and soften leaves. Cook mushrooms in water, drain and chop. Sauté onion in fat, add cooked mushrooms and fry for about 10 minutes. Add dill and hard boiled eggs, chopped fine. Place a tablespoon (15 mL) of filling into cabbage leaf, roll up and lightly tuck in ends. Arrange rolls in greased casserole, cover with sour cream and grated cheese. Bake in preheated moderately hot oven 350°F (180°C) until cabbage is cooked and cheese has completely melted through.

ZESTY CARROTS
Príchutná mrkva

6 large carrots
2 tablespoons (30 mL) onions, finely chopped
2 tablespoons (30 mL) horseradish
½ cup (1 dL) mayonnaise
¼ teaspoon (1.25 mL) salt
¼ teaspoon (1.25 mL) pepper
¼ cup (½ dL) fine, dry bread crumbs
2 tablespoons (30 g) butter, melted

Cut carrots into circles or julienne strips. Cook in water until tender, crisp. Drain well, reserving ¼ cup (½ dL) liquid. Transfer carrots to baking dish. In a small bowl, combine onion, horseradish, mayonnaise, salt, pepper and reserved liquid. Pour over carrots, spreading evenly. Toss bread crumbs with melted butter and sprinkle on top. Bake at 350°F (180°C) for 15 minutes.

Serves 6.

Anne Katanik
Etobicoke, Ontario
Canada

QUICK AND EASY CORN PUDDING
Rýchly kukuricový nákyp

1 stick (115 g) margarine, melted
1 can (approximately 400 g) kernel cream corn
1 can (approximately 400 g) whole kernel corn
1 egg, slightly beaten
½ cup (1 dL) sour cream

Melt margarine in medium saucepan. Remove from heat. Add corn, egg and sour cream. Stir all ingredients till thoroughly moistened. Bake at 350°F (180°C) for 30 minutes or till firm and browned.

Serves 4-6.

Dr. Lindy Kona
Chicago, Illinois U.S.A.

BAKED EGGPLANT
Zapekané baklažány

3 eggplants, peeled
Salt
4 tablespoons (60 mL) oil
2-3 carrots, cut into small pieces
1 stalk celery, chopped
2 onions, minced
7 tomatoes (cut each into four pieces)
4 cloves garlic, minced
Salt, pepper, to taste
Parsley flakes

Sprinkle salt on peeled eggplant and let stand half hour. In 2 tablespoons (30 mL) hot oil, fry celery and carrots; add onion, garlic, and sauté until onion is soft. Add quartered tomatoes, pepper, and salt. Simmer until juice from tomatoes thickens.

Meanwhile, brown eggplant, both sides in 2 tablespoons (30 mL) hot oil. In another baking dish which has been oiled, layer eggplant with vegetables. Sprinkle parsley flakes and bake in hot oven 375°F (190°C) until eggplant is tender.

Anna Škovierová
Očova, Slovakia

COOKED LETTUCE
Šalát

3 slices bacon
Milk (enough to cover lettuce)
Salt to taste
Water to wilt lettuce and to thin flour mixture
Vinegar to taste
1 head lettuce
3 tablespoons (30 g) flour

Fry bacon. Pour off half the fat. Pour boiling water over lettuce to wilt. Boil wilted lettuce in milk. Brown flour in remaining bacon fat. Add some water and vinegar to thin. After browned and mixed, add to lettuce and milk. Bring to boil. Add salt to taste.

Joan Jurishica
Milwaukee, Wisconsin U.S.A.

HAM AND MUSHROOM STUFFED PEPPERS
Šunka s hribami plnená paprika

6 medium green peppers
1 pound (450 g) fresh mushrooms, cleaned and finely chopped
1 onion, minced
1 cup (¼ L) cooked ham, chopped into small pieces
½ cup (1 dL) bread crumbs
1 tablespoon (15 mL) chopped parsley
½ clove garlic, minced
3 tablespoons (45 g) butter
Salt and pepper to taste
1 cup (¼ L) tomato sauce

Sauté onion in melted butter until transparent and soft. Add ham, bread crumbs, mushrooms, parsley, garlic, salt and pepper to taste. Simmer about 5 minutes. To prepare peppers: remove tops and seed peppers. Parboil peppers for a minute or two, just to loosen the skin. Fill peppers with mushroom mixture. Place peppers in a greased casserole, cover with tomato sauce and bake in preheated oven 350°F (180°C) for 15 minutes. Can be served as a main dish or a vegetable side dish.

Serves 6.

Martha Sarosy Zetts
Canfield, Ohio   U.S.A.

BAKED CHEESE POTATOES
Zapekané zemiaky so syrom

2-2¼ pounds (900 g-1 kg) potatoes
2 tablespoons (30 g) butter
¼ cup (50 g) cheese, grated
1¼ cups (2.5 dL) sour cream
2 eggs
Pepper, salt, to season

Cook potatoes in jackets, cool, peel, and cut into quarters. Mix with grated cheese. Season with salt and pepper, and place on greased baking sheet. Mix eggs with sour cream and pour over potatoes. Bake in preheated oven 350°F (180°C) until cheese is completely melted and egg mixture is well blended into potatoes.

POTATO CROQUETTES
Šklbanky s makom

2³/₄ pounds (1200 g) potatoes
Salt
Water
²/₃-1 cup (150 g) grits flour
3 ounces (80 g) fat
¹/₃ - ¹/₂ cup (60 g) poppy seed
³/₄ cup (1³/₄ dL) powdered sugar
Fat for deep frying

Cook peeled potatoes, drain; cover with flour. With a spoon, make an opening through flour permitting all steam to escape. Cover and let welt for 10 minutes. With a wooden spoon, blend potatoes, salt, and flour. Mix into smooth dough. Dip a spoon into melted fat, scoop up potato mixture, form a ball and drop into hot fat to brown. Serve with sprinkle of poppyseed and powdered sugar.

Anna Škovierová
Očova, Slovakia

VEGETABLE CASSEROLE
Zeleninová kastriola

16 ounces (450 g) (1 can) white corn, drained
16 ounces (450 g) (1 can) yellow corn, drained
16 ounces (450 g) (1 can) French style green beans, drained
¹/₂ cup (1 dL) chopped onion
¹/₄ cup (¹/₂ dL) green pepper chopped
1 cup (¹/₄ L) cheddar cheese, shredded
¹/₂ cup (1 dL) sour cream
16 ounces (450 g) (1 can) cream of mushroom soup
¹/₂ stick (60 g) margarine, melted, to drizzle on top
Cheese Crackers

Mix all ingredients and put in a casserole dish. Crumble cheese crackers on top. Bake at 325°F (165°C) until brown.

Marcy Pekarcik-Butorac
Fountain Valley, California
U.S.A.

SAUERKRAUT
Kyslá kapusta

Cabbage, about 50
 pounds (22.5 kg)
1$^1/_2$ cups (300 g) salt,
 pure granulated

Remove the outer leaves and any undesirable portions from firm, mature, heads of cabbage; wash and drain. Cut into halves or quarters; remove the core. Use a shredder or sharp knife to cut the cabbage into thin shreds about the thickness of a dime.

In a large container, thoroughly mix 3 tablespoons (45 mL) salt with 5 pounds (2$^1/_4$ kg) shredded cabbage. Let the salted cabbage stand for several minutes to wilt slightly; this allows packing without excessive breaking or bruising of the shreds.

Pack the salted cabbage firmly and evenly into a large clean crock or jar. Using a wooden spoon or tamper or the hands, press down firmly until the juice comes to the surface. Repeat the shredding, salting, and packing of cabbage until the crock is filled to within 3-4 inches (8-10 cm) of the top. Cover cabbage with a clean, thin, white cloth, such as muslin, and tuck the edges down against the inside of the container.

Cover with a plate or round paraffined board that just fits inside the container so that the cabbage is not exposed to the air. Put a weight on top of the cover so the brine comes to the cover but not over it. Formation of gas bubbles indicates fermentation is taking place. Fermentation is usually completed in 5-6 weeks.

To store: Heat sauerkraut to simmering. Do not boil. Pack hot sauerkraut into clean, hot jars and cover with hot juice to $^1/_2$ inch (1.5 cm) from top of jar. Adjust jar lids. Process in boiling water bath, 15 minutes for pint ($^1/_2$ L) jars, and 20 minutes for quart (1 L) jars. Start to count processing time as soon as hot jars are placed into the actively boiling water.

Yields 16-18 quarts (15-17 $^1/_4$ L)

In memory of my grandfather,
Joseph Zvara

Sandra Sarosy Duve
Slovak World Congress
Vice President U.S.A. West
Colorado Springs, Colorado
U.S.A.

SAUERKRAUT AND ONIONS
Kyslá kapusta s cibuľou

16 ounces (450 g) sauerkraut
1 onion, chopped
Water
Black pepper
¼ pound (112 g) salt pork

Rinse sauerkraut in colander to remove all additives, then put into 2 quart (2 L) pot with a little water. Cook slowly over medium heat. Add chopped onion and black pepper. Mix together. Meanwhile, using a small saucepan, cube salt pork and sauté until pieces are cooked and browned. Add to sauerkraut when it has browned, mixing together. Good with boiled klobása.

Samuel Sosnicky
Union, New Jersey U.S.A.

GREEN TOMATOES
Zavarené zelené paradajky

Liquid proportion:
4 cups (1 L) water
1 cup (¼ L) vinegar

Spice solution per jar:
1 teaspoon (5 mL) salt
1 teaspoon (5 mL) sugar
2-3 pieces garlic
½ teaspoon (2.5 mL) celery salt

Green tomatoes

Proportion is 4 to 1. Wash and sterilize jars - quart size (1 L). Fill each jar with green tomatoes. Prepare vinegar, water solution. Into each jar add spice mixture. Fill jars with water and vinegar solution. Put on jar rings and tops, not completely tight. Wrap each jar in cloth. In a large kettle, bring water to a boil. Boil 5 to 8 minutes. Remove jars from pot carefully to cool. When cool enough to handle, finish sealing.

My mother's recipe for pickling green tomatoes.

Anna Sosnicky
Union, New Jersey U.S.A.

GREEN TOMATO RELISH
Zelené paradajky (mleté)

4 quarts (4 L) green tomatoes
1 quart (1 L) onions
12 peppers (red and green)
¼ cup (½ dL) salt
Water to cover

3½ cups (7 dL) diluted vinegar
3½ cups (700 g) sugar
1 tablespoon (15 mL) celery seed
1 tablespoon (15 mL) mustard seed
1 teaspoon (5 mL) allspice
1 teaspoon (5 mL) cloves
1 teaspoon (5 mL) cinnamon

Grind tomatoes, onions and peppers in food chopper. Add salt and water. Let stand overnight.
Drain
Bring vinegar, sugar and spices to a boil. Add vegetables and bring to a boil again. Boil 2 or 3 minutes. Pour into hot jars.
Seal.

Betty Williams
Youngstown, Ohio   U.S.A.

BETTY'S TOMATO SAUCE
Rajčiaková omáčka - Betková

1 large can (28 ounces) (794 g) spiced plum tomatoes
1 large onion, diced
6 strips bacon, diced
2 cloves garlic, minced
¼ cup (½ dL) olive oil
Freshly ground peppercorns, to taste
½ teaspoon (2.5 mL) salt
1 tablespoon (15 mL) marjoram

Sauté bacon until golden brown. Add onion, garlic and oil. Mix well. Add remaining ingredients. Simmer ½ hour. Break up tomatoes while cooking. Pour over cooked pasta and mix well. Sprinkle with grated cheese.

Enjoy!

Betty Kominar
Slovak Domovina Dancers
Windsor, Ontario, Canada

SOUPS

Polievky

BARLEY-BEET SOUP
*Jačmeňová polievka
s cviklou*

- 2 pounds (900 g) beef bones
- 2 bay leaves
- 1-2 teaspoons (5-10 mL) salt, to taste
- 8 whole peppercorns
- 6 cups (1½ L) water
- 1 pound (450 g) rutabaga, diced
- 3 cups (1½ pounds) fresh beets (675 g) diced
- 1 onion, chopped
- 2 cups (½ L) celery, chopped
- 1 cup (¼ L) parsley root and leaves, chopped
- 1 pound (450 g) cabbage, shredded
- 2½ cups (1 pound) (450 g) carrots, diced
- 2½ cups (1 pound) (450 g) potatoes, peeled and diced
- ¾ cup (¾ L) pearl barley
- 1 can (14½ ounces) (406 g) tomatoes with liquid, cut up
- ¼ cup (½ dL) vinegar
- Fresh dill
- Sour cream, optional

In a soup pot or Dutch oven, place beef bones in water. Cover and bring to boil. Skim foam. Add bay leaves, salt and peppercorns. Cover and simmer for about 2 hours. Remove bay leaves and discard bones. Add all vegetables except tomatoes. Add barley and bring to boil; reduce heat. Cover and simmer 50 minutes or until barley is cooked and vegetables are almost tender. Stir in tomatoes with liquid, add vinegar; heat through. Upon serving, garnish with dollop of sour cream. Sprinkle with dill.

Yields 16 servings.

Anne Zvara Sarosy
Slovak World Congress
Women's Committee Chairperson
Campbell, Ohio U.S.A.

BARLEY SOUP
Jačmeňová polievka

1-1½ pounds (450-675 g) soup meat, cubed
1 large onion, diced in large pieces
8 cups (2 L) water
1 teaspoon (5 mL) salt
1 teaspoon (5 mL) parsley
2 medium potatoes, diced
1 cup (¼ L) barley
6 carrots, cubed
4 stalks celery, sliced
⅛ teaspoon (.625 mL) pepper
1 quart (1 L) canned tomatoes

In a large soup pot brown meat and onion. Add water and simmer for one hour. Add parsley, salt, barley, pepper, carrots, potatoes and simmer for one hour. Add celery and tomatoes; stir well and simmer until celery is tender.

A Sokol - Sbor 26
Campbell, Ohio U.S.A.

BEAN AND VEGETABLE SOUP
Fazuľová a zeleninová polievka

1 cup (¼ L) dried white beans
½ cup (1dL) smoked bacon, diced
2 cloves garlic, minced
1 onion, chopped
1 leek, sliced thin
2 carrots, sliced thin
4 fresh tomatoes, peeled and chopped, or 2 cups (½ L) canned tomatoes
1½ cups (3½ dL) coarsely chopped cabbage
Salt
Pepper

Rinse through beans. In large bowl, soak beans overnight in cold water to cover. Next day add enough water to the soaking liquid to make 6 cups (1½ L). Fry bacon in soup pot until crisp. Set aside the crisp bacon. Add garlic, onion, leek, and carrots to reserved fat. Cook over low heat for about 15 minutes. Add a little more fat if necessary. Stir in tomatoes, soaked beans and reserved liquid. Partially cover with lid and simmer about 1 hour or until the vegetables and beans are tender. Add the cabbage and cook 15 minutes more. Season with salt and pepper to taste, and sprinkle with crisp bacon bits.

Mary Kovachik Busek
Poland, Ohio U.S.A.

BEAN SOUP-ROMANIAN STYLE
Polievka fazul'ová (Rumunská)

- 1 pound (450 g) pinto beans
- 1 pound (450 g) carrots, diced
- 1 large onion, chopped
- 3 stalks celery, diced
- 10 cups (2½ L) water
- 2 chicken bouillon cubes
- ¼ teaspoon (1.25 mL) black pepper
- ½ teaspoon (2.5 mL) paprika
- ½ teaspoon (2.5 mL) salt, to taste
- 3 medium potatoes, diced
- 8 ounces (¼ L) sour cream
- 3 tablespoons (30 g) flour
- 2 tablespoons (30 g) corn oil
- 5 tablespoons (75 mL) white vinegar

Sort and wash beans and soak for 12 hours; change water at least once. Drain off water and add 10 cups (2½ L) fresh water, onion, bouillon, pepper and paprika. Bring to boil and simmer 20 minutes. Add carrots and celery and bring to boil, then simmer 40 minutes. Add potatoes and simmer until all vegetables are tender.

Roux: Combine flour and oil in fry pan and cook over low heat until brown, stirring constantly about 10 minutes. Let cool. Slowly add 1 cup (¼ L) liquid soup to roux, then add to rest of soup. Simmer 10 minutes. Add 1 cup (¼ L) soup liquid to sour cream slowly to thin and warm sour cream. Add to rest of soup. Add vinegar and salt if desired. Enjoy!

Serves 8.

Bradley J. Stanciu
Chicago, Illinois U.S.A.

YOUNG GREEN BEAN SOUP
Polievka z fazuľkových strukov

1½ cups (300 g) young green beans
5 cups (1¼ L) water
1 cup (200 g) potatoes
1½ tablespoons (20 g) fat
2 tablespoons (20 g) flour
1½ tablespoons (20 g) onion
1 clove garlic
Salt
1 cup (2 dL) sour cream or milk
2 tablespoons (20 g) flour
Sugar
Vinegar

Cut washed beans and put in boiling water. When half cooked, add cup up potatoes.
Roux: In a frying pan, melt fat and add flour. Cook until lightly browned. Add grated onion and garlic. Fry lightly. Add to soup. Salt to taste. Cook until tender.
In a separate bowl, mix flour into sour cream or milk. Pour into soup and let it just come to a boil. According to taste, add vinegar to sour, or sugar to sweeten soup.

In memory of
Dorothy Sarvaš Zvara
Campbell, Ohio U.S.A.

GREEN BEAN SOUP WITH BUTTERMILK
Fazuľová polievka zo strukov

2 cups (½ L) fresh green beans
1 medium onion, chopped
1 egg
2 tablespoons (20 g) flour
½ quart (½ L) buttermilk
½ pint (¼ L) sour cream
Salt and pepper
Note: a 16 ounce can (454 g) of green beans may be used in place of fresh beans

To prepare fresh beans, wash, snap off ends and cut into pieces. Place in pot and cover with water. Add salt, pepper and chopped onion. Cover and simmer until beans are tender. Beat egg and add flour, mixing well. Add buttermilk and sour cream into egg mixture. Stir into beans and simmer for 10 minutes.

Mary Roman
Youngstown, Ohio U.S.A.

SLOVAK SOUR LIMA BEAN OR POTATO SOUP
Slovenská kyslá fazuľková polievka/ Zemiaková polievka

1 quart (1 L) milk
1 quart (1 L) water
1 teaspoon (5 mL) salt
¼ teaspoon (1.25 mL) pepper
4 tablespoons (40 g) flour
1 cup (¼ L) milk
2-15 ounce cans (425 g each) lima beans, with liquid
1 medium onion, sliced
¼ cup (60 g) butter
2 tablespoons (30 mL) white vinegar
½ teaspoon (2.5 mL) paprika

Note: For potato soup, pare and cut up 6 medium potatoes; cook until tender in 1 quart (1 L) water, then add milk and continue as directed for lima bean soup.

Combine milk, water, salt and pepper in a kettle. Bring to just below boiling point. Meanwhile, blend flour and 1 cup (¼ L) milk until smooth. Add beans with liquid, to kettle. Stir in flour-milk mixture. Bring to a boil, then simmer 3 minutes; remove from heat and cover. Brown onion well in butter. Add to soup. (Or drain butter into soup and serve onions on the side, to be added, to taste, to individual soup bowls.) Gradually stir vinegar into soup. Sprinkle with paprika.

Yield 8-10 servings.

Submitted by:
Dr. Edward Tuleya
Middletown, Pennsylvania

Pauline Urban Archer
Seven Hills, Ohio   U.S.A.

U. S. SENATE'S FAVORITE BEAN SOUP
Senátorová fazuľová polievka

1 pound (450 g) navy, Great Northern or pea beans
5 quarts (5 L) water
1 large smoked ham hock
2 onions, chopped
2 cloves garlic, minced
3 potatoes, cooked and mashed
1 cup (¼ L) celery, diced
Salt and pepper, optional

Wash beans and cover with water. Bring to a boil and let boil 2 minutes. Remove from heat, let stand for 1 hour. Bring again to boil. Simmer covered for 2 hours or until beans begin to mush. Add all ingredients but salt and pepper, and simmer 1 hour longer. Remove bone, cut up meat and return to soup. Season to taste. For smaller quantity, reduce recipe in half. Left over soup can be placed in freezer.

Submitted by:
Joseph (Jay Dee) Vrable
Campbell, Ohio U.S.A.
Editor, Struthers, Campbell and Lowellville Journals
Jednota News, correspondent

RED BEET SOUP
Polievka cviklová

½ pot of water
2 carrots, cut up
2 pieces of celery
1 medium onion, cut
1 jar (1 L) chopped red beets, and juice
6 whole cloves
6 whole peppers, seeded and cut in large pieces
½ bay leaf
3 potatoes, cut up
4 tablespoons (40 g) flour
½ can evaporated milk or
8 ounces (225 g) sour cream

Add all ingredients to pot. When carrots and potatoes are cooked, add: 4 tablespoons (40 g) flour mixed with ½ can of evaporated milk or small container, 8 ounces (225 g) sour cream. Add to soup and let it just come to a boil.

Valeria Miller
Philadelphia, Pennsylvania U.S.A.

BEEF BOUILLON WITH BAKED BEEF DUMPLINGS
Bujón s pečenými haluškami

Soup:
- 1 pound (450 g) beef shank for soup
- ½ pound (225 g) soup bones
- 1 ½ quarts (1.5 L) cold water
- Salt, to taste
- ½ cup (100 g) carrots, diced
- ½ cup (100 g) celery, diced
- 1 onion, diced
- 1 clove garlic
- 3-4 peppercorns
- Parsley flakes

Halušky:
- ½ cup (100 g) beef, roasted or baked
- ½ clove garlic, minced
- 1 tablespoon (15 g) minced onion
- Salt, pepper, to taste
- 1 egg, beaten
- ¾ cup (105 g coarse) flour

Soup: Cut meat into cubes and place with soup bones into soup kettle. Add water, cover, and simmer slowly for 1 hour.

Add vegetables, salt, garlic and peppercorns. Simmer an additional hour, covered. Bring to boil and drop dumplings (halušky) into soup. Serve with sprinkled parsley.

Halušky: Grind meat with garlic and onion, season with salt and pepper. Add beaten egg, mix and let stand for a while. Add flour to mixture and mix into a dumpling dough. With a teaspoon, drop pieces of dough into boiling soup. Let cook until dumplings come to top.

An old Slovak recipe.

BEEF SOUP WITH LIVER DUMPLINGS
Hovädzia polievka s pečenými haluškami

Soup:
1 pound (450 g) beef or soup bones
1 stalk celery, chopped
2 carrots, chopped
1 onion, chopped
Parsley, chopped
6 cups (1½ L) water

Dumplings:
¼ pound (115 g) beef liver
1 slice bread
1 onion
2 tablespoons (30 g) bread crumbs
1 tablespoon (10 g) flour
1 clove garlic, minced
1 egg
Pinch of marjoram
Salt and pepper
Parsley flakes

Soup: Place meat or bones in soup pot, add water and bring to boil. Skim off foam. Add chopped vegetables and simmer until done. Remove meat or bones, add salt to taste.

Dumplings: In the meantime, soak bread in water, squeeze out liquid. Combine bread, liver, onion; grind finely. Into the ground mixture, add bread crumbs, flour, minced garlic, egg, marjoram, salt and pepper; mix well. Into a pot of boiling salted water, drop liver mixture through a spaetzle maker, and cook for 10 minutes. Place in a colander and pour cold water over top; drain well. Add the dumplings (halušky) to soup. Sprinkle with parsley flakes.

Maria Sarvaš Kováčiková
Pod Krivan, Slovakia

BEEF SOUP
Hovädzia polievka

2 pounds (900 g) beef chuck
Soup bones
5 quarts (4³/₄ L) cold water
¹/₂ teaspoon (2.5 mL) black pepper
¹/₂ teaspoon (2.5 mL) paprika
4 carrots, cut into 1 inch (2.5 cm) pieces
4 parsley roots, cut into 1 inch (2.5 cm) pieces
4 stalks celery, cut into 1 inch (2.5 cm) pieces
2 medium onions
1 potato
Parsley greens
Noodles, cooked, drained

Wash meat and bones. Add meat and bones to a large pot. Cover with water. Let come to boil and skim thoroughly. Add seasonings and simmer slowly for 1 hour. Add cleaned vegetables; tie parsley greens together, and add to soup. Cover and let simmer for approximately 2 ¹/₂ hours or until meat is done. Add potato to soup last ¹/₂ hour of cooking. Add cooked drained noodles and serve. Vegetables may be served with meat. Chill over night and discard grease hardened on top of soup.

Robert J. Dvoroznak
Bay Village, Ohio U.S.A.

HAM BONE-CABBAGE SOUP
Kapustová (šunková kosť) polievka

8 quarts (8 L) water
Ham bone
Leftover ham (cut-up into small pieces
1 onion, chopped
¹/₂ cup (1 dL) butter
3 tablespoons (45 mL) flour
1 cup (250 mL) water
2 medium heads cabbage, chopped
1 can (16 ounces) (450 g) stewed tomatoes
3 medium potatoes, cubed
Salt, pepper to taste
1 teaspoon (5 mL) paprika

In heavy pot, simmer 8 quarts (8 L) water, ham bone, cut-up ham, cabbage, onion, and stewed tomatoes, covered, for 2 hours. Add cubed potatoes and continue simmering until potatoes are soft.
In frying pan, melt butter. Add flour and brown, stirring constantly. Add paprika. Slowly add 1 cup (250 mL) water and cook until thick, stirring often. Add thick mixture to soup and simmer, covered, for 20 minutes. Season to taste.

Serves 10-12. Slovak recipe

CABBAGE SOUP
Kapustnica

- 2 pounds (900 g) pork shoulder, cut into bite size pieces
- 1 cabbage, shredded
- 10 3/4 ounces (305 g) (1 can) condensed tomato soup
- 1 onion, diced
- 28 ounces (794 g) sauerkraut, reserve liquid
- 1 tablespoon (15 mL) paprika
- 1 teaspoon (5 mL) garlic powder
- 1/4 teaspoon (1.25 mL) pepper
- 1 teaspoon (5 mL) salt
- 2 tablespoons (30 mL) oil
- 2 cups (1/2 L) sour cream

In a large heavy soup pot, sauté pork and onion in oil. Add shredded cabbage, sauerkraut and seasonings. Cook and stir until cabbage is slightly wilted. Add tomato soup and 1 can of water. Simmer for one hour adding as much water as you like. Add juice from sauerkraut. Simmer another 1/2 hour. Just before serving, stir in sour cream. You may continue cooking over low heat, but do not boil.

In memory of Bessie Kuris

Kim Katanik Kuris
Ontario, Canada

ENDIVE SOUP
Čakanková polievka

- 3/4 pound (340 g) endive, chopped
- 2 tablespoons (30 mL) butter
- 1 medium onion, minced
- 4 potatoes, cubed small
- 4 cups (1 L) meat or vegetable stock
- 1 small carton sour cream
- 1 tablespoon (10 mL) flour
- 1 egg yolk, beaten
- Salt and pepper to taste

Wash endive, drain, cut into noodle size. In melted butter, sauté onion, add endive, salt, pepper and potatoes. Cover with stock and simmer until tender. Mix cream, beaten egg yolk and flour until well blended; add to soup. Adjust seasoning and serve.

Anna Škovierová
Očova, Slovakia

TOSSED CABBAGE AND POTATO SOUP
Šajtľáva

½ head cabbage
1½ quarts (1½ L) water
Salt
Bay leaf
4-5 potatoes, peeled and cubed
1 tablespoon (15 mL) lard
1 onion, medium small, chopped
2 tablespoons (20 g polohrubej) flour
Paprika

Separate cabbage leaves and tear into smaller pieces. Cook cabbage in salted water, adding bay leaf. Peel and cube potatoes, add to cabbage and cook until tender. In the meantime, in a frying pan, sauté chopped onion in melted fat until transparent. Add flour and cook until flour starts darkening. Remove from heat, add paprika, according to taste and color, and mix. Pour water, or cabbage soup liquid and mix into a zápražka-roux of gravy consistency. Add roux to soup and cook 5 minutes longer. Serves 4 - lunch or supper.

PhDr. Zora Mintalová
Slovenské Národné Múzeum
Martin, Slovakia

CREAM OF TOMATO SOUP
Smotanová rajčiaková polievka

4 cups (1 L) milk or light cream
½ cup (1 dL) dry bread crumbs
½ onion, stuck with 6 cloves
Parsley sprig
½ bay leaf
2 teaspoons (10 g) sugar
2 cups (½ L) fresh or canned tomatoes, chopped
¼ teaspoon (¾ g) baking soda
4 tablespoons (60 g) butter
Salt and pepper, to taste

Put milk or cream in pot, add bread crumbs, onion with cloves, parsley, bay leaf, and sugar. Simmer gently over medium heat about 5 minutes. Remove from heat and discard onion with cloves and bay leaf. Add tomatoes and baking soda, simmer gently for 15 minutes or until fresh tomatoes are cooked. Purée vegetables and liquid and return to pot. Add butter, salt and pepper to taste, and reheat until soup is very hot.

Martha Sarosy Zetts
Canfield, Ohio, U.S.A.

CARAWAY SOUP
Rascová polievka

1 tablespoon (15 mL) caraway seeds
1 teaspoon (5 mL) salt
6 cups (1½ L) boiling water
4 tablespoon (½ dL) butter
4 tablespoons (40 g) flour
1 egg, beaten

In a medium size soup pot combine seeds, salt and water. Simmer for about 10 minutes. Strain, if you like, to remove seeds. In another saucepan, brown butter lightly in the flour. Remove from heat and while stirring with a whisk, stir in caraway liquid. Return to heat and when soup returns to a boil, simmer for another 5 minutes before stirring in beaten egg. Continue boiling gently for 3 more minutes before serving.

Janet Badham
Whitby, Ontario, Canada

SLOVAK CARAWAY SOUP
Slovenská rascová polievka

Soup:
3 heaping tablespoons (30 mL) flour
3 heaping tablespoons (45 mL) butter or oleo
½ teaspoon (2.5 mL) paprika
2 tablespoons (30 mL) caraway seeds
1 celery stalk, chopped
1 teaspoon (5 mL) chopped parsley
8 cups (2 L) cold water
Salt, pepper, to taste

Dumplings:
1 egg
1 tablespoon (5 mL) water
3 tablespoons (30 mL) flour

Soup: Brown flour in butter or oleo; add paprika and brown for 10 seconds. Slowly add cold water mixing well. Bring to a boil. Add caraway seed, celery, parsley, salt and pepper. Boil ½ hour.
Dumplings: Beat egg with water; add flour and beat until smooth. Just before serving soup, drop this mixture by teaspoonful into soup. Cook 5 minutes. It will resemble stringy dumplings.

In memory of
Mary Zvara Cverna
Lorain, Ohio U.S.A.

CROUTON SOUP WITH SHEEP CHEESE
Demikát

Dried bread cubes
³/₄ cup (150 g) sheep cheese
1 small onion, finely chopped
Caraway seeds, pressed
Chives or dill, finely chopped
1 quart (1 L) boiling, salted water or liquid from cooked potatoes
1-2 teaspoons (5-10 mL) sweet cream, butter (optional)

In a large soup bowl, or tureen, cut up old bread into small cubes, add sheep cheese mixed with finely chopped onion, caraway seeds, finely chopped chives or dill. Pour boiling, salted water (or use liquid reserved from boiling potatoes) over the bread mixture. Mix well. Cover and let steep for a few minutes so that the water soaked bread becomes somewhat spongy, but not soggy. This wholesome and substantial food was served for either lunch or supper.

Serves 4-6.

PhDr. Zora Mintalová
Slovenské Národné Múzeum
Martin, Slovakia

SHEEP CHEESE DILL SOUP
Bryndzová polievka s kôprom

¹/₂ pound (200 g) potatoes
Salt
Caraway seeds
2¹/₂ cups (6 dL) water
³/₄ cup (150 g) sheep cheese
1 cup (2 dL) milk
Dill or chives

Peel potatoes, cube, and cook in salted boiling water. Add caraway seeds (amount according to taste). In the meantime, in a bowl mix sheep cheese with milk. Add chopped dill; may substitute with chives. Add cheese mixture to cooked potatoes, mix, and remove from heat.

Serves 4-6 for lunch or dinner.

PhDr. Zora Mintalová
Slovenské Narodné Múzeum
Martin, Slovakia

CHICKEN SOUP
Kuracia polievka

1/2 chicken, cut up
2 celery stalks, chopped
2 carrots, chopped
1 onion, chopped
1 parsley root and leaves, chopped
1 whole tomato
2 cloves garlic
1/4 teaspoon (1.25 mL) turmeric or pinch of saffron
Salt, pepper, to taste
Parsley flakes

Fill a large pot with 3 quarts (3 L) cold water and add chicken which has been washed and cut up. Bring to boil; skim top removing foamy residue. Do this several times until liquid is clear. Reduce heat and add remaining ingredients and simmer for about two hours. Remove chicken and tomato. Adjust seasonings in soup. Remove skin and bones from cooled chicken; return meat to soup, and reheat. Serve with cooked noodles or rice. Sprinkle with chopped parsley flakes.

Dobrú chuť!
Toronto, Canada

CHICKEN SOUP
Kuracia polievka

1 soup chicken, approximately 5 pounds (2 1/4 kg)
4 quarts (3 3/4 L) water
4 carrots, cleaned and cut into 1 inch (2.5 cm) lengths
1 parsley root, cleaned and cut into 1 inch (2.5 cm) lengths with greens
1 onion
4 stalks of celery, cut into 1 inch (2.5 cm) lengths
1 tablespoon (15 mL) black pepper
1 teaspoon (5 mL) salt (optional)

Cook chicken in water; skim top very carefully when starting to boil. Skim top of soup 2 or 3 times to remove all foam. Add all vegetables and seasonings. Simmer until chicken is tender, approximately 1 1/4 hours. Serve with cooked, strained noodles.

Robert J. Dvoroznak
Bay Village, Ohio   U.S.A.

DILL-BUTTERMILK SOUP
Kôprová cmarová polievka

1 quart (1 L) buttermilk
1 cup (¼ L) sour cream
4 tablespoons (40 g) flour
1 egg yolk, beaten
Vinegar
Salt
3 tablespoons (45 mL) dill, chopped
4 eggs

Cook dill in about 1 quart (1 L) water for 10-15 minutes. Mix flour, egg yolk and sour cream. Add this mixture and buttermilk to dill water. Cook about 20 minutes. Add salt and vinegar to taste. Before serving, add poached egg in each serving dish. Sprinkle with additional finely chopped dill.

Poached egg: Boil water to which was added 1-2 tablespoons (30-45 mL) vinegar, for a few minutes. Break one egg at a time and with a soup spoon drop egg into boiling water. Cook 4-5 minutes. Remove egg with slotted spoon and add to soup. Serves 4.

Emily Danko, Canada

DILL SOUP
Kôprová polievka

2 tablespoons (30 g) butter
3 tablespoons (30 g) flour
4 cups (1 L) water or soup stock
Pinch of caraway seed
½ cup (1 dL) sour cream
2 egg yolks
1 stalk fresh green dill
1 bread roll or day old bun, rožok or croutons
1 tablespoon (15 mL) oil
Salt to taste

To make a roux (zápražka), brown flour lightly, add melted butter and brown. Add roux to water or soup stock, caraway seed and dill, which has been washed and finely chopped. Cook for 20 minutes. Meanwhile, beat egg yolks into sour cream and pour into hot soup. Remove from heat immediately. Season with salt to taste. Cut bun into small pieces and brown in hot oil. (Omit this procedure if croutons are used.) Serve by placing croutons or cut up rožok in soup dish and ladle hot soup over top.

Emily Danko, Canada

SOUR EGG SOUP
Kyslá vajíčková polievka

2 tablespoons (30 mL) butter
1 tablespoon, heaping (10 mL heaping) flour
1 teaspoon (5 mL) caraway seeds
2 quarts (2 L) water
1 teaspoon (5 mL) salt
Dash of black pepper
5 eggs
1 cup (¼ L) sour cream
¼ cup (½ dL) vinegar

In a soup pot, lightly brown flour in butter; add caraway seeds and brown another minute. Add water and seasonings. Bring to a full boil. Break eggs individually into a dish and carefully slip eggs into soup; cook until eggs are hard-boiled. Mix sour cream with vinegar and add to soup. Stir; bring to a full boil. Remove from heat and serve.

Serves 5. In memory of Julia Torma Ruszczyk

Kathy Ruszczyk Malone
Colorado Springs, Colorado U.S.A.

FISH CHOWDER
Rybacia polievka

1 pound (450 g) cod (treska) or halibut filets (druh ryby)
3 slices bacon, diced
⅓ cup (¾ dL) celery, chopped
⅓ cup (¾ dL) onion, chopped
2 cups (½ L) potatoes, diced
⅔ cups (1½ dL) water
2 teaspoons (10 mL) salt
3 cups (¾ L) milk
1 1/2 cups (3½ dL) peas, fresh or frozen
1½ teaspoons (7.5 mL) Worcestershire sauce
3 tablespoons (30 g) flour
1¼ cups (3 dL) light cream

Cut fish into bite size pieces. Sauté bacon until crisp, drain. Sauté onion and celery in drippings until tender, but not brown. Add potatoes, fish, water and salt. Bring to boil. Cover and simmer 15 minutes or until potatoes and fish are tender. Stir in milk, peas, bacon and Worcestershire sauce. Combine flour and cream, add to mixture. Cook over medium heat, stirring constantly until smooth and thickened and mixture comes to a boil. Upon serving, sprinkle with chopped parsley or paprika. Yields 7½ cups.

Catherine Timko
Slovak Domovina Dancers
Windsor, Ontario, Canada

MOM'S LETTUCE SOUP
*Šalátová polievka
(alebo omáčka) Mamičkiná*

½ stick (½ dL) margarine or butter
½ onion, medium size, chopped fine
2 tablespoons (20 g) flour
1 tablespoon (15 mL) fresh dill, chopped fine
1 clove garlic, minced fine
2 cups (½ L) water
1 small can evaporated milk
Salt and pepper, to taste
Home grown lettuce, washed and chopped into small pieces (approximately same amount as a head of lettuce or 1 head loose leaf lettuce)
1½ tablespoons vinegar and/or 4-8 tablespoons (½ -1 dL) sour cream

In a 2-3 quart (3 L) pan, sauté onion in fat. Add flour. This is the zápražka. Keep mixing until light brown. Do not let it burn. Add dill, garlic and mix well. Add water and stir until mixture thickens. Add milk, bring to a boil and boil for a few minutes. Add lettuce and let come to a boil, again. Boil a few minutes more, add salt and pepper to taste. Do not over cook. The lettuce will get very dark.

For a zesty, sour taste, add vinegar and/or sour cream. If the soup is too thick add a little water.

Boiled potatoes, cubed small, are a good side dish with the soup.

This was my mother's recipe that she cooked often like so many other Slovak mothers.

In memory of my husband, Frank
Margaret A. Kluka
Barberton, Ohio   U.S.A.

MUSHROOM BARLEY SOUP
Hríbová jačmeňová polievka

- 3 tablespoons (45 mL) butter
- 2 onions, chopped
- 1 large clove garlic, minced
- 5 cups (1¼ L) water
- ½ cup (1 dL) barley
- 2 teaspoons (10 mL) soya sauce
- 1 teaspoon (5 mL) salt
- ½ teaspoon (2.5 mL) thyme
- ½ teaspoon (1.25 mL) nutmeg
- ½ cup (1 dL) whipping cream
- 2 cups (½ L) sliced mushrooms

In a medium size saucepan, cook onions and garlic in butter for 5 minutes. Add water, barley and seasonings. Cover, then bring to a boil and simmer for one hour. Add mushrooms and simmer for another 25 minutes. Turn heat to low, add cream and cook another 5 minutes.

Yields 6 servings.

In memory of
Mary Coleman
Guelph, Ontario, Canada

BUTTERED MUSHROOM SOUP
Maslová hríbová polievka

- 1 pound (450 g) mushrooms
- 4 quarts (3¾ L) water
- 1 teaspoon (5 mL) salt (or more to taste)
- ½ teaspoon (2.5 mL) pepper (or more to taste)
- 1 stick (1 dL) oleo or butter
- ¼ cup (35 g) flour

(Served on Christmas Eve)

Clean mushrooms and chop. In a large pot, add water, mushrooms, salt and pepper and cook for 15 minutes. In the meantime, make a roux by melting oleo or butter, add flour; continue stirring until browned. Add to soup and continue cooking for 20 minutes longer, or until mushrooms are tender.

Serves 6-8.

Mrs. Robert Hnat
Youngstown, Ohio U.S.A.

MUSHROOM CREAM SOUP
Hubová smotanová polievka

5 tablespoons (75 g) butter
2 large carrots, chopped
2 onions, minced
6 cups (1½ L) boiling water and 6 bouillon cubes or 6 cups (1½ L) chicken stock
1 teaspoon (5 mL) dill
2 teaspoons (10 mL) salt
⅛ teaspoon (.625 mL) pepper
1 bay leaf
2 pounds (900 g) potatoes, diced
1 pound (450 g) fresh mushrooms, chopped
1 cup (¼ L) half and half cream
¼ cup (35 g) flour

In a kettle, melt 3 tablespoons (45 mL) butter and sauté onions and carrots for 5 minutes. Stir in boiling water, dill, salt, pepper and bay leaf. Cover and simmer until the carrots and potatoes are tender. Remove bay leaf.
Sauté mushrooms in remaining butter for 5 minutes. Add to the soup. Combine half and half with the flour and stir in the soup until slightly thick.

This is one of my favorite recipes, especially with fresh picked mushrooms.

Mary C. Sassak
Monessen, Pennsylvania   U.S.A.

LENTIL SOUP WITH PRUNES
Šošovicová polievka so sušenými slivkami

1¾ cups (350 g) lentils
¾ cup (150 g) prunes
⅓ cup (80 g) oil
⅓ cup (50 g) flour
½ cup (100 g) milk
Vinegar
Salt
Sugar

Sort out lentils and soak in water, about 4 cups (1 L) the day before. The next day, cook lentils until half cooked. Add prunes, cook until soft and done. Prepare a light roux (zapražka) by heating oil in pan, add flour, stirring until lightly browned. Add roux to soup and cook a few minutes longer. Add sugar, salt and vinegar to taste. Serves 4 - lunch or dinner.

Dr. Zora Mintalová
Slovenské Národine Múzeum
Martin, Slovakia

SOUR MUSHROOM-BARLEY SOUP
Hríbová-jačmeňová kyslá polievka

½ pound (225 g) dried mushrooms
1 pint (½ L) fresh mushrooms, washed and sliced
1 cup (¼ L) barley
4 quarts (4 L) water
1 quart (2-#2 cans) (1 L) sauerkraut juice
1 medium onion, chopped fine
¼ cup (½ dL) butter
¼ teaspoon (1¼ mL) pepper
1 tablespoon (15 mL) salt

Wash dried mushrooms in warm water and dry well. Cook mushrooms in 1 quart (1 L) water until done (about 45 minutes from boiling point). Strain in colander and save liquid. Chop mushrooms fine. Repeat same method for fresh mushrooms but cook only 25 minutes from boiling point. Save liquid. Chop mushrooms fine. Simmer barley in 1 quart (1 L) water for 1 hour. Strain in colander and rinse in cold water. Mix sauerkraut juice, liquid from dry and fresh mushrooms and final 1 quart (1 L) water in large pot. Bring to boiling point. Add mushrooms, barley, onion sautéed in butter, and seasonings. Simmer covered for 20 minutes. (If a more sour soup is desired, use more sauerkraut juice and less water).

Serves 8.

A traditional Slovak Christmas Eve (Štedrý Večer) Sour Mushroom Soup

MUTTON GOULASH SOUP
Polievka gulášová barania

1 pound (400 g) mutton or lamb, cut into 1 inch (2½ cm) pieces
¼ cup (50 g) smoked bacon, chopped
½ cup (100 g) chopped, onion
2 cups (400 g) potatoes, cubed
2-4 tomatoes, chopped
2 green peppers, diced
¼ cup (50 g) carrots, grated
¼ cup (50 g) celery, grated
⅛ cup (20 g) parsley, chopped
2 teaspoons (10 mL) paprika
Salt
Caraway seed
10 cups (2½ L) water

Fry chopped bacon, add onion and sauté until lightly golden. Add paprika and mix. Add mutton, carrots, celery, tomatoes, peppers, parsley, pinch of caraway seed, and season with salt. Cover with water and cook until meat is tender. Add cubed potatoes and cook longer until potatoes are done. Serve with rye bread.

Maria Sarvaš Kováčiková
Pod Krivan, Slovakia

MUTTON PEA SOUP
Baraninová-hrachová polievka

1 cup (200 g) peas
½ pound (225 g) mutton
8 cups (2 L) water
1 onion, chopped
2 tomatoes, cut into pieces
2 carrots, sliced circular
1 stalk fresh dill
1 bay leaf
3 whole peppercorns
Salt

In a small kettle, add enough water to cover peas and cook until semi-soft. Drain, and set aside. Cut meat in small cubes, add water and cook slowly. When meat is beginning to soften, add onion, tomatoes, carrots, dill, bay leaf and peppercorns. Add drained peas to soup mixture. Cook until tender. Salt to taste.

Košice, Slovakia

CAMP ONION SOUP
Táborová cibuľová polievka

2 tablespoons (30 mL) margarine or butter
4 large white Vadalia or Spanish onions
32 ounces (1 L) beef consommé or 4 cups (1 L) water and 6 beef bouillon cubes
2 cups ($1/2$ L) water
6 slices bread
6 slices Swiss cheese

Skin onions and cut in half, and again in $1/4$-$1/2$ inch pieces. In a large frying pan, melt the butter and add onions. Cook on very slow, low heat, mixing so as not to burn, 20-30 minutes. Heat the liquid. Bring to a boil. Drain fat off of onions and add onions to liquid. Continue simmering for an additional 1-2 hours.

Pour hot onion soup into oven-proof bowls. Fill $3/4$ to top. Add $3/4$ inch (2 cm) thick, dark toast on top of soup. Put Swiss cheese on toast and place bowls in 425°F (220°C) oven or under broiler until cheese melts. Serves 6.

Steve Bacon
Poland, Ohio   U.S.A.

ORAVA SOUP
Oravská polievka

1 pound (450 g) smoked ribs
8-9 cups (2 L) water
4 potatoes
1 tablespoon (15 mL) lard
1 onion, minced
2 cloves garlic, crushed
1 teaspoon (5 mL) paprika
1 cup ($1/4$ L) sour cream
1 egg yolk
Salt, pepper to season

Rinse ribs with hot water. Place in pot, add water and cook for 30-40 minutes. Peel potatoes, cube, and add to soup. In frying pan, sauté minced onion until golden. Add garlic and paprika to fried onion. Add onion mixture to soup. Cook until potatoes are done. Remove ribs and debone. Cut up meat into small pieces and add to soup. Beat egg yolk into sour cream and add to soup at end of cooking. Do not boil. Season with salt and pepper to taste.

Orava, Slovakia

BABA'S CREAM OF POTATO SOUP
Babičkiná smotanová zemiaková polievka

6 hard boiled eggs, diced
2 cups, heaping, (½ L) celery, diced
1 large onion, diced
3 tablespoons (45 mL) melted butter
10 cups (2½ L) water
Salt and pepper, to taste
8 medium potatoes, diced
1 quart (1 L) milk
3 eggs, beaten
1 pint (½ L) sour cream
½ cup (70 g) flour

Hard boil eggs, cool, peel and dice. In a large pot, sauté onion and celery in butter until golden in color. Add 10 cups (2½ L) of water and bring to a boil. Add diced potatoes. When potatoes are soft, add salt and pepper to taste. Add milk; simmer slowly on low heat. Meanwhile, in a small bowl, beat 3 raw eggs, stir in sour cream. To this mixture, stir in flour, using a fork, to form a thick paste. Slowly add this paste to the pot of simmering ingredients while mixing constantly. Texture of soup will be slightly lumpy. Watch carefully and continue stirring so that this rich mixture does not scorch. When mixture comes to a slow boil, cook on low for 5 minutes. Turn off burner and fold in diced cooked eggs. Soup tastes best if you allow standing time before serving.
Serves 10.

This soup has been part of our family's traditional Christmas Eve Holy Supper since 1913.

Justine Wesnak
FSWFE - Director of Membership
NSS - Advisory Board President
Whitehall, Pennsylvania U.S.A.

DILLED POTATO SOUP
Kôprová polievka

2 tablespoons (30 mL) butter
1 large onion, chopped to make 1 cup (250 mL)
4 large potatoes, peeled and sliced thin to make 5 cups (1¼ L)
1¼ cups (3 dL) half and half cream
1½ teaspoons (7.5 mL) salt
1 teaspoon (5 mL) dried dill
¼ teaspoon (1.25 mL) pepper
Thin red onion rings and fresh dill for garnish (optional)

In a 4 quart (3¾ L) saucepan, melt butter over medium low heat. Add chopped onion, and cook 4-6 minutes or until soft, stirring frequently. Add potatoes and 2 cups (½ L) cold water, bring to boil. Cover and cook over medium heat 20 minutes until potatoes are fork-tender. In food blender, coarsely purée potato mixture in two or more batches. Return puréed mixture to saucepan; stir in cream, salt, dried dill, and pepper, and bring to boil. Pour into bowls. Garnish each with red onions and fresh dill, if desired.

Serves 6.

Ilonka Martinka-Torres
Castro Valley, California   U.S.A.

POTATO SOUP
Zemiaková polievka

4 cups (1 L) chicken broth, or 4 cups (1 L) water and 4 chicken bouillon cubes
4 medium size potatoes, peeled and diced
1 small onion, finely chopped
1 carrot, finely chopped
1 stalk celery, finely chopped
2 tablespoons (20 g) flour
2 tablespoons (30 mL) cold water
3 tablespoons (45 mL) sour cream (Fresh dill-garnish)

In soup pan, bring broth to a boil. Add potatoes, onion, carrot, celery. Bring soup to boil again, cover and simmer over low heat for 20 minutes. Mix together flour and water to form paste. Stir sour cream into paste. Add this mixture to hot soup. Stir until blended. Simmer for 5 minutes or until soup has slightly thickened. Garnish with dill.

An European Recipe

SLOVAK PUMPKIN SOUP
Slovenská tekvicová polievka

1 fresh pumpkin (½ to 2 pounds) (225 g-900 g)
3 cups (¾ L) water
Salt, to taste
¼ cup (½ dL) butter
½ cup (1 dL) onion, chopped
Flour
12 ounces (355 g) evaporated milk, half and half, or cream

Rinse pumpkin. Cut in half and remove seeds. Peel and cut into pieces to grate. Add grated pumpkin to a pot. Cover with water, about 3 cups (¾ L). Salt to taste. **Roux:** Sauté chopped onion in butter. Add a little flour to make a paste. Add to pumpkin and boil about 15 minutes. Add milk and simmer about 10 minutes. Add pepper to taste. Serve warm with crackers.

Sister Mary Veronica, VSC
Bedford, Ohio   U.S.A.

SLOVAK SPINACH SOUP
Špenátová polievka

2¼ pounds (1 kg) spinach
10 ounces (285 g) carrots
2 tablespoons (20 g) flour
1 cup (¼ L) sweet cream
4 tablespoons (½ dL) butter
⅓ pound (145 g) sausage
Salt, pepper to season
Sugar to taste
¼ teaspoon (1.25 mL) nutmeg
Water

Wash spinach and dice. Cook in slightly salted water just enough to cover spinach. In a skillet, dice carrots (circles) and sauté in half the butter. Add a small amount of water, cover and cook carrots until tender. Add carrots to spinach. Mix flour and cream into smooth paste, add to soup and cook a few minutes longer. Season with salt, pepper, sugar, and nutmeg. Cut sausage into small circles, or chop into small pieces, and fry in remaining butter. Add to soup. **Note:** frozen spinach can be substituted, however, use only half the amount. For thicker soup, add more flour to cream (zátrepka.)

Anna Škovierová
Očova, Slovakia

SAUERKRAUT, LENTIL, MUSHROOM SOUP
Kapustnica so šošovicou a hubami

¼ cup (50 g) lentils
1 tablespoon (15 mL) dried mushrooms
Bay leaf
Caraway seeds
1½ cups (300 g) sauerkraut
2 ounces (60 g) smoked bacon, chopped
1½ tablespoons (20 g) onion, chopped
¼ cup (30 g hladkej) flour
½ teaspoon (2.5 mL) paprika
Black pepper

Sort through lentils, wash, soak in water 12 hours prior to cooking. Soak dried mushrooms to soften before cooking.

The following day, in a kettle of water, about 1 quart (1 L), add lentils, mushrooms, caraway seeds and bay leaf, cooking until lentils are half-cooked. Add sauerkraut to soup.

Chop bacon, fry with chopped onion until bacon becomes crisp and onion is lightly browned. Add flour to make a roux (zápražka), continue cooking until flour is lightly browned. Add paprika and mix. Add enough water to roux to make a gravy consistency. Stir until smooth and well-blended. Add roux to soup, continue cooking until lentils are tender. Add black pepper to taste.

4 servings - lunch or dinner.

PhDr. Zora Mintalová
Slovenské Národné Múzeum
Martin, Slovakia

SAUERKRAUT SOUP WITH SAUSAGE, MUSHROOMS AND PRUNES
Kapustnica s klobásou, hubami a slivkami

1/4 pound (100 g) smoked side of pork
1 1/2 cups (300 g) sauerkraut
2 tablespoons (30 g) lard
1/4 cup (40 g) onion, chopped
1/4 cup (30 g hladkej) flour
Paprika
1 tablespoon, heaping (10 g) dried mushrooms
1 ounce (30 g) prunes, pitted
Black pepper
Bay leaf
1/2 clove garlic, pressed
1/4 pound (100 g) homemade smoked sausage (klobása), thinly sliced
1 cup (2 dL) thick sour cream
Salt to taste

Place smoked pork in boiling water and cook slowly. When pork is half done, add sauerkraut that has been finely chopped; cook until meat is tender and well done. In the meantime, melt fat, sauté onion until transparent. Add flour making light roux (zápražka). Add paprika, amount according to taste and color, and mix. Pour warm water over roux, stirring into a smooth gravy-like consistency. Set aside. Cook dried mushrooms in water until tender. Set aside. Cook prunes in water until soft. Set aside. Remove pork from sauerkraut, debone and cut into small cubes. Set aside. To the cooked sauerkraut soup add black pepper, bay leaf, pressed garlic, cooked mushrooms with liquid. Thicken sauerkraut with prepared roux, mix well and simmer for 25 minutes. Add cooked prunes, smoked sausage, which was cut into thin round slices, cubed pork, and cook briefly. Add sour cream, stirring well. Cook a few minutes longer; do not boil. Remove from heat.

Dobrú chuť!

Serves 4-6 for lunch or dinner.

PhDr. Zora Mintalová
Slovenské Národné Múzeum
Martin, Slovakia

CREAMY VEGETABLE SOUP
Smotanová zeleninová polievka

1 pound (450 g) green or yellow beans
1 pound (450 g) carrots
1 pound (450 g) potatoes
1 onion
1 teaspoon (5 mL) salt
4 tablespoons (40 g) flour
1 cup ($1/4$ L) cold milk
2 cups (500 mL) carton sour cream
1 cup ($1/4$ L) fresh, frozen, or canned peas
1-$1^1/_2$ teaspoons (5 - 7.5 mL) salt
$1/4$ - $1/2$ teaspoon (1.25 - 2.5 mL) pepper
Milk

Wash and dice beans, about $1/2$ inch ($1^1/_4$ cm). Peel and slice carrots and potatoes. Add chopped onion, 1 teaspoon (5 mL) salt. Add water to cover vegetables. Boil till tender, about $1/2$ hour. Mix flour with milk thoroughly. Blend flour/milk mixture into sour cream using whisk or mixer. Mix well. Add vegetables. Add peas, salt and pepper, according to taste. Add milk to desired thickness.
Simmer an additional $1/2$ hour.

Note: Use 5 quart (5 L) soup pot. Fill to about half with vegetables and water.

Irene Timko
Slovak Domovina Dancers
Slovak World Congress
Heritage, Culture Commission, Sec.
Windsor, Ontario, Canada

VEGETABLE SOUP
Polievka so zeleninou

2 pounds (900 g) lean stewing beef
1 veal shin bone with some meat on it
3 quarts ($2^3/_4$ L) water
1 bunch carrots
$1/2$ bunch of celery
1 medium onion, diced large
1 quart jar (1 L) tomatoes
6 or more potatoes, cubed
2 cans tomato soup or 1 quart 1 L) tomato juice
$1/2$ bay leaf (optional)

Rinse meat and bone well and add to water. Let boil slowly so you can skim the foam well. Add bay leaf, if desired, for more flavor and continue boiling slowly until meat is almost tender, about one hour. Wash and clean carrots; slice. Wash, scrape and dice celery. Add cut up onion, tomatoes, and potatoes. Add tomato soup or tomato juice. Let boil until vegetables are done.

Anne Pavucek
Philadelphia, Pennsylvania, U.S.A

ROUX SOUP
Zapražená polievka

4 tablespoons (60 mL) butter
4 tablespoons (40 g) flour
3 cups (³/₄ L) water, hot
1 egg, slightly beaten
1 teaspoon (5 mL) salt

Melt butter at medium heat; add flour and salt. Stir constantly until roux is dark (as cinnamon), about 5 minutes. Remove from heat; add water, slowly stir until soup comes to a boil. Remove from heat. Continue stirring while slowly pouring beaten egg into soup. The egg will curdle and cook immediately. That's it. Enjoy!

Preparation time: 15 minutes
Serves three.

This is a soup my mother used to make for us especially when we were home from school with a cold. Next to chicken soup, this was supposed to cure all ills and make you feel good all over. We loved it. My family enjoys it anytime. This is a nice recipe for today's busy home-maker who will still be able to serve her family the same delicious hot soup her mother or grandmother did.

Mary F. Kopsic
Youngstown, Ohio U.S.A.

BASIC WHITE SAUCE
Omáčka

2 tablespoons (30 mL) butter
2 tablespoons (30 mL) flour
1 cup (250 mL) milk
Salt, pepper to taste

Melt butter in frying pan and add flour, stirring until golden, about 2 minutes. add warm milk, seasoning, and cook several minutes longer. Remove from heat and cover pan to prevent from thickening film forming over top of sauce.

-Editor

THICKENING SOUP - ROUX
Zápražka, Zhustenina, Zátrepka

Roux is prepared from flour, (or cornstarch) and fat, (lard, butter, oil, margarine, bacon fat or meat drippings). Use amount of flour equal to amount of fat.

Slovak cooks begin by partially frying the flour, without fat, to help evaporate some of the flour's moisture. In this way the flour may lose its uncooked flavor and smell. The longer the flour is fried, the more intense the color will become. Fat is gradually whisked in - continue to fry according to degree of desired color. Cold liquid is added into hot roux (zápražka) and hot liquid into cold zápražka. The preferred method is the first, adding cold liquid into hot, partially fried flour which mixes smoothly, avoiding lumps.

The consistency of zápražka depends upon the amount of liquid. The intensity of color is determined by length of cooking. The color of the zápražka identifies its usage.

light zápražka - utilized in preparation of white soups, sauces or gravy

light brown zápražka - utilized at the end of cooking to thicken soups, sauces and gravies

dark brown zápražka - utilized in preparation of dark sauces, gravy or stews

To thicken with zátrepkou (uncooked flour mixed with water) is not recommended. Soups thickened in this manner tend to be pasty or gummy.

Liquids used in roux preparation: Water, milk or cream
Additions: Minced onion, paprika

Onion is added along with the shortening so as to cook to transparent or slightly golden. Paprika is added at end of frying for additional flavor and color intensity. When adding paprika, remove from heat to prevent burning.

Other soup thickenings:
Potato thickening -
Grate three tablespoons of raw potato for each cup of soup and simmer until the potato is absorbed, about 15 minutes.

Egg yolk thickening -
The standard measurement is one egg yolk beaten with 1 teaspoon (5 mL) of milk or cream to each cup of soup. To prevent curdling, add a little hot soup to egg yolk mixture, whisk briskly, and then pour into the pot of hot soup, stirring until thickened. Do not boil.

-Editor

MAIN DISHES

Hlavné Jedlá

BEEF SKILLET FIESTA
Hovädzia miešanina

1 pound (450 g) ground beef
1 tablespoon (15 mL) oil
¼ cup (½ dL) onion, diced
1 teaspoon (5 mL) chili powder
¼ teaspoon (1.25 mL) pepper
2 teaspoons (10 mL) salt
1 can (1 pound) (454 g) stewed tomatoes, with juice
1 can (12 ounces) (336 g) whole corn, do not drain
1¼ cups (3 dL) beef stock or 2 bouillon cubes in 1¼ cups (3 dL) hot water
½ cup (1 dL) green pepper, thinly sliced
1⅓ cups (2¾ dL) instant rice

Brown meat in oil over high heat in large skillet. Add onion and reduce heat to medium, cooking until onion is tender. Add green pepper and cook till tender. Season to taste. Add tomatoes with juice, corn with liquid, and bouillon. Bring to boil. Stir in rice. Remove from heat and let stand 5 minutes. Fluff and serve.

Marcella Straka
Hellertown, Pennsylvania U.S.A.

CABBAGE BEEF CASSEROLE
Kapusta s hovädzinou - kastriola

- 1 pound (450 g) ground beef
- 2 medium sized onions, diced
- 1 medium sized head green cabbage, coarsely sliced
- 1/4 teaspoon (1.25 mL) pepper
- 2 medium sized carrots, thinly sliced
- 2 1/2 teaspoons (12.5 mL) salt
- 3/4 cup (1 3/4 dL) regular, long grain rice
- 1 can (14 ounces) (419 g) beef broth

In 5 quart (5 L) Dutch oven or sauce pot, over high heat, cook ground beef and onions until pan juices evaporate and meat is well-browned. Remove pot from heat. Add cabbage, carrots, pepper and salt; toss, then mix well.

Pour rice into 3 quart (3 L) casserole; spoon ground beef mixture on top of rice; pour beef broth and 1/2 cup (1 dL) water over mixture. Cover casserole and bake in 350°F (180°C) oven for 1 hour.

To serve, stir ground beef mixture with rice to mix well.

Makes 6 servings.

Kay Krajewski
Garfield Heights, Ohio U.S.A.

SAUERBRATEN
Sviečková

5 pounds (2¼ kg) top or eye round of beef
1 large onion
4 cloves garlic
4 medium size carrots
1 parsnip, bottom and top
3 ribs celery
3-4 bay leaves
Paprika
Salt, pepper to taste
Water

Roux:
¼ pound (115 g) margarine
Flour
1 onion, chopped
Water

½ pint (¼ L) heavy cream
Vinegar, to taste
Sugar, to taste

Dumpling - Knedl'a:
4 cups (560 g) flour
4 eggs
¼ pound (115 g) butter or margarine, melted
1½ cups (3½ dL) milk
5 slices white bread
2 packages (7 g each) dry yeast
1 teaspoon (5 mL) sugar
¼ teaspoon (1.25 mL) salt

In a large cooking pan cover meat with water and add vegetables and seasonings: onion, garlic, carrots, whole parsnip, celery, bay leaves, paprika, salt and pepper. Boil until meat is tender, approximately 1 hour. Remove meat and let it cool. When cooled, cut in small pieces. Remove bay leaves and discard. Purée all vegetables with cooking liquid in a blender. Return meat to cooking pan and pour puréed liquid over meat.

Roux: In a separate pan make a roux. Melt margarine and add one chopped onion and flour. Stir; when yellowish in color, add enough water to make a gravy-like paste. Cook slowly. Place this mixture in blender and blend to make a smooth gravy. Add to vegetable and meat mixture. Warm thoroughly and add ½ pint (¼ L) heavy cream, vinegar along with sugar to create sweet-sour taste. This is best served with a dumpling, "knedl'a".

Dumpling - knedl'a: Dissolve yeast in ½ cup (1 dL) of milk. Add sugar, salt and sprinkle with a little flour. Let rise in a warm place. Bread slices are left to dry for 3-5 hours, then cut in small squares.

(continued)

SAUERBRATEN
Sviečková
(Continued)

Mix flour with eggs and butter. When yeast rises add to flour mixture. Let rise again. After the second time, add bread cubes, mix well and on floured board make two long dumplings (knedl'e). This dumpling is not boiled, it is steamed. There are many ways this can be done. There are utensils on the market now. However, in the "old" days our mothers used a pan with cover and used a clean white "dish towel" fastened by a string. They cooked the dumpling (steamed) for 10-15 minutes. Remove and put on a wax paper.

Dobrú chuť!

Nina Holy
Slovak World Congress,
Vice-President, U.S.A., East West Orange, New Jersey U.S.A.

STEAK LOUISE
Hovädzí rezeň-Lujza

6 pieces filet mignon ½ inch (1.25 cm) thick
1 large onion, chopped
¼ pound (115 g) butter
8 ounces (225 g) fresh mushrooms, sliced
½ can brown gravy
2 tablespoons (30 mL) heavy cream
2 jiggers Cognac
Mustard
1 teaspoon (5 mL) Diablo sauce (escoffieo)
1 teaspoon (5 mL) Worcestershire sauce

Sauté onion in butter for 3 minutes and add a little mustard on steak with fork, one side only. Add steak to pan, add salt, pepper to steak. Brown quickly on both sides. Add mushrooms, Sherry or Cognac. Remove steak to plate, add Worcestershire sauce, gravy, Diablo sauce and heavy cream. Return steak to pan. Heat and serve.

Louise Talafous
Jersey City, New Jersey U.S.A.

SLOVAKIAN BARBECUE ROAST
Slovenská zbojnícka pečienka

5 beef cutlets, about 1/2 inch (1 cm) thick (size of pork chops)
5 pork cutlets (same size as beef
1 larger onion, full sliced rings
4 slices smoked bacon (cut each slice into 3 pieces)
Salt

Lightly salt all pieces of meat on both sides.

Note: Layer all ingredients in vertical, upright position. The arrangement in the roaster will resemble a large shish-kabob or a rolled roast.

Into a roaster, place 1 slice beef, upright, vertically; next to beef slice place 1 full slice onion, next to onion place 1 piece of bacon, upright also. Then take 1 slice of pork and repeat procedure as with beef. Alternate between beef and pork slices until all ingredients are placed against each other in vertical position. Sprinkle top slightly with black pepper.

Note: Roaster should be deep enough to permit enough space for meat stacked vertically. Cover with air-tight lid and roast in preheated 350°F (180°C) oven for about 1 1/2 hours. Do not baste or add any liquid. Serve with rice and any type of vegetable salad.

Serves 5.

Antonia Kralik
Berwyn, Illinois U.S.A.

BREADED BAKED CHICKEN LEGS OR PORK CHOPS
Bravčová, kuracia pečeň

6 chicken legs or thighs or pork chops
1 egg, beaten
Bread crumbs
Oil for frying
Salt, pepper to taste

Dip meat in egg. Roll and cover meat in bread crumbs. Fry golden brown on both sides. Place in roaster, salt and pepper. Cover and bake at 350°F (180°C) for 45 minutes or until meat is tender.

Dorothy Rygiel
New Jersey   U.S.A.

BROCCOLI CHEESE-RICE WITH CHICKEN
Kuracina s karfiolom na ryži

3/4 pound (340 g) chicken, skinned, boneless, diced
2 teaspoons (10 mL) vegetable oil
1 can (10 3/4 ounces) (305 g) broccoli cheese soup
1 can (13 3/4 ounces) (407 mL) chicken broth
3/4 cup (1 3/4 dL) water
1/2 teaspoon (2.5 mL) dried thyme
1/4 teaspoon (1.25 mL) pepper
1 1/2 cups (3 1/2 dL) rice
2 cups (1/2 L) broccoli, cut up into florets
1 red or green pepper, cut into strips

Brown chicken in cooking pot. In bowl, combine soups, water, thyme, and pepper; blend together. Add to chicken and bring to boil. Stir in rice. Cover and add vegetables; simmer till vegetables are tender.

Sandra Joyce
Slovák Domovina Dancers
Windsor, Ontario, Canada

CHICKEN CASSEROLE
Kuracia kastriola

2 cups (½ L) cooked breast of chicken
4 hard cooked eggs, chopped coarsely
2 cups (½ L) cooked rice, not instant, 2/3 cup (1½ dL) raw rice yields 2 cups (½ L)
1½ cups (3½ dL) chopped celery
1 small onion, minced fine
3¼ ounces (91 g) slivered almonds
1 teaspoon (5 mL) salt
2 tablespoons (30 mL) lemon juice
1 cup (¼ L) Hellman's mayonnaise (no substitute)
2 cans (10¾ ounces) (304 g) cream of mushroom soup
Buttered bread crumbs for topping

Toss together chicken, rice, eggs, celery, onions and almonds. Mix together mayonnaise, soup, lemon juice and salt; add to rice mixture. Put into buttered casserole (3 quarts-3 L) or large flat baking dish. Cover and refrigerate over night. Remove from refrigerator about an hour before baking. Top with buttered crumbs. Bake at 350°F (180°C) for about 45 minutes, uncovered.

In memory of husband Jim Koscak
Columinist reporter
   "Thought you'd like To Know"
Slovak Catholic Sokol - FALCON

Marge Koscak
Parma, Ohio   U.S.A.

CHICKEN PAPRIKA
Kuracî paprikáš

1 onion, chopped
4 tablespoons (60 mL) oil
1 tablespoon (15 mL) paprika
1 teaspoon (5 mL) black pepper
1 teaspoon (5 mL) salt (optional)
5 pounds (2¼ kg) chicken
1½ cups (3½ dL) water
½ pint (¼ L) sour cream

Skin and disjoint chicken. Brown the onions in the oil; add chicken and seasonings; brown 10 minutes. Add water; cover and let simmer until tender (approximately 1 hour). Remove chicken and debone. Add sour cream to drippings in pan and mix well. Add dumplings and chicken. Heat through and serve.

Dumplings:
3 eggs, beaten
3 cups (420 g) flour
½ cup (70 g) all purpose flour

Dumplings: Mix all ingredients together and beat with a spoon. Drop batter by teaspoonful in boiling water. Cook about 10 minutes, drain and rinse with cold water. Drain well and add to chicken paprikaš.

Serves 4 to 6.

Robert J. Dvoroznak
Bay Village, Ohio   U.S.A.

CHICKEN PAPRIKA
Paprikáš kurací

1 broiler-fryer (3-3½ pounds) (1.3-1.5 kg) chicken
½ cup (70 g) flour
¼ teaspoon (1.25 mL) pepper
1 cup (¼ L) chopped onion
1 cup (¼ L) chicken broth
½ cup (1 dL) sour cream
1½ teaspoons (7.5 mL) salt, (divided)
⅛ cup (30 g) butter
2 tablespoons (30 mL) paprika
1 cup (¼ L) light cream
¼ cup (½ dL) bacon pieces
¼ cup (½ dL) green pepper

Combine all flour, except 2 tablespoons (20 g), salt, and pepper in plastic bag. Shake chicken in bag until coated. In a large kettle, sauté onion in butter until light golden brown. Add paprika, ½ teaspoon (2.5 mL) salt, and chicken broth. Bring to a boil. Lower heat, place chicken in pan. Coat each side. Cook covered for 30 minutes or until tender. Remove chicken and place on greased pan. Keep warm in oven at about 250°F (120°C).

Stir light cream into pan after chicken is removed. Add bacon and pepper to gravy. Make a paste of the 2 tablespoons (20 g) flour and sour cream. Slowly stir into pan. Simmer, stirring constantly over low heat until thickened. **DO NOT BOIL**. Place chicken on platter and serve with gravy on the side. Serve with halušky.

Serves 6.

Joan Jurishica
Milwaukee, Wisconsin U.S.A.

CHICKEN PAPRIKA

Kurča na paprike s haluškami

2 tablespoons (30 mL) lard
2¹/₂-3 pounds (1.1-1.3 kg) fryer chicken, cut up
2 medium onions, chopped
1 clove garlic, chopped
1 large tomato, chopped
¹/₂ cup (1 dL) water
2-3 tablespoons (30-45 mL) paprika
1 teaspoon (5 mL) salt
¹/₄ teaspoon (1.25 mL) pepper
1 large green pepper, cut into ¹/₂ inch (1¹/₂ cm) strips
1 cup (¹/₄ L) sour cream
3 tablespoons (45 mL) heavy cream

Dumplings:
8 cups (2 L) water
1 teaspoon (5 mL) salt
3 eggs, well beaten
¹/₂ cup (1 dL) water
2 cups (280 g) flour
2 teaspoons (10 mL) salt

Heat the lard in a heavy 12 inch (30 cm) skillet or Dutch oven until hot. Cook disjointed chicken over medium heat until brown on all sides, about 15 minutes. Remove chicken. Cook and stir onions and garlic in lard until onions are tender. Drain lard from skillet. Stir in tomato, water, paprika, salt and pepper; loosen brown particles from bottom of pan. Add chicken. Heat to boiling; reduce heat and cover tightly to simmer for 20 minutes. Add green pepper, cover and cook until thickest pieces of chicken are done, 10-15 minutes more. Remove chicken and place on heated platter or in warm oven. Skim fat from pan, stir in sour cream and heavy cream. Heat till just hot. Serve chicken with dumplings and sour cream sauce.

Dumplings: Heat 8 cups (2 L) of water and 1 teaspoon (5 mL) salt to boiling in a large kettle. Mix eggs, ¹/₂ cup (1 dL) water, 2 cups (280 g) flour and 2 teaspoons (10 mL) salt; drop dough by teaspoonfuls into boiling water. Cook uncovered, stirring occasionally about 10 minutes. Drain and serve with sour cream sauce.

In authentic chicken or veal paprikáš recipes, the usage of sweet and sour cream is never forgotten. Today, more often than not, the cream is omitted and milk is substituted for a less rich dish.

Martha Sarosy Zetts
Canfield, Ohio   U.S.A.

CHICKEN PAPRIKA
Kuraci paprikáš

3 pounds (1¹/₃ kg) chicken, remove skin, cut in pieces
1 onion, chopped
Salt, pepper, paprika, to taste
1 cup (140 g) flour, for dredging and thickening
Oil for frying
1 cup (¹/₄ L) or more, chicken stock
1 teaspoon (5 mL) paprika
1 pint (¹/₂ L) sour cream

Fry onion in oil until transparent. Sprinkle chicken with salt, pepper and paprika. Dredge chicken in flour and brown on all sides in pan. Use as much oil as needed. Add ¹/₂ cup (1 dL) of stock and 1 teaspoon (5 mL) paprika. Simmer 15 minutes. Add remaining stock. Keep covered until chicken is tender. Blend 3 tablespoons (45 mL) flour and sour cream. Add to chicken. Simmer 3-4 minutes. Pour sauce and chicken over homemade halušky.

Serves 4-6.

Olivia Kona
Beaconsfield, Quebec, Canada

CHICKEN SOUFFLE
Kuraci nákyp

10 slices bread (more can be used)
2 cups (¹/₂ L) diced cooked chicken
¹/₂ cup (1 dL) mayonnaise
1 cup (¹/₄ L) mixed diced vegetables (green pepper, celery, onion)
Salt, pepper
4 eggs, well beaten
3 cups (³/₄ L) milk
1 can (10³/₄ ounce) (304 g) cream of mushroom soup
¹/₂ cup (1 dL) grated sharp Cheddar cheese
Paprika

Cube bread and spread on buttered 9x13 inch (22x32 cm) pan. (Reserve some for top.) Mix chicken, mayonnaise, vegetables, salt, and pepper, and spread over bread. Cover with rest of bread cubes. Beat eggs well and pour over bread. Refrigerate for a few hours. Spread with soup, sprinkle with cheese and paprika. Bake at 325°F (160°C) for 1 hour.

Marge Koscak
Parma, Ohio U.S.A.

CHICKEN AND RICE
Kuracina s ryžou

1 chicken, using bony pieces, neck, feet, wings, gizzard, liver
1 onion, diced
2 tablespoons (¼ dL) shortening
2 teaspoons (10 mL) paprika
2 cups (½ L) water
1 cup (¼ L) carrots, diced
½ cup (1 dL) parsley root, diced
Parsley greens
½ cup (1 dL) celery, diced
Salt, pepper, to taste
1 cup (¼ L) rice
2 tablespoons (¼ dL) shortening or other fat

Cut up chicken into serving pieces. Brown onion in shortening, add paprika and meat; brown. Add 2 cups (½ L) water, salt and pepper. Cook until meat is partly done. Add carrots, parsley root and greens, and celery. Cook until meat and vegetables are tender. Wash rice thoroughly. Melt 2 tablespoons (¼ dL) shortening in skillet and add rice. Sauté for a few minutes. Add to meat and cook until rice is done, adding water as needed to prevent burning.
Note: Duck may be substituted for chicken.

In memory of
Julia Torma Ruszczyk

Kathy Ruszczyk Malone
Colorado Springs, Colorado
U.S.A.

CREAM OF CHICKEN PAPRIKA
Paprikáš kurací

3½-4 pounds (1.5-1.8 kg) chicken cut up, skinned and deboned
1 teaspoon (5 mL) margarine or butter
¼ cup (½ dL) onion, chopped
¼ teaspoon (1.25 mL) salt
¼ teaspoon (1.25 mL) pepper
¼ teaspoon (1.25 mL) paprika
2 cans (8 ounces each) (224 g each) tomato sauce
1 whole egg
½ cup (1 dL) sour cream
3-3½ cups (¾ L) milk
2 tablespoons (20 g) flour
1 cup (2 dL) water

Drop Spoon Noodles:
2 cups (280 g) flour
½ teaspoon (2.5 mL) salt
2 whole eggs

In a skillet, melt margarine or butter and sauté onion slightly. Add chicken, salt, pepper and paprika, and fry about 45 minutes. Add water as needed during frying to prevent chicken from sticking and burning. Add 1½ cans (336 g) tomato sauce and 1 cup (2 dL) water. Simmer for 5-10 minutes. Bring to boil, remove from heat and mix occasionally. In a 3 quart (3 L) bowl, prepare and mix egg, sour cream, milk and flour; beat well. Add slowly to chicken while stirring; simmer until heated. (Do not allow to boil or overcook as the mixture will curdle). Serve with noodles.

Noodles: In a bowl, mix flour, eggs, and salt together. Continue mixing until dough comes out smooth. You can add ½ cup (1 dL) water to make smoother dough. In about 3 quarts (3 L) pot of boiling water, scrape batter off the edge of the bowl, with a tablespoon, into the boiling water, adding one tablespoon at a time. Boil noodle dumplings for about 15-20 minutes or until cooked. Serve with the chicken paprika.

Mary Skyba
Murray Hill, New Jersey U.S.A.

KONA GLAZED FRUITED CHICKEN
Kuracina v broskyňovej glažúre, Rodina Konová

1 can (29 ounces) (822 g) peaches
²/₃ cup (1¹/₂ dL) mayonnaise
1 package (7 ounces) (196 g) herb stuffing
2 slices toasted white bread, sliced into small cubes
1 broiler-fryer chicken, cut in parts
Salt and pepper
8 ounces (¹/₄ L or 224 g) orange marmalade
Parsley

Drain fruit, set aside. Reserve ²/₃ cup (1¹/₂ dL) fruit liquid. Stir reserved liquid into mayonnaise. Stir constantly over medium heat until mixture boils. Add stuffing and cubed bread. Spread stuffing in 13x9x2 inch (33x23x5 cm) pan. Put chicken on top of stuffing. Sprinkle chicken with salt and pepper. Brush chicken with additional mayonnaise. Bake in 350°F (180°C) oven for one hour. Arrange peaches around chicken. Brush chicken with melted orange marmalade. Bake 15 minutes longer. Garnish with parsley and serve.

Serves 4.

One of the favorite family recipes.

Martha Mistina Kona
Slovak World Congress
Heritage and Culture Commission, Chairperson
Wilmette, Illinois U.S.A.

NO PEEK CHICKEN
Kuracina (pečená na ryži)

1 chicken, cut up or 8 pieces of your choice
1 cup (200 g) uncooked, converted rice
1/2 cup (1 dL) celery, chopped
1 can (10³/4 ounces) (305 dL) cream of mushroom soup
1 can (10³/4 ounces) (305 dL) cream of chicken soup
2¹/2 cups (6 dL) boiling water
1 chicken bouillon cube
1/2 package onion soup mix
Oleo for braising

In a skillet, heat oleo and brown chicken lightly on both sides. Spread uncooked rice in bottom of a 9x13 inch (23x33 cm) pan; add soups, celery, bouillon cube, water, and onion soup mix. Place chicken on top. Cover with foil. Bake in preheated oven 300°F (150°C) for two hours. Do not open foil while cooking. Very delicious!

Josephine Kopachko
Smock, Pennsylvania U.S.A.

ROAST CHICKEN
Sliepka pečená

5 pounds (2¹/4 kg) chicken
4 tablespoons (60 mL) butter
Salt
1 teaspoon (5 mL) paprika or turmeric

Wash chicken in salted water and pat dry. Rub melted butter and sprinkle with salt and turmeric or paprika. Place chicken in roasting pan, breast side up, in preheated oven 325°F (165°C) and bake for about 2 hours or until tender. If chicken browns before cooking time, cover and complete roasting. Baste often to avoid drying.

Optional: Small peeled potatoes can be placed around chicken at midpoint of roasting.

ROAST CHICKEN
Kurča dusené s rezancami

3½ pounds (1½ kg) chicken, cut into pieces
½ cup (1 dL) oil
1½ cups (300 g) onion, finely chopped
2 tablespoons (30 mL) paprika
2 tablespoons (30 mL)) salt
1½ cups (300 g) green pepper, cut into strips
½ cup (100 g) celery, chopped
1 cup (240 mL) tomato, sliced

Noodles:
1¼ pounds (500 g) noodles
¼ pound (115 g) bacon, chopped, or butter
½ pound (225 g) cottage cheese
1 cup (¼ L) sour cream
1 tablespoon (15 mL) dill, finely chopped

Cut chicken into serving pieces, rinse and set aside. In a skillet, sauté onion in hot oil until golden yellow. Remove from heat and add paprika. Add chicken pieces, salt and small amount of water. Cover and let brown. Simmer for about 20 minutes or until half done. Add pepper, tomato and celery and continue cooking until done.

Noodles: Cook noodles in boiling salted water. Strain and drain thoroughly. Melt butter over noodles. (If using bacon, chop finely and fry. Mix noodles into bacon bits and fat). Sprinkle cottage cheese and heat in casserole. When ready to serve as side dish with chicken, dot noodles with sour cream and garnish with fresh dill.

Marta Kovačiková
Zvolenská Slatina, Slovakia

SOUR CREAM CHICKEN BAKE
Pečená kuracina v kyslej smotane

1 chicken, cut up or use chicken breasts or thighs
1/3 cup (3/4 dL) oil
1/2 cup (70 g) flour
1 teaspoon (5 mL) salt
1 teaspoon (5 mL) paprika
8 small potatoes, pared and halved
3/4 cup (1 3/4 dL) onion, chopped
1 can (10 3/4 ounces) (305 g) cream of chicken soup
1 cup (1/4 L) sour cream

Combine flour and seasonings. Dredge cut up chicken in flour and brown in hot fat in skillet. Remove chicken. Place potatoes in the skillet. Add chopped onion and pour soup across top. Transfer this potato mixture into a casserole and place browned chicken on top. Cover and bake till chicken and potatoes are done-about 1 hour in 325°F (160°C) oven. When done, pour sour cream over the chicken/potato bake; return to oven for about 10 minutes. Serve with a salad. This is a delicious meal. It is an old family recipe.

Makes 6 servings.

Margaret Mowery
Akron, Ohio   U.S.A.

ROAST DUCK
Kačica pečená

5 pounds (2 1/4 kg) duck
Salt and pepper

Wash duck in salted water and pat dry. Make small slits in duck to allow fat to escape. Sprinkle with salt and pepper and place duck, breast side up, in shallow roasting pan. Roast in preheated oven 450°F (230°C) basting every 15 minutes. Turn duck at intervals and continue roasting, basting often until done. Let stand, covered, for 10-15 minutes before carving.

EASTER CHEESE
Syrek

6 eggs
2 cups (½ L) milk
½ teaspoon (2.5 mL) salt

Pour milk into top of double boiler and break one egg at a time into milk. (Make sure each yolk is broken). Add salt and mix slowly. Do not cook over direct flame. Stir constantly, and when mixture begins to look like scrambled eggs, pour mixture into cheese cloth and tie tightly. Press and squeeze liquid from cheese while molding into round shape. When cool (not cold) carefully remove cheese from bag to avoid breaking. Put in refrigerator and chill.

Serves 1-5.

Marcella Straka
Hellertown, Pennsylvania, U.S.A.

EASTER CHEESE
Syrek

6 eggs
1 quart (1 L) milk

Lightly beat 6 eggs in a heavy saucepan. Add milk. Using a wooden mixing spoon, stir mixture over a very low heat until curds form and liquid gets clear (about 1 hour). Pour in cheesecloth and squeeze tightly; hang up and let drain for about 4 hours. Take out of cheesecloth and refrigerate in covered bowl. The cheese will be about the size of a softball.

From the kitchen of my mother, Elizabeth Gasper Evans.

Marlene G. Evans
Disputanta, Virginia U.S.A.

SUNDAY BRUNCH EGG CASSEROLE
Nedeľné raňajky - vajíčková kastriola

3 cups (¾ L) seasoned croutons
1½ pounds (675 g) bacon, fried and crumbled
6 eggs, beaten
3 cups (¾ L) Cheddar cheese, grated
3 cups (¾ L) milk
⅛ teaspoon (.6 mL) basil
⅛ teaspoon (.6 mL) thyme
⅛ teaspoon (.6 mL) marjoram
¼ cup (½ dL) fresh parsley
¾ teaspoon (3.75 mL) salt
Dash onion powder, pepper

Set aside ¾ cup (1¾ dL) cheese and ¾ cup (1¾ dL) bacon. Pack croutons and cheese in 9x13 inch (23x33 cm) baking dish. Cover with bacon and parsley. Mix eggs, milk and seasonings in medium bowl. Pour over top of above ingredients. Top with reserved cheese and bacon. Refrigerate overnight. Bake at 350°F (180°C) for 1 hour.

Serves 8-10.

Lindy A. Kona
Chicago, Illinois U.S.A.

SLOVAK QUICHE
Quiche Slovaquienne

1¼ cups (3 dL) crushed crackers
4 medium onions
8 ounces (225 g) mild cheese, grated (Monterey Jack)
4 ounces (115 g) Slovak bryndza cheese, grated
1 tablespoon (10 g) light flour (Wondra)
1 teaspoon (5 mL) salt
⅔ cup (1½ dL) melted butter
3 eggs
1 cup (¼ L) scalded milk
Chopped chives
Dash of sweet paprika

Combine cracker crumbs with ⅓ cup (¾ dL) butter and press into a 9 inch (23 cm) pie plate or quiche dish. Slice onions into thin rings and sauté in ⅓ cup (¾ dL) butter until tender and transparent. Arrange in crumb crust. Stir flour and salt into cheese. Beat eggs until light, combine with milk and stir into cheese. Pour mixture over onions and bake in a moderately slow oven 325°F (165°C) until set, 30-40 minutes. Top with chopped chives, sprinkle with paprika.

Thomas Klimek Ward
Honorary Consul of the Slovak Republic
Chicago, Illinois U.S.A.

BREADED CARP
Vyprážaný kapor

(Fish for Christmas Eve)

Carp
Salt
Flour
1 egg, beaten
Bread or cracker crumbs
Cooking oil
Lemon, sliced in circles
Parsley

Clean carp, remove skin and wash. Cut into serving portions, salt and let stand a while. Coat the fish with flour, then dip in beaten egg, and lastly in bread or cracker crumbs. Fry in hot oil until both sides are golden. Place on tray, garnish with circles of lemon. Add fresh parsley or parsley flakes. Serve with the traditional Christmas Eve fruit compote of cooked dried prunes, pears, apples, raisins and almonds.

Traditional holiday recipe from Slovakia

CHRISTMAS EVE CARP IN TOMATO SAUCE
Kapor na rajčiakoch
(Jedlo na Štedrý Večer)

2 pounds (1 kg) carp
1 cup (¼ L) sour cream
½ cup (1 dL) tomatoes, puréed
1 large onion
2 cloves garlic
Parsley flakes
1 lemon
1 teaspoon (5 mL) sugar
1 teaspoon (5 mL) paprika
Salt
Pinch of pepper

Clean and wash carp; place in clay-type casserole baking dish. Whisk sour cream into puréed tomatoes. Add sugar, salt, pepper, paprika, parsley flakes and some lemon rind. Mix, and pour over carp. Bake in oven 325°F (165°C) basting frequently. Place lemon wedges around dish. Serve in baking dish as the main course.

Traditional Slovak recipe

FRIED FISH IN BEER BATTER
Ryby pražené obaľované s pivom

Fish fillets
12 ounces (3½ dL) beer at room temperature
2 cups (½ L) pancake flour
¼ teaspoon (1.25 mL) salt
¼ teaspoon (1.25 mL) pepper
Cooking oil

Pour beer (use approximately 6 ounces (1¾ dL) of beer for the batter), in a glass and let it get flat for 1 hour prior to mixing batter. Mix all ingredients into a thin batter. Use fish fillets, cleaned, with no skin on them. Set a wire rack over wax paper about 18 inches (45 cm) long. Dip fillets in batter, set on rack for 15 to 20 minutes. Batter will set, slightly. Heat oil in skillet to hot temperature. Fry each piece about 4 minutes on each side. Put fish back on rack over paper towel to drain fat.

Steve Bacon
Poland, Ohio U.S.A.

BEEF GOULASH
Hovädzí guláš

2 pounds (900 g) beef, cubed
1 onion, chopped
½ green pepper, chopped
3 tablespoons (45 mL) fat
1½ tablespoons (22 mL) paprika
2 tablespoons (20 mL) flour
4 cups (1 L) water
4 cubes beef bouillon
1½ cups (3½ dL) potatoes, cubed
½ cup (1 dL) sour cream
¾ teaspoon (3.75 mL) crushed marjoram
1 clove garlic, minced
Salt, pepper to taste

In a heavy pot, sauté onion in hot fat until golden. Add green pepper, garlic and paprika. Add beef cubes that have been sprinkled with flour. Season with salt, pepper and marjoram. Add water and beef bouillon cubes. Simmer until meat is done, about 1 hour. Add potato cubes and cook until done, about 20 minutes. Remove from heat and add sour cream. Garnish with parsley to serve.

Serves 6.

Recipe from Slovakia

PEASANT BEEF GOULASH
Sedliacky hovädzí guláš

2 pounds (900 g) stewing beef, cubed
2 pounds (900 g) pork shoulder roast, cubed
Water
2 tablespoons (30 g) butter
2 tablespoons (30 g) oil
2 large onions, chopped
3 large carrots, chopped
2 green peppers, chopped
2 teaspoons (10 mL) salt
8 whole peppercorns
1 large tomato, diced
3-4 large potatoes, cubed
1 clove garlic, minced
1 tablespoon (15 mL) parsley, finely chopped
2 red peppers, chopped

Place cubed meat in a large soup pot. Cover with cold water and bring to a boil. Simmer for 5 minutes. Drain well. Rinse meat in more water and blot dry. Using half the butter and oil, brown cubed meat. Set aside. In a separate saucepan, heat rest of butter and oil and brown onion. Sprinkle with paprika and cook 10 minutes over low heat while stirring. Transfer to soup pot and add 1 cup ($^1/_4$ L) of cold water. Cover and stew for 20 minutes. Add celery, carrots, peppers and enough water to barely cover. Cook for 30 minutes. Stir in salt, peppercorns, tomato, potatoes and cook until potatoes are tender. Lastly, with heat off, add red peppers and cover allowing peppers to soften in hot goulash. Just before serving, sprinkle with chopped parsley.

Serves 10.

Margaret A. Dvorsky
Slovak World Congress
Executive Vice President
Keswick, Ontario, Canada

BEST BEEF STEW EVER!
Najlepšia dusená hovädzina vždycky!

2 pounds (900 g) lean stewing beef
¼ cup (35 g) flour
2 tablespoons (30 mL) oil
2 teaspoons (10 mL) salt
¼ teaspoon (1.25 mL) basil
¼ teaspoon (1.25 mL) pepper
2 (8 ounce) (225 g) cans tomato paste or tomato sauce
2 cups (½ L) hot water
6 of each of the following: small carrots, onions, potatoes, pared and quartered
1 cup (¼ L) celery, sliced

Cut beef into 1 inch (2.5 cm) cubes and coat with flour. In a large heavy sauce pan or skillet, brown beef in hot oil. Stir in water, tomato paste or sauce, and seasonings. Cover and simmer for 1½ hours. Add vegetables and simmer until done, about 45 minutes.

Serves 6.

Benjamin Gombar
Saginaw, Michigan   U.S.A.

BEEF STROGANOFF
Hovädzia kastriola

2 pounds (900 g) round steak, cut in strips
3 teaspoons (15 mL) oil
1½ cups (3½ dL) chopped onion
1 clove garlic, mashed
2 tablespoons (20 g) flour
1½ cups (3½ dL) sliced celery
8 ounce can (224 g) tomato sauce
10 ounce can (280 g) mushrooms, undrained
1 teaspoon (5 mL) salt
¼ teaspoon (1.25 mL) pepper
1 cup (¼ L) sour cream
1 teaspoon (5 mL) Worcestershire sauce

Brown meat in oil in large fry pan. Add onion and garlic and cook until soft. Stir in flour. Add celery, tomato sauce, mushrooms and liquid, sour cream, salt, pepper and Worcestershire sauce. Mix thoroughly. Turn into greased 2 quart (2 L) casserole. Bake uncovered at 300°F (150°C) for 2 hours. Stir every half hour. May need to cover for last half hour. May be made day before and reheated.

Serves 6.

Irene Timko
Slovak Domovina Dancers
Slovak World Congress
Heritage, Culture Commission, Sec.
Windsor, Ontario, Canada

MOM'S SAUERKRAUT GOULASH
Mamičkin kapustný guláš

1½ pounds (675 g) lean pork and veal cubes
1 onion, minced
3 tablespoons (30 g) flour
1 large can (766 g) sauerkraut
1 pint (½ L) sour cream
1 tablespoon (15 mL) oil, for frying
Pepper, salt, paprika, caraway seed, to taste
1 cup (¼ L) stock

Sprinkle meat with pepper, salt and paprika. Sauté onion until transparent. Add meat. Stir fry or slow cook for 1 hour or until tender. Rinse sauerkraut. Add to meat. Add stock and simmer for 30 minutes. Mix sour cream and flour together. Add to simmering meat and sauerkraut. Cook for 2-3 minutes.

Serves 4.

Olivia Kona
Beaconsfield, Quebec, Canada

BAKED LAMB - EASTER
Pečená jahňacina

1¼ - 1½ pounds (600 g) lamb meat
2 ounces (60 g) lard, fat
3 cloves garlic
Salt

Before baking lamb, remove skin and fat, and par boil meat a few minutes. Remove meat from hot water immediately and immerse in cold water, washing meat quickly and thoroughly. This process eliminates the strong pervasive quality of lamb.

Salt meat, rub well with garlic and let stand about 20 minutes. In a roasting pan, heat the fat and place meat in pan to bake.
In a preheated oven, bake at 350°F (180°C) until tender and done, basting frequently.
When baked, slice and serve with baked or mashed potatoes, or with cabbage.
Lamb was eaten most frequently at Easter.

Serves 4-6.

PhDr. Zora Mintalová
Slovenské Národné Múzeum
Martin, Slovakia

ROAST LEG OF LAMB
Pečená baranina

6 pounds (2¾ kg) leg of lamb
4 garlic cloves, cut in half
½ teaspoon (2.5 mL) rosemary
Salt, pepper, for seasoning
Oil
Parsley Sprigs

Wash meat and pat dry. Rub with oil, insert garlic slivers into meat. Sprinkle with salt, pepper, and rosemary. With fat side up, place lamb in a shallow roasting pan and roast in a preheated oven 350°F (180°C) for about 2 hours or until done, about 30 minutes per pound. Add parsley sprigs when serving.

DOUGH COVERED MEAT BALLS
Fašírky obalené v ceste

3 cups (600 g) mashed potatoes
1¹/₂ cups (210 g) flour
1 egg, beaten slightly
1 cup (200 g) cooked, left over meat, finely ground
¹/₂ cup (100 g) smoked bacon, chopped
1 onion, chopped
Salt, pepper
1 tablespoon (15 mL) fat

Use any left over cooked meat such as chicken, pork, ham or cooked ground beef. Sauté chopped onion in fat until lightly golden. Add half of the onion to finely ground meat, season with salt and pepper. Cook potatoes in skins, peel and mash. Add flour and egg. Knead into dough.

Take a spoonful of meat and roll dough around, forming a ball. Cook in boiling salted water until tender. Fry chopped bacon, add remaining onion and sprinkle meat balls upon serving.

A. Lakota
Teplická, Bratislava
Slovakia

GRANDMA'S SLOVAK PORK CHOPS
Starej mamky Slovenské bravčové kare

Oil for frying
1¹/₂ pounds (675 g) pork chops
¹/₂ cup (70 g) flour
1 large can (about 766 g) sauerkraut, stewed
4 tart apples, peeled and chopped
Salt, pepper, garlic, marjoram, to taste

Pound pork chops thin. Sprinkle with seasonings. Dredge chops in flour. Brown in oil in frying pan. Place chops in baking pan with apples and sauerkraut. Bake at 350°F (180°C) for 20 minutes.

Serves 4-5.

Olivia Kona
Beaconsfield, Quebec, Canada

EASTER MEAT LOAF
Veľkonočná plnina-sekanina

2 pounds (900 g) boneless veal
1 pound (450 g) boneless pork
6 eggs, well beaten
1 teaspoon (5 mL) salt
¼ cup (½ dL) fresh chives, chopped
1 loaf bread (day-old preferred), crumbled
Pepper, to taste
1 small cake (21 g) yeast
1 cup (¼ L) milk

Boil meats, covered with water, until tender. Drain and cool. Grind meat in a coarse grinder. Add salt, chives, and crumbled bread. Dissolve yeast in milk, add beaten eggs. Add this mixture to the meat mixture and blend together to consistency of moist meat loaf. Bake in greased 8x13 inch (20x33 cm) pan at 400°F (205°C) for 1 hour or until top is brown and crusty. Cut into squares and serve either hot or cold.

Sister M. Annette, V.S.C.
Pittsburgh, Pennsylvania, U.S.A.

EASTER MEAT LOAF
Veľkonočná mäsová sekanica

1 pound (450 g) pork shoulder
2 pounds (900 g) boneless veal
½ pound (225 g) ham or smoked meat
1 tablespoon (15 mL) salt
Pepper, to taste
1 tablespoon (15 mL) marjoram
1 medium onion
Fresh parsley
½ cup (1 dL) celery
¼ cup (½ dL) chives
2 medium cloves garlic
¼ pound (115 g) saltine crackers
6 eggs, beaten
Butter

Cook all meat, salt, pepper and marjoram in large kettle until well done. Cool and drain reserving broth. Grind meat, onion, parsley, celery, chives and garlic. Soak crackers in broth. Drain through a colander. Reserve broth. Combine meat and crackers in large bowl. Add eggs, mix well. Place in a buttered loaf pan, dot with butter. Bake at 350°F (180°C) for 1 hour or until golden brown. If loaf appears too dry, add some of the reserved broth over top.

Michael V. Hrifko
Union, New Jersey, U.S.A.

MEAT LOAF WITH CHEESE FILLING
Mäsový bochník

1 pound (450 g) ground meat, pork and beef
2 slices bread
3 eggs
½ cup (1 dL) milk
½ cup (100 g) dry cheese, grated (Edam)
½ pound (225 g) dry cottage cheese or farmer's cheese
1 clove garlic, minced
1 small onion, minced
Seasoned salt, freshly ground pepper, to taste
Parsley flakes, chopped
2 tablespoons (20 g) butter
Bread crumbs

Soak bread in milk, squeeze out liquid; mix bread into meat. Add 2 eggs, grated cheese, garlic, onion, salt and pepper; mix well.
In a bread loaf pan which has been greased with butter and coated with bread crumbs, layer one half of the meat mixture in bottom of pan.
Combine cottage cheese with remaining egg. Piquantly season with salt and pepper. Add chopped parsley, and mix well.
Spread cottage cheese over layer of meat. Spread remaining meat mixture over cottage cheese. Dab a little butter across top and bake in hot oven 375°F (190°C) until done.

Anna Škovierová
Očova, Slovakia

BEGGAR'S PORRIDGE
Žobrácka kaša

2¼ pounds (1000 g) hog head
1⅛ pounds (500 g) lungs and heart
2½ tablespoons (40 g) lard or fat
¼ cup (50 g) onion, chopped
Garlic, minced, to taste
½ cup (100 g) rice
Marjoram, pinch
Salt and pepper, to taste

In a kettle, cook (cleaned and washed) hog head, lungs and heart in enough water to cover meat. When done, debone meat and grind all cooked ingredients.
Sauté onion and minced garlic in lard or other fat.
In a small sauce pan, cook rice adding enough water to cover.
Combine meats, onion, garlic, rice, marjoram, and salt and pepper to taste. Mix well, adding some liquid from cooked meat to make a moist mixture. Bake in a greased baking dish until thoroughly baked through.

This kaša was customarily prepared throughout villages during the winter season when piglets were being slaughtered.
Žobrácká kaša belongs to the so-called "slaughtering" specialties along with the various types of klobásy.

PhDr. Zora Mintalová
Slovenské Národné Múzeum
Martin, Slovakia

HAM
Hrianky

All fat left over from a holiday ham, cubed
All lean meat left over from same ham
1 sliced onion, medium size
1 small bunch watercress, chopped
1 large onion, chopped
Red pepper (paprika)

Render the cubed fat in a fry pan until nearly done. Add sliced onion and continue to fry until onion is golden. Add ham meat into the fry pan and stir to heat everything evenly. Ham needs not be cooked; only heated. Remove the ingredients from the pan leaving only the drippings. Mix chopped onions and watercress, and put over bread. Add the meat over the bread and lightly pepper. Eat as an open-face sandwich.

After the holiday ham was served, the fat and leftover meat was separated and cubed in preparation to make "hrianky". "Hrianky" means something heated. Nowadays this preparation can be frozen and stored for future use. This was good at any time, but especially as a Sunday breakfast, which was usually prepared by the father of the family. This was a specialty always, even now in the John Sterbinsky family. The watercress would be picked in the woods near a spring of fresh water. Our Dad planted hot peppers, and at harvest time dried them and crushed them into paprika.

George Sterbinsky
Edwardsville, Pennsylvania
U.S.A.

HAM AND BACON - HOME CURING
Šunka, slanina - domáca, zasolená a udená

Our parents did not have a refrigerator in their homes in Europe so they prepared their meats for storage by salt curing. Every year during the late fall they would purchase a hog, if they did not raise one during the year, and they would process the meat to meet their needs for the winter.

The hams and bacon were rubbed with ground garlic and salt. This was called a "dry process". Every other day for 3 to 4 weeks this meat was removed from the wooden tub and alternated from bottom pieces to the top, and top pieces to the bottom. In this way no piece would be too long in the accumulated water at the bottom. When the meat was cured by the salt treatment, it was cleaned, dried and smoked.

After this process is complete, the meat can be hung at room temperature, in the cellar, for many months and still be edible.

George Sterbinsky
Edwardsville, Pennsylvania
U.S.A.

FRIED HAMBURGERS
Pražené fašírky

1 pound (450 g) ground pork
2 cups ($1/2$ L) bread crumbs
1 large onion, minced
1 egg, beaten
Salt, pepper to taste
Oil, for frying

Mix meat with 1 cup ($1/4$ L) bread crumbs, onion, salt and pepper. Add beaten egg and mix together. Mold $1/2$ cup (1 dL) meat mixture into an oblong size patty. Roll gently in remaining 1 cup ($1/4$ L) bread crumbs. Fry hamburgers in $1/2$ inch ($1 1/4$ cm) hot oil on medium flame till golden brown on both sides.

Makes 6 servings.

Dorothy Rygiel
New Jersey   U.S.A.

GOVERNOR GEORGE V. VOINOVICH'S PORK CHOPS WITH APPLES
Bravčové rezne s jablkami

8 loin pork chops
Salt
Pepper
½ cup (1 dL) apple juice or cider
3 tablespoons (45 mL) catsup
½ cup (1 dL) soy sauce
½ cup (1 dL) brown sugar
2 tablespoons (30 mL) cornstarch
½ teaspoon (2.5 mL) ginger
2 apples, Golden Delicious

Bake pork chops with salt and pepper in single roasting pan, uncovered for 30 minutes at 350°F (180°C). Turn chops over.

Combine juice, catsup, soy sauce, brown sugar, cornstarch and ginger. Cook over medium heat until thickened. Spoon some juice from roasting pan into sauce to thin.

Core apples; cut into rings. Place one ring on each chop; pour sauce over. Bake 30 minutes longer. Baste several times.

Serve with rice and broccoli.

I am sure the Slovak World Congress Cookbook will be a fitting dedication to the observance of Slovakia's independence.

As your fraternal brother, I would like to thank you for this opportunity to be a part of Slovak-American history in the State of Ohio and the United States of America. It is truly a pleasure to see the heritage and traditions of our common Slavic ancestries preserved in this cookbook for future generations.

Best wishes and God bless you, the members, and families of the Slovak World Congress.

The Honorable
George V. Voinovich, Governor
State of Ohio, U.S.A.

PORK ROAST WITH SAUERKRAUT AND DUMPLINGS
Pečená bravčovina v kyslej kapuste s haluškami

1 pork roast
Caraway seeds
Salt
Sauerkraut
Onion
Sugar

Dumplings:
3 large potatoes
1 egg
1 teaspoon (5 mL) salt
1 cup (140 g) flour

Pork Roast: Score fat, sprinkle caraway seeds and seasoned salt over roast. Pour a little hot water over pork and roast in moderate oven.

Sauerkraut: Drain, cook for an hour in small amount of water. Add caraway seeds. Thicken with grated potato juice. Leave covered.

Dumplings: Grate potatoes. Drain juice and reserve for thickening sauerkraut. Combine grated potatoes, egg, salt and flour. Use more flour if necessary. In a large pot filled with boiling water, drop mixture by tablespoonful. Cook the large dumplings for 15 minutes (for smaller dumplings, cook 10 minutes).

In a frying pan, pour drippings from roast and sauté minced onion, until brown. Add a little sugar and combine with sauerkraut.

In memory of husband,
Jim Koscak.

Marge Koscak
Parma, Ohio   U.S.A.

MINCEMEAT COUNTRY-STYLE RIBS
Rebrovina

4 pounds (1³/₄ kg) country style ribs
1 teaspoon (5 mL) salt
1 onion
Water as needed
1¹/₂ cups (3¹/₂ dL) prepared mincemeat
1 can (10¹/₂ ounces) (294 g) condensed beef broth
1 beef bouillon cube
1 cup (¹/₄ L) water
2 tablespoons (30 mL) vinegar

Place ribs in pot, cover with water. Add salt and onion. Bring to boil. Lower heat and cook for 1¹/₂ hours or until tender. Drain the ribs. Place ribs in roasting pan. Combine minced meat, vinegar, broth and bouillon cube, dissolved in water, and mix well. Pour over ribs in pan. Bake uncovered 30 minutes at 350°F (180°C). Baste occasionally. Serve with potatoes and vegetables of your choice.

Makes 4-6 servings.

I won first prize for this recipe in the 1979 Pioneer Press Cook-off competition.

Martha Mistina Kona
Slovak World Congress
Heritage and Culture Commission, Chairperson
Wilmette, Illinois U.S.A.

SAUERKRAUT WITH HOMEMADE SAUSAGE
Kapustnica s klobásou

(An European recipe prepared for Christmas Eve)

1 pound (450 g) sauerkraut
¼ pound (115 g) dried mushrooms
Head of carp (from Christmas Eve fish)
2 tablespoons (40 g) fat, oil or lard
1 tablespoon (10 g) flour
1 onion, chopped
Salt, pepper, to taste
1 teaspoon (5 mL) paprika
1¼ cups (3 dL) sour cream
Homemade sausage

Chop sauerkraut into smaller bits; cover with water, add salt, and simmer. Wash mushrooms, rinse with hot water, chop into small bits. Add mushrooms to sauerkraut. Cook the head of a carp separately in a pan of water. When cooked, strain liquid into sauerkraut; debone carp and chop meat into bits. Add carp to sauerkraut and simmer. Heat fat, add flour and onions and sauté until browned. Remove from heat, add paprika; mix into sauerkraut. Stir in sour cream to sweeten the taste of sauerkraut. Serve with homemade cooked sausage.

FRANKFURTERS WITH SAUERKRAUT
Parky s kyslou kapustou

½ cup (1 dL) margarine
1 pound (450 g) sauerkraut
1 large onion, chopped
3 tablespoons (45 mL) brown sugar
1 teaspoon (5 mL) caraway seeds
8 frankfurters

In a skillet, melt margarine, add onions and caraway seed; sauté until golden and tender. Add brown sugar and sauerkraut. Make spiral slashes lengthwise across each frankfurter, arrange on top of sauerkraut, cover and simmer for 20-25 minutes. Serve on sausage rolls; or serve with mashed potatoes.

European Slovak recipe

PORK SAUSAGE
Hurka

1 pork liver, whole, raw
3 pounds (1^1/$_3$ kg) pork butts (do not use lung, spleen and the lacy, veil-like lining of butchered hog)
6 pounds (2^2/$_3$ kg) rice
6 medium onions
1 tablespoon (15 mL) marjoram
^{3}/$_4$ tablespoons (30 mL) ground allspice
2 tablespoons (30 mL) black pepper
3 tablespoons (45 mL) salt
25 feet (about 8 meters) hog casing, well cleaned

Boil pork butts until done; cool. Boil rice until well done.
Finely grind pork and liver and put in pot with rice. Grind onion and add to pot. Sprinkle all seasonings over above mixtures and mix thoroughly.
Stuff mixture into hog casings and tie ends. Boil hurka for approximately 45 minutes. Can be eaten cold or hot.

George Sterbinsky
Edwardsville, Pennsylvania
U.S.A.

SAUSAGE
Klobása

- 5 pounds (2¼ kg) ground pork butts, grind coarse
- 3 or 4 cloves garlic, medium size
- 3 tablespoons (45 mL) salt
- 3 teaspoons (15 mL) black pepper
- 1 teaspoon (5 mL) red pepper
- 10 feet (3 meters) hog casings, well cleaned

Chop or grind garlic to a fine consistency; sprinkle seasoning over the ground pork. Spread ground garlic evenly over the ground pork. Mix thoroughly by hand. Put meat mixture into a sausage stuffer and fill the hog casing. Tie sausage ends with string. When the klobása is made, it can be smoked in a "smoker" or smokehouse.

Preparation for eating: Simmer in boiling water for approximately ½ hour. Sausage can be eaten hot or cold. If preferred not smoked, prepare the same way for eating, or make patties instead of using sausage casing.

Our Sokol pioneer, Frank Sterbinsky, was an apprentice butcher as a teenager in Slovakia, then Austria-Hungary. He butchered hogs in Slovakia and in this country with his brother, John, not only for their own families, but also for other families in their neighborhood. They also made klobásy, hurky, and presmong (hog headcheese) (tlačenka-sviňačina). They cured their own hams and bacon and taught the neighbors and others these curing skills. These recipes were traditional tastes and are in use by their children and grandchildren, particularly the sons and grandsons of John Sterbinsky.

George Sterbinsky
Edwardsville, Pennsylvania, U.S.A.

SAUERKRAUT AND SAUSAGE
Kyslá kapusta s klobásou

- 32 ounces (896 g) sauerkraut, drained
- 2 pounds (900 g) sausage, cut into 1 inch (2.5 cm) chunks
- 1 tablespoon (15 mL) bacon fat
- 1 medium onion, chopped
- 1/8 teaspoon (.6 mL) caraway seeds
- 1 small apple, peeled and chopped
- 1 1/2 tablespoons (22.5 mL) brown sugar
- 1 potato, peeled and diced
- 1/8 teaspoon (.6 mL) red pepper, crushed
- 2 cloves garlic, minced
- 1 cup (1/4 L) beer or wine

Heat oven at 350°F (180°C). Grease roasting pan with bacon fat. Combine all ingredients except sausage. Mix well and roast for 1 hour. Add sausage and roast for 20-25 minutes longer.

Note: The sauerkraut and sausage taste much better when reheated the next day.

Optional: Sauerkraut can be rinsed first, then drained.

Benjamin Gombar
Saginaw, Michigan U.S.A.

SENATOR MIKE DE WINE'S FAVORITE SAUSAGE, GRAVY AND BISCUITS
Senátora Michala obľúbená klobása v omáčke na biskvite

1 pound (450 g) bulk sausage
½ cup (70 g) flour
2-3 cups (½-¾ L) cold milk
Margarine
Biscuits

Brown sausage in heavy skillet. Leave some bits to stick to bottom and brown. This gives good flavor and color to gravy. Remove browned sausage to plate. Leave about ¼ cup (½ dL) of drippings in skillet. If sausage is lean, add enough margarine to make the needed liquid.

To drippings, add the flour and stir over medium heat until bubbly. Add cold milk and stir over medium heat until thickened. Add reserved sausage to gravy and simmer 5-10 minutes more. Serve over hot biscuits.

Michael De Wine
United States Senator, Ohio
U.S. Senate Office
Washington, D.C. U.S.A.

SLOVAK POTATO SAUSAGE
Slovenské droby-zemiaková klobása

10 pounds (4^1/$_2$ kg) potatoes
1 pound (450 g) beef casings
1 pound (450 g) slab bacon
2 pounds (900 g) pork shoulder
2 pounds (900 g) smoked picnic ham, boiled
3 medium onions
2 tablespoons (30 mL) garlic salt
2 tablespoons (30 mL) black pepper
2 tablespoons (30 mL) marjoram (majoranka)
30-6 inch (15 cm) lengths of white cotton string

To prepare casings: Wash casings inside and out, cut into 15 inch (38^1/$_2$ cm) lengths. Tie one end of each casing with a length of string. Set aside.

Grind bacon (using second from smallest grinder) and fry. Remove from frying pan with slotted spoon and place in a large kettle. Grind onions (using same grinder) and fry in skillet with bacon grease. Add onions and grease to bacon. Grind pork shoulder, fry and add to the above. Grind smoked picnic ham (boil ham before hand, do not use canned or luncheon ham) and add to the above, mixing well.

Wash and peel potatoes, quarter them and grind. Add to the above mixture. Add seasonings and mix well. Stuff casings solid, gently but firmly, leaving no air pockets. Work quickly because potatoes will start to turn dark when exposed to air. Tie off other casing end.

Bring a large kettle of water (filled a little more than half way) to a boil. When boiling, reduce heat to a low simmer. Prick all sausages about four or five times with a needle (this keeps them from bursting while simmering). Place about 5 or 6 sausages at a time in the kettle, cover, and let simmer slowly for about 20-25 minutes. When all sausages are cooked, spread out and let cool. Place in freezer bags or paper and freeze until needed.

To cook: Place sausage in very lightly greased baking dish and bake at 325°F-350°F (160°C-180°C), about 30 minutes on each side, so they cook slowly but the casings get nice and crusty.

Magdalena Jahelka Klimek
Lockport, Illinois U.S.A.

SLOVAK SAUSAGE
Slovenská klobása

10 pounds (4½ kg)
    boneless pork butts
For every 5 pounds
    (2¼ kg) pork, use
    1 pound (450 g) beef.
    If pork is fatty use
    2 pounds (900 g) beef
3 tablespoons (45 mL) salt
3 tablespoons (45 mL) sugar
2 tablespoons (30 mL)
    black pepper
1 teaspoon (5 mL) or more,
    garlic powder
1½ tablespoons (22.5 mL)
    marjoram
1 cup (140 g) powdered dry
    milk (optional)

Coarsely grind meat. Combine all ingredients and add to meat, mixing well. Let marinate over night in the refrigerator. Mix again and stuff into rinsed casings. Sausage will stuff much easier by adding about 1 cup (¼ L) cold water.) Tastes great fresh or smoked. Klobása tastes best when roasted in oven at 350°F (180°C) for not longer than 40 minutes.

Note: powdered soy bean filler can be substituted for powdered dry milk.

Benjamin Gombar
Saginaw, Michigan U.S.A.

SLOVAK KLOBÁSY AND SAUERKRAUT (COOKED WITH BEER)
Slovenská klobása s kapustou (varená s pivom)

2 pounds (900 g) klobásy
2 large cans (2-764 g)
    sauerkraut, drained
Salt, pepper to taste
Garlic and onion salt
1 cup (¼ L) tomato
    juice (V-8)
1 can (12 ounces)
    (355 mL) beer, any brand
1 tablespoon (15 mL)
    butter
2 tablespoons (20 g) flour

Arrange sauerkraut in a roaster or Dutch oven or a heavy 9x13 inch (23x33 cm) pan; add beer to cover, add seasonings, and tomato juice. Cover and simmer 1 hour. Melt butter in a small skillet, stir in flour and brown well. Add 1 cup (¼ L) juice from sauerkraut, cook and stir until thickened. Stir back into sauerkraut, add klobásy; simmer covered 1½ - 2 hours.

Mrs. Joseph F. Kopachko
Smock, Pennsylvania U.S.A.

A SLOVAK TEXAN'S KIELBASA, CABBAGE, POTATO SUPPER
Slovenská Teksanská večera, klobása, kapusta so zemiakmi

1½ or 2 kielbasa links
1 medium onion, sliced
1 medium head cabbage
4 medium size potatoes
Salt and pepper to taste
1 cup (¼ L) water

Slice or quarter washed head of cabbage into electric skillet. Arrange on top of cabbage, onion, kielbasa links and sliced potatoes. Salt and pepper cabbage and potatoes to taste. Add 1 cup (¼ L) water. Cover and cook until cabbage and potatoes are completely cooked.

Note: Depending on your electric skillet, enough water should be added just to keep ingredients steaming and moist.

Yields approximately 6 servings.

Mary Kay Ritchie
Garland, Texas U.S.A.

BREAD STUFFING WITH SAUSAGE
Chlebová plnka s klobásou

6 stalks celery, sliced very thin
2 medium onions, diced
¼ cup (½ dL) fresh parsley, chopped
1 egg
½ pound (225 g) bulk "country" sausage
½ pound (225 g) "country" sausage, in casings
(Do Not Use Italian Sausage)
2 loaves of dried bread
2 cups (½ L) chicken broth
½ stick (60 g) margarine
Pinch of sage
Pinch of thyme

Break bread into 1 inch (2.5 cm) squares. Brown bulk sausage and drain, saving some grease to lightly sauté the onions and celery. In a large container, add bread, browned sausage, egg, celery, onions, parsley, margarine, thyme, sage, and chicken broth. Stir all ingredients until mixed thoroughly. Place in a 4 quart (4 L) casserole baking dish, patting mixture down to eliminate air pockets. Place remaining sausage, in casings, on top of stuffing and cover with a lid. Bake at 350°F (180°C) for 1 hour, or until the top sausage is done.

Serves 8.

Robert J. Dvoroznak
Bay Village, Ohio   U.S.A.

BETTY'S STUFFED CABBAGE
Betkiná plnená kapusta

1 large or medium cabbage
2 large onions, chopped
2 tablespoons (30 mL) fat
1½ pounds (675 g) ground chuck
¼ pound (115 g) ground pork
1 teaspoon (5 mL) salt
½ teaspoon (2.5 mL) pepper
½ cup (1 dL) rice
2 eggs
1 can (10 ¾ ounces) (305 g) tomato soup, undiluted
1 quart (1 L) tomato juice
1 cup (¼ L) tomato sauce

Brown onions in melted fat in skillet. Cover rice with water and partially cook. Mix ground chuck and pork, add salt and pepper, eggs, onions and partly cooked rice. Mix well. Remove core from cabbage to loosen leaves. Place in large pot filled with water and let boil till leaves soften and come off. Cool cabbage leaves. Place small amount of meat mixture in each leaf, roll up and tuck in ends. Arrange cabbage rolls in greased baking dish, add tomato juice, sauce and soup, bake in preheated oven about 1½ hours at 325°F (160°C).

Betty Williams
Youngstown, Ohio   U.S.A.

DOROTHY'S STUFFED CABBAGE
Dorotkiné holubky

1½ pounds (675 g) ground meat (half beef and half pork)
3½-4 pounds (1½ - 1¾ kg) cabbage
2 cups (½ L) cooked rice
1½ large onions, minced
½ pound (225 g) margarine
24 ounces (672 g) tomato sauce
4 whole bay leaves
8 whole all spice
Salt and pepper

Loosen core of cabbage and steam in boiling water until semiwilted. (If using microwave oven, place cabbage in bowl with 3 inches (7½ cm) water and cover with plastic wrap. Microwave on high for about 20 minutes. Keep loosening cabbage leaves from core as they get tender.)

Melt margarine and sauté onion until golden. Mix ground meat, cooked rice, onion, salt and pepper. Place tender steamed cabbage leaf in palm of hand with core stem lengthwise. Fill leaf with 1 tablespoon (15 mL) meat mixture at base of leaf and roll. Tuck in both loose ends. Place in roaster in alternating rows. Cover stuffed cabbage with tomato sauce. Tuck bay leaves and allspice among cabbage rolls. Cover roasting pan and bake at 350°F (180°C) for about 3 hours or until pierced easily with fork.

Dorothy Rygiel
New Jersey   U.S.A.

STUFFED CABBAGE
Plnená kapusta

1 1/2 pounds (675 g) ground beef
1 pound (450 g) ground pork
1 head cabbage
4 tablespoons (60 mL) fat (oil, lard, or bacon fat)
2 cups (1/2 L) tomato soup and 16 ounces (450 g) can tomatoes or sauce
1 cup (1/4 L) uncooked long grain rice
1 large onion, minced
2 cloves garlic
1 tablespoon (15 mL) paprika
Salt, pepper
2-3 tablespoons (1/4 dL) milk
4 cups (1L) sauerkraut, rinsed

Cut out core of cabbage and loosen leaves. In a deep pot place cabbage in boiling, salted water and simmer (10-15 minutes) until leaves soften slightly. (Do not overcook). Separate cabbage leaves and trim off spine. In a heavy skillet, sauté onion until softened. Add paprika, garlic, rice, and simmer for a few minutes, covered, adding a few tablespoons of water as needed. Add ground meat, salt, pepper, milk and mix well. Fill cabbage leaves with rice/meat mixture by rolling leaf over meat and tucking in ends. In a pot, layer bottom with sauerkraut and place rolls, seam side down. Alternate layers of kraut and rolls and if any cabbage is left over, shred and add to top layer. Cover with tomato soup, sauce or canned tomatoes. Add enough water to barely cover rolls. Simmer slowly for 1 1/2 to 2 hours, or until rice and meat are done. Rolls may also be baked in roaster or baking dish by placing holubky in alternate layers with sauerkraut and covering with tomato liquid. Bake in 300°F (150°C) oven for 1 1/2 to 2 hours or until rice and meat is tender.

Serves 8-10.

DeSanto Family
Poland, Ohio U.S.A.

STUFFED CABBAGE
Plnená kapusta na cibuli a v paprike

5 pounds (2 1/4 kg) ground chuck
1-1 1/2 pounds (675 g) onions, grated
3/4 pound (340 g) white rice
2 tablespoons (30 mL) Accent (seasoned salt)
1 cup (250 mL) hot water
5 eggs
Garlic powder
Salt

Mix all the above ingredients together.

3 heads cabbage
1 1/2 pounds (675 g) chopped onions
1 teaspoon (5 mL) salt
2 green peppers, chopped
1 teaspoon (5 mL) garlic salt
1 large can (780 g) sauerkraut
1 large can (780 g) tomato purée sauce
2 tablespoons (30 mL) sugar

After scalding and separating cabbage leaves, roll meat mixture into larger leaves. Set aside. Chop excess cabbage leaves or small leaves. In bottom of electric roaster, put 1/2 of chopped cabbage, 1/2 can sauerkraut and juice, 1/2 of the chopped green peppers, 3/4 of the chopped onions, salt, sugar, and garlic salt. Add cabbage rolls on top of this mixture. Over cabbage rolls, layer remaining onions, peppers, sauerkraut, and chopped cabbage. Do not add more salt or sugar. Pour purée sauce on top. Cover just to top of cabbage with hot water. Cook till tender.

Note: Rolls can be cooked in large cooking pot on top of stove on low heat to prevent leaves from coming undone.

Gerry Benya
Farrell, Pennsylvania U.S.A.

STUFFED CABBAGE
Holubky

¾ pound (340 g) ground chuck
¼ pound (115 g) ground sausage
1 egg
3 tablespoons (45 mL) rice
2 tablespoons (¼ dL) butter
1 small onion
1 clove garlic
1 tablespoon (15 mL) ketchup
1 head cabbage
1 can tomato sauce
Dill pickle juice, (optional)

Combine meat, salt, pepper and rice. Sauté onion and garlic in butter until nice and brown. Add onion mixture and ketchup to meat and mix well. Cover cabbage leaves and cook in boiling water about 5 minutes. Drain. Place small handful of meat mixture in a cabbage leaf. Roll up and tuck in ends. Place rolls in bottom of Dutch oven. Pour tomato sauce and add enough water to cover rolls.

For an exciting new taste, add dill pickle juice.

Simmer for about 2½ hours or bake in 350°F (180°C) oven for 2 hours.

In memory of
Mrs. Katherine Sarosy Machuga

Helen Machuga Livesay
Struthers, Ohio   U.S.A.

STUFFED CABBAGE
Holubky

3 pounds (1¹/₃ kg) head of cabbage
1 can (16 ounces) (450 g) sauerkraut (optional: drain juice)
12 ounces (336 g) ground beef
12 ounces (336 g) ground turkey (optional)
1 tablespoon (15 mL) butter or margarine
3 cans (8 ounce each) (3-224 g) tomato sauce
1 small onion, diced
1¹/₂ cups (3¹/₂ dL) rice
1 tablespoon (15 mL) salt
Pepper to taste
3 nice slices pork shoulder, well trimmed and cut in small pieces

Place butter or margarine in fry pan, add onion and cook until tender. Combine the ground meat, rice, onion, salt and pepper and half a can of tomato sauce. Mix all ingredients together and set aside. Boil the cabbage slowly and remove the rough outer leaves as they become loose, and allow to cool. In a large Dutch oven, place the leftover leaves and half a can of sauerkraut on the bottom. Take a small portion of the meat mixture, approximately 1 tablespoon (15 mL), and place in center of cabbage leaf. Roll up loosely and place over sauerkraut in Dutch oven. Proceed with all the cabbage leaves, and place side by side in pot. Add the pork and cover the leaves with the rest of the sauerkraut. Add the tomato sauce, cover and bring to a boil. Lower the heat and allow to simmer for approximately 1¹/₄ hours until meat and cabbage are tender.

Mary Skyba
Murray Hill, New Jersey U.S.A.

STUFFED CABBAGE
Plnená kapusta

1 large head of cabbage
1½ pounds (675 g) ground round
½ pound (225 g) lean ground pork
3 cups (¾ L) uncooked rice
46 ounces (1.36 L) tomato juice
1 teaspoon (5 mL) salt
Dash of pepper

Core cabbage and put in boiling water for 5 to 10 minutes. Separate leaves with a fork and set aside in a bowl. Mix uncooked rice, meat, salt and pepper in a separate bowl. Open a leaf of cabbage and starting at the end where the core was, fill with a large spoonful of filling and roll into a ball. Proceed as above until all filling is used. Then put cabbage rolls (and remaining cabbage, if any is left, chopped up) in a large pot, cover with juice and cook on slow heat (after rolls reach boiling point) for 40 minutes.

Helen Klimek Ward
Lockport, Illinois U.S.A.

STUFFED CABBAGE
Holubky

1 pound (450 g) ground chuck
1 pound (450 g) ground pork
1 head cabbage
1 medium onion, chopped
3 tablespoons (45 mL) bacon drippings
1 teaspoon (5 mL) salt
1 teaspoon (5 mL) paprika
1 teaspoon (5 mL) parsley
1 cup (¼ L) rice
1 clove garlic, chopped fine
1 quart (450 g) canned tomatoes
1 can (450 g) sauerkraut
1 quart (1 L) tomato juice
Bacon or klobásy
Water
Bay leaf

Sauté onion in bacon drippings; add minced garlic, stir well and cook until tender. Add salt and paprika. To meat mixture, add the sautéed onion, garlic, and parsley and rice. Mix well.

Core cabbage and boil until partially cooked. Drain and separate leaves. Trim thick veins off of cabbage leaves with a sharp paring knife. Cut any remaining torn or small pieces of cabbage into small pieces and put in the bottom of the cooking pot.

Place about ½ cup (1 dL) of the meat mixture into a cabbage leaf and roll up tightly tucking in the ends. The amount of meat used per leaf will depend upon the size of the cabbage leaf.

Pour half of the tomatoes into the cooking pot over the shredded cabbage. Line the pot with the rolled holubky. Rinse sauerkraut with water and squeeze off the excess. Put sauerkraut over top of rolls. Add strips of smoked bacon or klobásy for flavor. Pour over top remaining tomatoes and tomato juice. Add water if necessary to provide enough cooking liquid. Add bay leaf for additional flavor. Cook over medium heat until liquid boils; reduce heat and simmer for 1½ hours.

Martha Sarosy Zetts
Canfield, Ohio U.S.A.

STUFFED CABBAGE ROLLS
Plnená kapusta

1 large head of cabbage
3 pounds (approx.) (1¹/₃ kg) ground chuck
2 teaspoons (10 mL) salt
1 teaspoon (5 mL) pepper
1 medium onion, chopped
4 tablespoons (60 mL) shortening
1 large can (27.3 ounces) (765 g) crushed tomatoes
1 large can (27.4 ounces) (766 g) sauerkraut, drained
1 large can (46 fluid ounces) (1.36 L) tomato juice
¹/₂ cup (1 dL) rice

Steam cabbage and separate leaves. Boil rice. Sauté onion in shortening until slightly browned. Add onions, rice, salt and pepper to ground chuck and mix well. Fill cabbage leaves, roll, and close in the ends. In a large pot, layer rolls, tomatoes and sauerkraut, repeating layers. If any meat mixture is left over, roll into large size meatballs and place on top of cabbage rolls. Pour tomato juice over rolls and cook on top of stove over medium low heat for about 2¹/₂-3 hours.

Regina Bires Ostrowski
Campbell, Ohio U.S.A.

MUSHROOM CABBAGE ROLLS CASSEROLE
Kapusta plnená s hríbami, kastriola

8 cabbage leaves
1¹/₂ cups (300 g) mushrooms, cleaned, cut up
¹/₂ cup (100 g) onion, chopped
²/₃ cup (120 g) rice
¹/₄ cup (50 g) butter
¹/₄ cup (50 g) tomato sauce
1 teaspoon (5 mL) salt
¹/₂ teaspoon (2.5 mL) paprika
Water

(A meatless dish served on Christmas Eve)

Pour boiling water over cabbage leaves to wilt. In a saucepan, cook rice in water until semi-cooked. In a frying pan, sauté onion in butter until transparent, add paprika, salt, mushrooms and mix well. Add rice and tomato sauce and simmer about 3-5 minutes. Place small amount of mixture into cabbage leaves. Roll up and arrange in greased casserole. Add a little water, cover and bake at 350°F (180°C) for 20-30 minutes, or until rice is completely cooked.

CREAMED STUFFED PEPPERS
Paprika plnená

6 large red sweet peppers
Tops of red peppers, chopped
3/4 pound (340 g) ground pork
3/4 pound (340 g) ground beef
1 medium onion, grated
2 cloves garlic, minced
1/2 stick (57 g) butter
1 tablespoon (15 mL) red paprika
1/2 cup (1 dL) rice
1/2 teaspoon (2 1/2 mL) pepper
1/2 teaspoon (2 1/2 mL) salt, to taste
2 quarts (2 L) tomato juice
1 cup (1/4 L) water
2 bay leaves
1/2 pint (1/4 L) sour cream
2 tablespoons (20 g) flour, or more, depending on how thick of a sauce you want
3 teaspoons (15 mL) sugar, or to taste for desired sweetness

Wash peppers and cut off the tops. Cut off the stems and finely chop the pepper tops. Set aside. Clean seeds out of peppers and wash.

Melt butter in a small frying pan. Add minced garlic and grated onion, finely chopped pepper tops and paprika. Fry lightly.

Mix ground pork and beef with rice, salt, pepper. Add onion mixture and mix well. Stuff peppers and place in a large cooking pot. Heat tomato juice and pour over peppers, add bay leaves and cook for about 1 1/2-2 hours, slowly, on low heat.

When nearly done, mix in a bowl, the sour cream and flour until smooth; add sugar to taste. Remove bay leaves from cooking pot. Take some of the juice from the peppers and add to the cream mixture; stir thoroughly; then pour over the peppers and bring to a low boil.

Delicious served with mashed potatoes or halušky. Pour gravy over top of potatoes or halušky and also over peppers.

In memory of my father,
John J. Sarosy
Sandra Sarosy Duve
Colorado Springs, Colorado
U.S.A.

STUFFED TURKEY
Plnená morka

1 turkey
¼ pound (112 g) smoked bacon strips
Salt
½ cup (125 mL) fat
14½ ounce can (411 g) broth

Stuffing:
½ cup (112 g) smoked bacon, chopped
½ cup (1 dL) onion, chopped
½ cup (112 g) smoked ham, chopped
4 eggs, separated
1 loaf dry bread or 4 cups (1 L) croutons
1 cup (2 dL) broth
1 teaspoon (5 mL) salt
½ teaspoon (2.5 mL) nutmeg
2 tablespoons (30 mL) parsley, chopped
2 tablespoons (30 mL) almonds, finely chopped

Rub turkey with bacon strips. Sprinkle with salt. Fill with stuffing; place turkey in roasting pan. Pour hot fat across top and add soup stock (broth). Roast in moderately hot oven 325°F (160°C) until golden brown and tender. Baste occasionally with juices during roasting period.

Stuffing: Fry chopped bacon. Add chopped onion and chopped ham. Fry together; cool. Soak bread, or croutons, in hot broth. Add beaten egg yolks, salt, nutmeg. Add parsley, almonds, and meat mixture. Mix well. Beat egg whites stiff, and lightly fold into the stuffing mixture.

Ján Lakota
Teplická, Bratislava
Slovakia

VEAL AND CARAWAY SEED GOULASH
Kmínový guláš

2 pounds (900 g) diced veal
1½ teaspoons (7.5 mL) caraway seeds
5 medium onions, sliced
5 medium potatoes cut into chunks
1 tablespoon (15 mL) salt
1 tablespoon (15 mL) lard or oil
Water
Flour

Melt lard or oil in pot then simmer sliced onions. Add caraway seed after 5 minutes. Add veal and simmer approximately 45 minutes or until bottom of pot is brown. Then add 4 cups (1 L) water, and simmer till meat begins to be tender. Add 8 cups (2 L) water and 1 tablespoon (15 mL) salt. Add potato chunks and simmer again. After meat and potatoes are fork-tender, add 1 cup (¼ L) water with 2 forkfuls of flour beaten up into it and add to the pot.

Serve with thick slices of rye bread and ice cold beer.

Ilonka Martinka-Torres
Castro Valley, California   U.S.A.

VEAL PAPRIKA STEW AND DUMPLINGS WITH EGGS
Tel'acie mäso na paprike-halušky s vajcom

2¼ pounds (1000 g) veal, cubed
½ cup (1 dl) oil
1 medium red onion, finely chopped
1 tablespoon (15 mL)\ paprika
1 green pepper, cut in thin strips
1 tomato, sliced thin
1 pint (½ L) sour cream
2 tablespoons (20 g) flour
Salt
Tomato, sliced horizontally for garnish
Yellow sweet pepper, sliced horizontally for garnish
Fresh parsley flakes

Dumplings:
3½ cups (490 g) flour, or a little more
5 eggs
Oil, butter or margarine
Salt

Sauté onion in oil until a nice golden yellow. Add the paprika stirring continuously and pour in immediately a little water. When water evaporates and onion turns golden brown, add meat, cut into cubes of equal size. Season with salt; cover and cook slowly. When the meat begins to become tender, add thin strips of green pepper and sliced tomato. In a separate bowl, blend sour cream and flour until smooth; add to simmering meat and stir in gently. Simmer for a few more minutes at moderate temperature until done and almost boiling.

Dumplings with eggs: Prepare dough for the dumplings by mixing flour, two eggs, a little water and some salt. Chop the dough into boiling, slightly salted water. When the dumplings are cooked, strain, rinse in tepid water and drain again. Beat and salt the remaining three eggs until light. Heat a little butter, margarine or oil in a pan, put in the dumplings, and when they are hot, add the beaten eggs. Keep mixture on the stove until it thickens like a soft omelette.

Drizzle sauce over dumplings and stew, garnish with sliced tomato and pepper rings. Sprinkle with fresh parsley flakes. A very elegant and delicious company dinner served with fresh asparagus spears and a cucumber salad in dilled vinaigrette dressing. Serves 4.

Sandra Sarosy Duve
Colorado Springs, Colorado, U.S.A.

SLOVAK VEAL ROLLS
Slovenské teľacie závitky

Veal steaks, sliced thin
Sliced processed cheese
Salt, to taste
Flour for dredging
Beaten egg
Fine bread crumbs
1 clove garlic
Oil
Chicken stock
Flour for thickening sauce
Paprika
Bacon slices

Sprinkle each steak with salt to taste. Cover each with a slice of bacon and top with a slice of cheese. Roll and fasten with wooden picks or skewers. Dip each roll in flour, then in beaten egg and then in fine bread crumbs. Place on rack and allow to chill in refrigerator for about one hour.

Heat oil in heavy skillet. Slice garlic and sauté in hot oil. Brown the rolls over moderate heat, on all sides, then remove to a baking dish. Remove garlic from drippings in skillet. Add flour and a little paprika and blend, allowing 2 tablespoons (20 g) flour for each cup of sauce desired. Add stock, using 1 cup ($1/4$ L) for each cup of sauce, and cook and stir until resulting sauce is smooth and thickened. Adjust seasonings.

Pour sauce over rolls, cover and bake in a 350°F (180°C) oven for about 1 hour, or until meat is tender. Serve at once with cooked rice or noodles.

Monica M. Chlumecky
Boca Raton, Florida   U.S.A.

HUNTER'S STEW
Poľovnícky guláš

- 1 pound (450 g) wild meat (venison, moose, elk), cut into ³/₄ inch (2 cm) cubes
- 1 cup (140 g) flour
- 3 cups (³/₄ L) dry red wine, white Chardonay, or Chablis
- 2 cans beef consommé, or beef stock, or 1 cup (¹/₄ L) water and 2 beef bouillon cubes
- ¹/₄ teaspoon (1.25 mL) black pepper
- ¹/₂ teaspoon (2.5 mL) red paprika
- ¹/₂ teaspoon (2.5 mL) salt
- 1 small onion, sliced
- 3 potatoes, medium, cut up
- 3 carrots, cut up
- ¹/₂ teaspoon (2.5 mL) ginger
- 3 tablespoons (45 mL) Worcestershire sauce
- 6 ounces (180 g) mushrooms
- 6 ounces (180 g) snow peas
- 3 tablespoons (45 mL) fat, for frying

Put flour in bowl and add dry spices. Dip cubed meat into the flour mixture and fry in hot skillet. Sear all sides of meat. Add wine, water and Worcestershire sauce in heavy skillet, bring to boil. Add carrots and potatoes. Then add meat after it has been drained of excess fat. Cook 1 hour, very slowly. Then add mushrooms, onions, and snow peas. Cook additional 10 minutes.

Serves 4 hungry people.

Steve Bacon
Poland, Ohio U.S.A.

Sister Cities
Youngstown, Ohio U.S.A. and Spišská Nová Ves, Slovakia

RABBIT IN WHITE WINE SAUCE
Zajac v bielej vínovej omáčke

1 rabbit
Salt, pepper
2 tablespoons (30 mL) mustard
1/4 pound (115 g) smoked bacon
1 can (14 1/2 ounces) (410 g) soup stock
3 tablespoons (30 g) flour
1 cup (1/4 L) white wine
Oil
2 tablespoons (30 mL) onion, minced
2 tablespoons (30 mL) tomato juice or ketchup
1 teaspoon (5 mL) paprika

Cut rabbit into serving portions, sprinkle with salt and pepper. Lightly spread mustard over each piece. Wrap meat in bacon strips, fasten with skewers. Brown quickly in hot oil; remove meat and sauté onion in hot fat until transparent. Add meat to onion. Add soup stock and tomato juice. Cover and cook until tender. Remove juice, and in small fry pan bring to boil. Add flour to make a roux. Add paprika and white wine and simmer a few minutes longer. Pour hot sauce over rabbit upon serving.

Anna Škovierová
Očova, Slovakia

WILD GAME
Divina

Recipe for all wild game, except fowl

Game meat
1 cup ($1/4$ L) vinegar
$1/2$ cup (1 dL) lemon juice
2 large onions
Water
1 cup ($1/4$ L) salt
$1/2$ cup (1 dL) flour
4 tablespoons ($1/2$ dL) oil
Salt, pepper, paprika for seasoning
8 strips bacon
1 can ($10 1/2$ ounces) (294 g) mushrooms
Potatoes, carrots, (optional)
1 pint ($1/4$ L) sour cream

Step #1: Cut up game into pieces. Marinate meat in glass container with mixture of vinegar, lemon juice, one large onion, sliced, and 1 cup salt. Add enough water to cover all the meat. Let stand for 24 hours in a cool place or refrigerator.

Step #2: Rinse marinated wild game. In hot oil, braise meat and place into a roaster.

Zápražka: Brown flour, add water to make a gravy, and pour over meat.

Add salt and pepper to season. Cut bacon into small pieces and brown. Chop one large onion and sauté in bacon until slightly brown; pour over wild game. Add mushrooms. Add carrots and potatoes (this would make a whole meal). Add desired amount of vegetables according to size of meat and serving portions.

Step #3: Bake in 350°F (180°C) oven for about 1 hour or until tender. Add sour cream. Sprinkle with paprika upon serving.

The Reverend Michael J. Chonko
New Castle, Pennsylvania U.S.A.

WILD MEAT HAMBURGERS
Jelenie-bravčové fašírky

1 pound (450 g) wild meat, (venison, moose, elk), ground
1 pound (450 g) pork, ground
1 medium onion
1/2 teaspoon (2.5 mL) ginger
2 tablespoons (30 mL) Worcestershire White Wine Sauce (Perrine's)
3/4 cup (180 mL) cornflake crumbs
1/2 teaspoon (2.5 mL) salt
1/2 teaspoon (2.5 mL) pepper
1 teaspoon (5 mL) paprika
1 tablespoon (15 mL) oil

Cut onion in half and pulverize in blender or dice on shredder. Put oil in frying pan. Add the onion. Cover with lid and fry and steam the onion until golden brown.
Put ground meat in bowl and add all spices and crumbs. Mix, then add the sautéed onion with the oil and mix again. Shape into burgers and fry.
This recipe can be used for meatloaf by deleting cornflake crumbs and substituting dry bread pieces. Also add 1 stalk of celery, diced. Bake at 325°F (165°C) for 1 hour.

Steve Bacon
Poland, Ohio U.S.A.

CALF LIVER
Teľacia pečeň

1 pound (450 g) calf liver
1 onion, sliced
2 tablespoons (30 mL) oil
Salt and pepper
2 tablespoons (20 mL) flour
2 eggs, beaten
3/4 cup (180 mL) bread crumbs

Sauté sliced onion in hot oil until transparent. Slice liver into serving portions. Sprinkle with salt and pepper. Coat with flour, then dip into beaten eggs, and cover with bread crumbs. Place into sautéed onions, and simmer until tender.

Martha Sarosy Zetts
Canfield, Ohio U.S.A.

CHICKEN LIVERS AND GIZZARDS
Kuracie pečienky aj puchorky

1/4 pound (115 g) bacon, cubed
1 1/2 pounds (675 g) gizzards, cubed
1/2 pound (225 g) livers, cut into larger cubes
1 large onion, sliced
3 ounces (90 mL) water
Salt and pepper, to taste

Render bacon in large fry pan. Add onion and cook till golden. Add gizzards and cook for 5 minutes, stir often. Add water, salt and black pepper, to taste. Bring to a boil; cover and simmer for 1/2 hour. Remove cover and cook at a higher heat to cook out water. Place the liver in the pan and cook as the water is boiling out. When water is boiled out, the mixture is ready to eat. Best eaten with fried eggs.

George Sterbinsky
Edwardsville, Pennsylvania
U.S.A.

HEADCHEESE
Tlačenka

1 hog head, thoroughly cleaned
1 hog heart
1 hog tongue
1 teaspoon (5 mL) red pepper
1 teaspoon (5 mL) marjoram
2 tablespoons (30 mL) black pepper
3 tablespoons (45 mL) salt
1 pint (1/2 L) hog blood
1 hog stomach

Cook head, heart and tongue until done and when meat falls off the head bones, slice the meat into long strips and place in a mixing pot.
Add seasonings and blood. Mix thoroughly. Stuff ingredients into the stomach casing and tie shut. Simmer the headcheese for 1 1/2 hours. Do not boil violently. Smoke headcheese in smoke house. Slice and eat cold.

George Sterbinsky
Edwardsville, Pennsylvania, U.S.A.

KIDNEYS WITH RICE
Obličky s ryžou

5 or 6 pork kidneys
Water
1½ cups (3½ dL) rice
1 onion, chopped
½ teaspoon (2½ mL) black pepper
1 teaspoon (5 mL) paprika
Salt
4 tablespoons (½ dL) lard

Cover kidneys with cool water and cook until done. Cool and slice. Cook well washed rice in salted water. In a fry pan, brown chopped onions in melted lard, about 5 minutes. Add seasonings and the sliced kidneys, cooking for about 10 minutes more. Add drained rice and heat through before serving.

In memory of
Julia Torma Ruszczyk

Kathy Ruszczyk Malone
Colorado Springs, Colorado U.S.A.

STUFFING
Plnka

Giblets
½ cup (115 g) butter
1 onion, minced
1 stalk celery, chopped fine
2 eggs
4 cups (1 L) dry bread crumbs
Salt, pepper
1 teaspoon (5 mL) paprika
Parsley, minced

Cook giblets, in enough water to cover, until done. Remove giblets, reserving liquid to add to stuffing. Grind or chop well. In skillet, sauté onion until golden. Add paprika. Stir in celery, parsley, bread crumbs and beaten eggs. Season with salt and pepper to taste. Add ground giblets, mix well. Add enough liquid to make a medium mixture (not too dry and not too mushy). Stuffing may be baked separately in a buttered baking dish at 350°F (180°C) for 20-30 minutes, or may be stuffed into poultry.
Note: Croutons, plain or herb, may be substituted for bread crumbs.

LARD - HOW TO RENDER
Ako vyškvárať sadlo

Trim the fat from the pork carcass and render it into lard as quickly as possible after slaughtering. Cook the leaf fat, backfat and fat trimmings. Caul and ruffle fats from internal organs yield lard of a darker color; if you use them, cook them separately. Remove fat, wash and chill promptly.

Cut fat into small pieces or grind it to hasten the rendering. Place in a large, heavy kettle and cook slowly, starting with a small quantity to make stirring easier. When the fat begins to melt, add more pieces, but do not fill kettle or it might boil over. Stir frequently and cook slowly to avoid sticking and scorching.

During the cooking, the brown cracklings, škvarky, will start to float. When the lard is almost rendered, they sink to the bottom of the kettle. Be careful not to let them stick and scorch. You can stop the cooking while the cracklings still float, but complete rendering removes more water and results in lard that keeps better. If moisture is eliminated by proper rendering, water souring should not develop during storage.

Let the lard cool slightly and settle before emptying the kettle. Pour lard carefully into empty cans (shortening or large coffee cans). Strain all the lard through three thicknesses of cheesecloth.

Store immediately in a cool place at near freezing or freezing temperature. Chilling it quickly produces a fine-grain lard.

This process was taught to me by my grandmother. I have obtained pork fat trimmings from a butcher and have been able to render fresh lard and make cracklings, škvarky. I have used small loaf pans, lined with aluminum foil, and poured the rendered lard into them to freeze into loaves. After freezing, remove lard block and foil; wrap lard in waxed paper and then heavy freezer paper. It is a time consuming process but results in a fine, white lard that produces the flakiest pie crusts. It is also maintaining the purity of a culinary tradition.

In memory of my grandmother,
Dorothy Sarvaš Zvara

Sandra Sarosy Duve
Colorado Springs, Colorado
U.S.A.

Co-editor

DILL GRAVY
Kôprová omáčka

White sauce
Green dill weed
2-3 tablespoons (45 mL) sour cream

To any basic white sauce, add chopped tender green dill weed. Add sour cream to taste. Simmer for approximately 10 minutes. Very good over mashed potatoes, meat loaf, or meat balls.

Millie Heban
Rossford, Ohio   U.S.A.

PAPRIKA GRAVY
Paprikova omáčka

3 tablespoons (45 mL) oil
2 tablespoons (30 mL) paprika
1 clove garlic, minced
1 teaspoon (5 mL) chicken stock
2 green peppers, diced
6 cups (1½ L) beef stock
1 onion, chopped
1 cup (¼ L) sour cream

Brown paprika in oil; add garlic, chicken stock, peppers, onion, and beef stock; simmer till onions and peppers are cooked down. Add sour cream and stir thoroughly. Simmer another 10 minutes. Strain and serve.

Robert J. Dvoroznak
Bay Village, Ohio   U.S.A.

DUMPLINGS
BASIC RECIPE
Halušky

1 cup (140 g) sifted flour
1½ teaspoons (7.5 mL) baking powder
½ teaspoon (2.5 mL) salt
2 tablespoons (30 mL) vegetable shortening, chilled
½ cup (1 dL) milk

Sift flour, baking powder, and salt together into a bowl. Cut in shortening, as for pie, until mixture resembles coarse meal. Add milk all at once and mix lightly just until dough holds together. Drop by rounded tablespoonfuls on top of gently boiling soup or stew. Simmer, uncovered, 10 minutes; cover and simmer 10 minutes longer so that steam will fluff up the dumplings.

BREADS

Chleby

SLOVAK BASIC DOUGH
Slovenské základné cesto

My Mother's recipe

- 2 packages (14 g) dry yeast
- 1 ¾ cups (4 dL) warm water
- 17 cups (2.38 kg) sifted all-purpose flour
- 4 ⅓ cups (1 L, ¾ dL) milk
- ¼ pound (115 g) margarine or oleo
- ¼ pound (115 g) butter
- 1 tablespoon (15 g) vegetable shortening
- 1 ⅔ cups (3¾ dL) sugar
- 2 tablespoons (30 g) salt
- 5 eggs, beaten

In a medium bowl, dissolve yeast in warm water. Add 2 cups (280 g) of the flour; cover and let rise until mixture fills bowl, about 30 minutes. Heat milk until very warm, but not scalding. Melt oleo, butter and shortening in warmed milk. Let cool. In a 10 quart (10 L) container, combine and mix 6 cups (840 g) of the flour with sugar and salt. Mix in milk mixture. Add yeast mixture, then beaten eggs. Gradually add remaining 9 cups (1.26 kg) of flour. Mix with hands, kneading until dough no longer sticks to hands. Cover and let rise until doubled, about 3 hours. Turn out on a lightly floured board. Form into roll; cut with a sharp knife into 9 or 10 pieces. Cover pieces with towels; let rise again until doubled. Use as desired for braided sweet bread, rolls, doughnuts, nut and poppyseed rolls, bobáľky or any similar purpose.

Pauline Urban Archer
Seven Hills, Ohio U.S.A.

Submitted by:
Dr. Edward Tuleya
Middletown, Pennsylvania U.S.A.

BRAIDED BREAD
Zapletaný chlieb

1 cup (¼ L) warm water
2 packages (¼ ounce) (14 g) dry yeast
2 cups (½ L) milk
1 stick (115 g) butter
1 cup (200 g) sugar
3 teaspoons (15 mL) salt
4 eggs
8-9 cups (1¼ kg) flour
1 beaten egg

Sprinkle yeast in warm water and let stand a few minutes. Stir until blended. Combine milk, butter, sugar and salt in a saucepan and heat until butter melts. Beat 4 eggs in bowl and gradually beat milk mixture into eggs. Cool to lukewarm. Add yeast mixture. Beat in enough flour to make a soft dough. Turn out on floured board and knead 10 minutes until smooth. Put in a greased bowl (grease top of dough) and cover. Let rise until doubled, about 1½ hours. Roll out on floured board. Cut in three large pieces, then cut each piece into three smaller pieces. Roll dough with hands to make ropes and braid. Let rise until doubled in greased bread pans. Brush top with beaten egg and bake at 350°F (180°C) for 40 minutes or until browned. Makes 3 loaves.

Ruth Williamson
Columbiana, Ohio U.S.A.

CHEESE ROLLS
Syrové chlebíky

2¼ cups (7.5 dL) milk
3 tablespoons (45 g) butter or margarine
5¾ - 6¼ cups (805-875 g) flour
2 packages (7 g each) active dry yeast
2 tablespoons (30 mL) sugar
2 teaspoons (10 mL) salt
2 pounds (900 g) cheese, grated (old fashion Cheddar)
2 egg yolks beaten with fork to spread on top of rolls

Heat milk and butter to 120°F (49°C). In large mixing bowl combine 3 cups (420 g) flour, yeast, sugar, salt and warmed milk. Mix well. Gradually add enough remaining flour to form a stiff dough. Knead until smooth and satiny, about 10 minutes. Place dough in greased bowl, turning once to grease top. Cover and let rise in a warm place until doubled, about 1 hour. Punch down and divide into 6 equal parts. Roll each portion out to about a 12 inch (30 cm) circle. Spread some grated cheese over dough and sprinkle a pinch of sugar over cheese and pat down. Roll like jellyroll, tucking in ends. As you roll, dampen edge with warm water. With hands roll so as to stretch roll in length. Place in an oiled 12x15 inch (30x38 cm) pan across end and down side of pan. Now repeat with each portion of dough in the same way putting roll in pan with the last until you use all the dough. With a fork, poke through each roll at 1 inch (2.5 cm) intervals. Brush rolls with oil and cover with wax paper. Let rise about 1 hour. Brush with egg yolk using pastry brush or with fingers. Bake in 350°F (180°C) oven for about 25 minutes.

I wrap mine in paper towels and let cool on wire rack. Rolls may be wrapped in foil after cooling and until ready to be sliced.

Makes 6 rolls.

Ruth Slatsky
Graysville, Alabama U.S.A.

CHRISTMAS BUNS
Vianočné opekance - bobáľky

Dough:
1 cake (21 g) yeast
1/4 cup (1/2 dL) water, lukewarm
2 cups (1/2 L) milk, scalded
2 tablespoons (30 mL) sugar
1 tablespoon (15 mL) butter
2-2 1/2 teaspoons (10-13mL) salt
6-7 cups (840-980 g) flour

Poppyseed topping:
1/2 cup (1 dL) poppyseed, ground
3/4 cup (1 3/4 dL) water
3 cups (3/4 L) milk
1 cup (200 g) sugar (Optional: substitute honey for sugar)
1 stick (115 g) butter

Dough: Dissolve yeast in water; set aside. Scald milk adding butter and sugar; cool to lukewarm. Combine yeast mixture with milk. Add flour and salt to liquids and work into a dough, soft and elastic but not sticky. Knead well on floured board, place in greased bowl, turn dough to grease top. Cover and set in warm place to rise until doubled in bulk. Punch down and let rise again. Place on floured board and cut into long strips. Roll each strip in palm of hands into a long pipe roll. Cut into small pieces and place on cookie sheet. Let rise 10-15 minutes. Bake at 375°F (190°C) for 15 minutes or until lightly browned. Cool. Place in colander and pour boiling water over top. Drain, and add poppyseed mixture.

Poppyseed topping:
Cook poppyseed in water until liquid evaporates. Mix frequently to prevent poppyseed from sticking to pan. Combine milk with sugar and boil to dissolve the sugar. Add butter, mix with poppyseed and pour over the opekance - bobál'ky.

Marcella Straka
Hellertown, Pennsylvania
U.S.A.

CHRISTMAS DUMPLINGS
Bobáľky

A Christmas Eve Tradition

Dough:
1½ cups (3½ dL) milk
2 tablespoons (30 mL) sugar
1 teaspoon (5 mL) salt
1/2 stick (60 g) butter
2 - ¼ ounce packages (14 g) dry yeast
Flour

Sauce:
15 ounces (426 g) raisins
Water
4 ounces (115 g) butter
½ cup (1 dL) honey
1 cup (¼ L) raisin juice
1 cup (200 g) ground poppyseed

Dough: Combine milk, sugar, salt and butter in a saucepan; heat only enough to melt the butter. Pour into a large mixing bowl and add dry yeast. Add a cup of flour (140 g) at a time until dough stiffens; knead about 10 minutes. Cover and let rise until it is nice and plump; punch down. Let rise again and then make into round balls about the size of a large marble. Let rise until double in size and bake in preheated 350°F (180°C) oven, about 20 minutes or until golden brown.

Poppyseed Sauce: Rinse raisins. Put in saucepan with 3 large glasses of water; simmer slowly until water turns brown. Drain the juice off and reserve liquid. (Raisins may be used for cookies.) In a large skillet, melt butter, add honey and 1 cup (¼ L) raisin juice; add prepared ground poppyseed. Continue stirring until mixture becomes a thick sauce. Put bobáľky in a colander and pour boiling water over top; soften and drain. Put bobáľky in a heat resistant container and pour hot sauce over the top. Let stand about an hour, mixing occasionally to thoroughly cover with sauce. Serve warm.

In memory of my mother, Elizabeth Gasper Evans.

Marlene G. Evans
Disputanta, Virginia   U.S.A.

CHRISTMAS EVE POPPYSEED BUNS
Opekance

Dough:
3½ cups (500 g hladkej) flour
¾ ounce (20 g) yeast
⅛ cup (20 g) sugar
1 cup (¼ L) milk
Salt
Fat for greasing

Topping:
⅜ cup (80 g) poppyseed
¼ cup (50 g) honey
⅜ cup (60 g) powdered sugar
2-4 ounces (60-115 g) butter

Crumble yeast into flour, add sugar, salt and mix. Add lukewarm milk to form a medium soft elastic dough. Knead dough well on a floured board. Place in a greased bowl, cover with cloth and let rise until double in bulk, about 1½ hours. Punch down and let rise again, about ½ hour.

On a floured board, divide dough into smaller pieces. Roll each piece into a long rope and cut into ¾ inch (2 cm) pieces. With a knife, gently push the cut pieces downward on to a greased cookie sheet. Let rise about 10 minutes. Bake at 350°F (180°C) for 15 minutes or until slightly golden. Let cool.

Place baked opekance in a colander. Pour boiling water over baked dough, drain well. Place in serving dish. Pour melted butter, honey and sprinkle with poppyseed and powdered sugar.

Opekance-a traditional Slovak dish prepared primarily for Christmas Eve supper.

Serves 4

PhDr. Zora Mintalová
Slovenské Narodné Múzeum
Martin, Slovakia

COTTAGE CHEESE SQUARES - POTATO DOUGH
Tvarohové rezy - zemiakové cesto

1½ cups (210 g) flour
1 cup (200 g) cooked mashed potatoes
Lemon rind
4 tablespoons (60 g) butter
2 tablespoons (30 g) sugar
1 egg yolk, beaten
3 tablespoons (45 mL) milk, lukewarm
¾ ounce (21 g) yeast

Filling:
⅓ cup (65 g) sugar
1 egg yolk, beaten
Lemon rind
2½ cups (500 g) cottage cheese
1 egg white, beaten
4 tablespoons (60 g) raisins
1 teaspoon (5 mL) vanilla

Glaze:
1 cup (112 g) powdered sugar
1 egg white, beaten
1 tablespoon (15 mL) rum

Dough: Crumble yeast into lukewarm milk, add sugar and set aside to rise.
Mix flour with mashed potatoes, add lemon rind, butter and egg yolk. Add yeast mixture and knead well. Place in greased bowl; keep warm while rising.
When dough has doubled, divide in half. Roll each piece to size of baking pan. Place one section on greased pan.

Filling: Combine all ingredients. Mix well, and spread filling evenly across dough. Cover with other half of dough.
Bake in preheated oven 350°F (180°C) until golden. When koláč has cooled, frost with rum icing.

Glaze: Mix powdered sugar, egg white and rum. Add either more sugar or drop of boiling water to make a smooth, thick consistency. Cut into squares or diamond shape bars.

Veronica Tuchek Seach
Campbell, Ohio U.S.A.

MARGIE'S COTTAGE CHEESE ROLLS
Margitkiné tvarohové koláčky

8 cups (1.12 kg) flour
1 cup (200 g) sugar
3 sticks (³/₄ pound) (336 g) melted oleo
½ cup (1 dL) warm water
2 packages (14 g) dry yeast
3 whole eggs, beaten
2 cups (½ L) warm milk
4 egg whites, beaten

Filling:
2 - 24 ounce (2-672 g) cottage cheese (1 large and 1 small curd)
2 - 8 ounce (2 - 224g) cream cheese, softened
2 tablespoons (30 mL) melted oleo,
2 teaspoons (10 mL) vanilla
2 cups (400 g) sugar
16 teaspoons (80 mL) tapioca
4 egg yolks

Filling: (Refrigerate filling overnight.) Mash softened cream cheese with potato masher; mix together with cottage cheese, oleo and vanilla. In a separate, large bowl, mix together sugar, tapioca, and egg yolks. Combine cheese mixture and tapioca mixture. Mix well and refrigerate, in a covered bowl, overnight.

Dough: Combine yeast and warm water. Set aside to make a bubble. Meanwhile, blend flour, sugar and 3 sticks melted oleo; mix as for pie crust. Add beaten eggs to warm milk; combine with flour mixture, and add yeast mixture last. Knead well and let rest 20 minutes. Make 8 to 10 balls and let rest 10 more minutes. Roll as long as a loaf of bread. Put filling down the center and cut sides into <u>strips</u> and overlap. Let rise ½ hour. Beat the 4 egg whites - spread over top just before baking. Bake at 350°F (180°C) for 25-30 minutes.

Makes 8-10 rolls.

Margaret Hurajt-Bodnar
Campbell, Ohio U.S.A.

CRACKLING BISCUITS
Škvarkové piškóty

2 potatoes (½ L) cooked, mashed
1 cake (21 g) yeast
1½ - 2 cups (3½ dL - ½ L) milk, warm
3 cups (420 g) flour
1 tablespoon (15 mL) salt
2 tablespoons (30 mL) sugar
1 pound (450 g) cracklings, ground
1 egg, beaten, for brushing

Dissolve yeast in milk. Mix all other ingredients except cracklings. Add yeast mixture and knead well. Let rise until doubled in bulk. Roll out on floured board and spread cracklings over dough. Fold over four ways. Let rise again. Roll out and fold over again four ways. Continue this rising and folding of dough three more times. Total rising time 3-4 hours. Roll out and cut with biscuit cutter. Place on cookie sheet. Brush tops with beaten egg. Bake in moderate oven, 350°F (180°C) for about 20-30 minutes.

Polly Torma
Trenton, New Jersey   U.S.A.

FILLED CRESCENTS - KIFFELS
Plnené rožky

½ pound (225 g) butter or oleo
3 cups (420 g) flour
3 egg yolks (save whites to brush kiffels)
¼ ounce (7 g) package active dry yeast
½ cup (1 dL) warm milk
1 tablespoon (15 mL) sugar
1 teaspoon (5 mL) vanilla

Filling:
Nut, poppyseed, lekvar, or apricot
Powdered sugar, optional

Cut butter or oleo into flour as for pie dough. Add egg yolks, yeast dissolved in the warm milk, sugar and vanilla. Mix well with hands. Divide dough into four balls. Roll each ball into a circle, cut into eight wedges.

Spread a teaspoon of your favorite filling on each wedge. Roll up and shape into a crescent. Place on greased cookie sheet and let rise for 30 minutes. Brush tops with beaten egg whites. Bake at 350°F (180°C) for 20-25 minutes. When cool, sprinkle with powdered sugar, if desired.

Mary Hatagan
Youngstown, Ohio   U.S.A.

EASTER BREAD
Páska

In memory of my mother, Sophie Duke

Basic Dough:
8 cups (1.12 kg) flour
2 tablespoons (30 mL) salt
1 cup (¼ L) warm water
1 tablespoon (15 mL) sugar
¼ pound (115 g) butter
½ cup (1 dL) sugar
2 cups (½ L) milk, boiling point
2 packages (14 g) dry, rapid rise yeast
3 eggs

Cheese Dough:
1-1 ounce (28 g) yeast cake
1 pound (450 g) dry cottage cheese
1 cup (¼ L) yellow raisins
4 egg yolks
1 cup (¼ L) sugar, or less, to taste
1 teaspoon (5 mL) salt
1 teaspoon (5 mL) lemon rind
1 teaspoon (5 mL) baking powder
½ cup (1 dL) milk
3 cups (420 g) flour, sifted

Basic Dough: Crumble yeast in ½ cup (1 dL) water and 1 tablespoon (15 mL) sugar. Set aside for 5 minutes. Pour boiling milk over sugar and butter, add balance of water. Cool to lukewarm. Sift flour into bowl, add salt, eggs, milk mixture and yeast. Knead dough until smooth and elastic. Cover. Let rise until doubled in bulk, about 2 hours, in a warm place.

Cheese Dough: Crumble yeast in warm milk to which 1 tablespoon (15 mL) sugar has been added and let stand 5 minutes. Mix cottage cheese with spoon until smooth. Add raisins and yeast mixture. Add unbeaten egg yolks, remaining sugar, salt, lemon rind, baking powder and flour, and knead well. Set aside to rise until doubled in bulk, about 2 hours. When basic dough has doubled in size, turn out onto lightly floured board and shape into four parts. Let stand on board, covered, for about 15 minutes. Take one part of dough and lightly punch around the edge so that the center is elevated. Take cheese dough and place around the elevated center, then lightly make an opening in the center. Join edges of center with the outside edges, press carefully so that the cheese dough is completely covered. Place into 9-inch (23 cm) tube pan and let rise for about 30 minutes. Cover dough to prevent drying. Just before placing into oven, brush top with egg yolk. Bake for 10 minutes at 325°F (160°C), increase temperature to 350°F (180°C) and bake for 40 minutes. Recipe may be cut in half. Makes 4 paskas.

Anna Marie Popernack
Bobtown, Pennsylvania   U.S.A.

FRAN'S FAVORITE ROLLS
Františkiné obľúbené žemle

2 cups (½ L) milk, scalded
½ cup (115 g) margarine
½ cup (1 dL) honey
2 eggs
1 teaspoon (5 mL) salt
2 packages (14 g) yeast
6-7 cups (840-980 g) flour
   (can be part whole wheat)
Butter, softened

Melt margarine in scalded milk. Let cool to lukewarm. Add in honey, eggs, salt, yeast. Stir in enough flour to make dough easy to handle (can still be slightly sticky). Knead a couple of turns on floured surface. Place in greased bowl. Cover and let rise until double (1½-2 hours). Punch down. Divide into 4 parts.

To make crescent rolls, roll out each ball into 12 inch (30 cm) circle. Spread with softened butter. Cut into 12 pie shaped wedges. Roll up from large end and shape into crescent. Place on baking sheet. (Note: at this point, after rolls are shaped but before they rise, they can be frozen. To bake, remove from freezer. Let rise 2-3 hours. Bake). Let rise 30 minutes or until double. Bake 15-20 minutes at 350°F (180°C).

Fran DeWine
Wife of U.S. Senator
Mike DeWine
Cedarville, Ohio   U.S.A.

SLOVAK RYE BREAD
Žitný chlieb

1 small potato, liquified
2 cups (½ L) water
½ tablespoon (7.5 mL) salt
1 tablespoon (15 mL) sugar

1¼ cups (175 g) rye flour, sifted

2 packages (14 g) dry yeast
½ cup (1 dL) warm water
½ teaspoon (2.5 mL) sugar

2½ tablespoons (37.5 mL) caraway seeds
1 tablespoon (15 mL) orange peel
1 tablespoon (15 mL) sugar
½ teaspoon (2.5 mL) salt
3¾ cup (525 g) white flour
1¼ cup (175 g) gluten flour
1 cup (¼ L) warm water

1 tablespoon (15 mL) bacon grease

2 egg yolks for glaze
Corn meal

Add together first four ingredients and boil for fifteen minutes. Then pour over rye flour and mix well and let set for a half hour. In the half cup (1 dL) of warm water, dissolve yeast and sugar. Add this to the above ingredients mixing well. Cover and let set overnight in the oven.

The following day, add the remaining ingredients up to the bacon grease and knead into a stiff dough. Now add the bacon grease and knead again until grease is absorbed into the dough. Flour top of dough lightly, cover and let rise until doubled in size. Place on floured board and shape into round loaf. In a 10 inch (25 cm) round cake pan, sprinkle corn meal on the bottom and rub into sides, then place loaf and let rise again until double in size. Glaze with beaten egg yolk and bake for one hour at 350°F (180°C).

Delicious! A Will County Fair blue ribbon winner.

Thomas Klimek Ward
Honorary Consul of the
Slovak Republic
Chicago, Illinois U.S.A.

Slovak American Cultural Society
Of The Midwest, Chairman
Naperville, Illinois

WATER-RISEN CRESCENTS
Kifle

7 cups (980 g) flour
2 tablespoons (30 mL) sugar
1 teaspoon (5 mL) salt
1 pound (450 g) shortening
4 eggs
1 cup (¼ L) milk, lukewarm
2 yeast cakes (42 g)
Sugar, ground nuts, for dusting

Lekvar or nut filling

Combine milk, sugar and salt in large mixing bowl; add yeast and stir until dissolved. Add eggs, shortening and flour; mix well. Knead until dough is smooth. Tie dough in cloth bag large enough allowing room for dough to rise. Set dough/bag in a pan and set this pan into a larger pan of lukewarm water, keeping water temperature constant.

Remove dough when doubled in bulk. Place on floured board; grease hands with lard and pinch off pieces of dough and flatten. Fill with nut or lekvar filling. Roll in sugar or nuts and bake for 25 minutes or until golden in 350°F (180°C) oven.

Polly Torma
Trenton, New Jersey U.S.A.

CHRISTMAS HOLIDAY LAYERED KOLACH
Štedrák-skladaný koláč

3½ - 3¾ cups (½ kg) coarse flour
1¼ cups (3 dL) milk
¼ pound (120 g) butter
½ cup (100 g) sugar
3 - ¼ ounce packages (21 g) yeast
3 egg yolks
2 tablespoons (30 g) butter, melted for brushing top of dough
1 egg yolk, beaten for brushing
1 lemon rind
1 teaspoon (5 mL) vanilla (vanilkový cukor)
Salt

Nut filling:
¾ cup (180 g) nuts, ground
1 cup (2 dL) milk
3 tablespoons (30 g) bread crumbs
¾ cup (80 g) powdered sugar
1 teaspoon (5 mL) vanilla (vanilkový cukor)
Lemon rind

Poppy Seed filling:
1 cup (200 g) ground poppyseed
1 cup (2 dL) milk
1¼ cups (120 g) powdered sugar
1 tablespoon (15 g) butter
1 teaspoon (5 mL) vanilla (vanilkový cukor)
Lemon rind

Cottage Cheese filling:
1½ cups (300 g) cottage cheese
¾ cup (80 g) powdered sugar
3 ounces (80 g) butter
2 tablespoons (30 g) raisins
2 egg yolks
2 egg whites, beaten stiff
1 teaspoon (5 mL) vanilla (vanilkový cukor)
Lemon rind

Lekvar filling:
1 cup (200 g) prune lekvar
Lemon rind

Dough: Dissolve yeast in part of the milk (lukewarm), add some of the sugar. Mix flour with butter, add the yeast mixture and remaining milk and sugar. Add egg yolks, vanilla, lemon rind and salt. Knead into medium consistency dough. Place in greased bowl, turning dough so that top is greased; cover and let rise until doubled. Divide dough into 5 equal pieces. On a floured board, roll one piece to thickness of finger. Place rolled dough on greased baking pan and

(Continued on next page)

CHRISTMAS HOLIDAY LAYERED KOLACH
Štedrák-skladaný koláč
(Continued)

spread with prune lekvar. Cover with another piece of dough rolled out to same size. Spread nut filling; cover with rolled dough; spread poppy seed filling, cover with dough, and spread cottage cheese mixture. Take the last piece of dough and roll out, cut into strips and lattice top. Brush with egg yolk and sprinkle with melted butter. Bake in moderate preheated oven 350°F (180°C) until golden brown.

Fillings: For lekvar, nut and poppy seed fillings, mix ingredients for each and simmer. For cottage filling, mix ingredients and spread over dough.

Throughout the regions of Slovakia, this old favorite is a very popular koláč with its generously layered fillings.

This traditional pastry is baked during the Christmas Eve and New Year holidays.

Ľudmila Šandorfi
St. Catherine's, Ontario, Canada

Marta Kováčiková
Zvolenská Slatina, Slovakia

FILLED ROLLS
Koláče

2 cups (½ L) milk
½ cup (100 g) sugar
2 packages (14 g) dry yeast
6 cups (840 g) flour, divided
3 large eggs
1 teaspoon (5 mL) salt
1 cup (¼ L) oil

Nut filling:
1 pound (450 g) ground nuts
1 cup (200 g) sugar
½ cup (1 dL) milk

Poppyseed filling:
1 pound (450 g) poppyseed
1½ cups (300 g) sugar
1 cup (¼ L) milk

Apricot filling:
1 pound (450 g) apricots, cooked, drained and chopped
½ cup (100 g) sugar

Prune filling:
1 pound (450 g) prunes, cooked and drained
¾ cup (150 g) sugar

Warm milk in saucepan to about 105° to 115° F (65°C). Add sugar and let dissolve. Add yeast and let stand until foamy. Place mixture in a large bowl and add 3 cups (420 g) flour. Beat until smooth. Add eggs and salt. Beat. Add oil and beat. Add 3 more cups flour (420 g). Mix and knead until smooth, about 10 minutes. Let rise until doubled. Divide into 6-8 rolls. Roll out and fill. Bake at 350°F (180°C) for 45 minutes.

Filling: For nut or poppyseed filling, heat ingredients slightly in a sauce pan.
For apricot or prune filling, mix ingredients.

Makes 6-8 rolls.

Ruth Williamson
Columbiana, Ohio U.S.A.

NUT ROLLS
Orechové koláče

Dough:
8 cups (1.1 kg) flour
2 teaspoons (10 mL) salt
1 teaspoon (5 mL) baking soda
2 cups (450 g) margarine
12 egg yolks, beaten
2 cups (½ L) sour cream
1 large cake yeast (1¾ ounce) (5 dkg)
4 tablespoons (60 mL) lukewarm water
1 tablespoon (15 mL) granulated sugar
Powdered sugar

Filling:
8 cups (2 L) ground nuts
2 teaspoons (10 mL) vanilla
3 cups (¾ L) powdered sugar
12 egg whites

Dough: Crumble yeast with granulated sugar in small bowl. Add warm water and let foam while mixing other ingredients. Measure flour in large bowl. Add margarine and mix as for pie dough. Add salt and baking soda, and mix well. Add sour cream, egg yolks and yeast mixture. Knead until dough and hand are no longer sticky and dough does not stick to the sides of the bowl. Refrigerate overnight. Divide dough into 12 balls and roll each out in powdered sugar into a rectangle ⅛ to ¼ inch (.31-.625 cm) thick. Spread with nut filling and roll up as for jelly roll. Place on greased cookie sheets and bake in preheated oven at 350°F (180°C) for 35-45 minutes or until golden brown.

Filling: Beat the egg whites till frothy. Add powdered sugar, vanilla, and fold in nuts.

Makes 12 rolls.

Kathy Ruszczyk Malone
Colorado Springs, Colorado

PRUNE FILLED ROLLS
Lekvárové koláčky

Dough:
2 cups (280 g) sifted flour
1 cup (224 g) cold butter, cut into small chunks
1 - 8 ounce package (224 g) cold cream cheese, cut into small chunks

Brushing:
1 egg yolk
1 teaspoon (5 mL) sugar

Lekvar Filling:
2 cups (½ L) pitted prunes
1¾ cups (4 dL) water, divided
¼ cup (½ dL) honey
2 tablespoons (30 mL) lemon juice
1 teaspoon (5 mL) cinnamon
Dash of ground cloves

Dough: Into large bowl, measure flour. Add butter and cheese, toss to coat with flour. With pastry blender or 2 knives, blend ingredients quickly, until mixture resembles coarse meal. Form dough into 3 equal balls. Wrap each and chill at least 2 hours. Preheat oven to 425°F (215°C). Grease cookie sheets. On lightly floured board, roll one ball of dough into a 12 inch (30 cm) square, fold into thirds. Turn dough over and fold into thirds again to make a 4 inch (10 cm) square. Roll out again into a 12x16 inch (30x40 cm) rectangle. With sharp knife, cut into twelve 4 inch (10 cm) squares. Transfer to prepared cookie sheets. Measure a scant tablespoon (15 mL) of prune filling onto center of each pastry square. Fold opposite corners together to overlap filling. Repeat rolling, cutting and filling with remaining chilled pastry dough and filling.

In cup, mix egg yolk and sugar, brush on pastry dough. Bake for 10 to 12 minutes or until lightly browned. Cool on wire racks.

Filling: In medium size saucepan over high heat, bring prunes and 1¼ cups (3 dL) water to a boil. Reduce heat to low, simmer 10 minutes, stirring occasionally. Pour prune mixture into container of electric blender, add remaining water, honey, lemon juice, cinnamon and cloves. Blend until smooth. Return mixture to saucepan. Cook and stir over low heat until mixture is the consistency of thick jam, about 15 minutes. Cool.

Ilonka Martinka-Torres
Castro Valley, California   U.S.A.

SLOVAK NUT ROLLS
Slovenské orechové koláče

1 large yeast cake (45 g) equal to 2 small cakes
³/₄ cup (1³/₄ dL) warm milk
³/₄ cup (150 g) sugar
6 cups (840 g) flour
4 egg yolks
1 teaspoon (5 mL) salt
1 cup (250 mL) sour cream
¹/₂ cup (125 mL) sweet butter, melted
¹/₂ cup (125 mL) sweet butter, softened
1 teaspoon (5 mL) vanilla
1 whole egg, beaten, for brushing on top

Filling:
4 cups (1 L) ground nuts
2 cups (400 g) sugar
4 tablespoons (60 g) butter
4 egg whites, beaten
Milk
1 teaspoon (5 mL) vanilla

In a small bowl, dissolve yeast in warm milk. Add 1 tablespoon (15 mL) of the sugar into yeast mixture and set aside to foam. In a large bowl, place 3 cups (420 g) flour. Make a well and add egg yolks, salt, sour cream, remaining sugar, ¹/₂ cup (125 mL) melted butter, vanilla, and yeast mixture. Blend together thoroughly and work in remaining flour until dough is smooth. Roll out on lightly floured board to ¹/₂ inch (1¹/₄ cm) thickness. Spread with ¹/₂ cup (125 mL) softened butter. Fold up and set aside to rise until doubled in bulk (about 2 hours). Divide dough into 5 balls. Roll out each ball separately on lightly floured board to ¹/₄ inch (.38 cm) thick or less. Spread on filling and roll up. Place on greased cookie sheet and brush with beaten egg. Bake at 350°F (180°C) for 25-30 minutes, or until browned.

Filling: Mix nuts, sugar, butter, beaten egg whites, and vanilla, with enough milk to moisten the mixture.

Makes 5 rolls.

Anne Zvara Sarosy
Campbell, Ohio   U.S.A.

SLOVAK NUT - POPPYSEED ROLLS
Slovenské orechové - Makové koláče

Dough:
1 quart (1 L) milk
3 teaspoons (15 mL) sugar
1 cake (56 g) yeast
10 cups (1.4 kg) flour
1 pound (450 g) shortening (may be part oleo or butter)
1 teaspoon (5 mL) salt
3 egg yolks
1 teaspoon (5 mL) vanilla

Poppyseed filling:
1 cup (¼ L) boiled milk
1 pound (450 g) ground poppyseed
2 cups (400 g) sugar
¼ cup (1.2 dL) raisins
½ teaspoon (2.5 mL) cinnamon

Nut filling:
3 pounds (1.35 kg) whole walnuts (shell and grind)
OR
18 ounces (504 g) shelled nuts (ground)
1½ cups (300 g) sugar
¼ cup (½ dL) raisins
1 teaspoon (5 mL) sugar
3 beaten egg whites
1 teaspoon (5 mL) cinnamon
Boiled milk, if necessary

Dough: Warm milk, then take ½ cup (1 dL) of warm milk and add sugar and yeast; set aside to foam. Set aside remaining warm milk. Sift flour and salt, and add shortening. Work with hands as for pie dough. Add egg yolks, remainder of warm milk, vanilla, and yeast mixture. Knead until dough leaves sides of bowl and hand (about 10 minutes). Cover bowl with towel and let rise 1 hour.
Divide dough into 8 equal parts. Roll each out and spread with filling. Roll as for jelly roll. Place two koláče on greased baking sheet, folded sides under, and let rise ½ hour.
Bake in preheated oven 375°F (190°C) for 30-35 minutes.

Poppyseed filling: Combine all ingredients into spreadable consistency.

Nut filling: Combine all ingredients. If necessary, add boiled milk to make a spreadable consistency.

Makes 8 koláče; 4 nut and 4 poppyseed.

Anna Sosnicky
Union, New Jersey U.S.A.

SLOVAK POPPYSEED ROLLS
Slovenské makovníky

1/2 cup (1 dL) sugar
4 cups (560 g) all purpose flour
2 yolks and 1 whole egg
3/4 - 1 cup (1 3/4 dL - 1/4 L) milk
1/4 pound (115 g) butter or margarine
1 teaspoon (5 mL) salt
1 package (7 g) dry yeast
1/4 cup (1/2 dL) warm water
1/4 teaspoon (1.25 mL) sugar
Sprinkle of flour

Butter, melted, or
Egg yolk, dissolved in milk (for basting rolls)

Poppyseed filling:
3 cups (3/4 L) ground poppyseed
3/4 cup (1 3/4 dL) sugar
1/2 cup (1 dL) milk
Rind of 1/2 lemon
Cinnamon
1 teaspoon (5 mL) vanilla extract
White raisins (optional)

Nut filling:
5-6 egg whites, beaten or 3/4 cup (1 3/4 dL) milk
1 cup (1/4 L) sugar
3 cups (3/4 L) ground nuts
Lemon rind
Vanilla extract
White raisins (optional)

Cheese filling:
1 package farmers cheese
1 egg yolk
1/2 cup (1 dL) sugar
Lemon rind
White raisins (optional)

Dough: Dissolve yeast in warm water with 1/4 teaspoon (1.25 mL) of sugar and sprinkle a little flour over top. Set aside to foam. Place eggs, sugar, salt and flour in a bowl. Add butter dissolved in milk. Add dissolved yeast mixture. Mix all ingredients and put in a bowl or pot to let rise in a warm place. When doubled in bulk, mix and let it rise a second time. Place on a floured board and make three rolls filled with desired filling.

Poppyseed filling: Place ingredients in a pan and gently boil 5-10 minutes. Keep mixing. Let it cool before using. Taste for sweetness and adjust if needed. Sprinkle with white raisins, if desired.

Nut filling: Mix all ingredients together and fill a roll. Sprinkle with white raisins, if desired.

Cheese filling: Mix all ingredients together. Add white raisins, if desired.

(Continued on next page)

SLOVAK POPPYSEED ROLLS
Slovenské makovníky

(Continued)

All three of the fillings, before rolling into a roll should be sprinkled with butter and if needed, additional sugar and/or cinnamon. After rolling, rolls should be basted with butter or an egg yolk dissolved in milk for a deep golden color when baked. Bake approximately 40 minutes at 375°F (190°C), or until done. Pierce a metal needle through the dough to test for doneness. This dough can be used for "babovka", and "rožky", small crescents, or for rolls.

Nina Holy
Slovak World Congress
Vice-President, East
West Orange, New Jersey
U.S.A.

KOLACH
Koláče

1 cup (225 g) butter, softened
1 cup (200 g) sugar
4 eggs
1 teaspoon (5 mL) salt
8 cups (1.12 kg) flour
1 ounce (28 g) compressed yeast
1 pint (½ L) lukewarm milk
Grated rind of ½ lemon

In a small bowl, crumble yeast, add lukewarm milk and a cup (140 g) of the flour; set aside, in a warm place, to rise.

Cream butter, add sugar and eggs, one at a time, beating well after each addition. Add the rest of the flour and the yeast mixture alternately. Mix well, adding any additional flour if dough is too sticky. Knead until dough is smooth and elastic. Set aside in a warm place to double in bulk.

Roll out for koláč or form into any desired shapes. After dough is filled, let rise again before baking. Bake in preheated moderate oven 350°F (180°C) until light golden brown.

Joan Jurishica
Milwaukee, Wisconsin U.S.A.

SLOVAK POPPYSEED ROLL
Slovenský makový rožtek

Dough:
6 tablespoons (³/₄ dL) butter or margarine
2 packages (14 g) active dry yeast
²/₃ cup (1¹/₂ dL) water
¹/₂ teaspoon (2.5 mL) salt
3¹/₃ cups (470 g) all-purpose flour
¹/₃ cup (65 g) sugar
1 large egg

Filling:
12¹/₂ ounces (350 g) prepared poppyseed filling
1 tablespoon (15 mL) grated orange peel
2 tablespoons (30 mL) milk
2 tablespoons (30 mL) sugar
¹/₂ - ³/₄ cup (1 dL-1³/₄ dL) raisins

Glaze:
¹/₄ cup (¹/₂ dL) confectioners' sugar
1 tablespoon (15 mL) water

Dough: In a 1 quart (1 L) saucepan over low heat, heat butter or margarine and water until very warm (120 - 130°F) (60°C).

In a large bowl, with mixer at low speed, beat yeast, salt, 1 cup (140 g) flour, ¹/₃ cup (³/₄ dL) sugar, and liquid ingredients until blended. At medium speed, beat 2 minutes. Beat in egg and 1 cup (140 g) flour; beat 2 minutes. Stir in 1 cup (140 g) flour.

On floured surface, knead dough until smooth and elastic, about 10 minutes, working in more flour (¹/₃ cup) (50 g) while kneading. Shape dough into a ball; place in a greased bowl, turning to grease top. Cover and let rise in warm place (80-85°F) (28°C), until doubled, about 1 hour.

Punch down dough; turn onto a floured surface, cover and let rest for 15 minutes. Grease large cookie sheet.

Roll dough into 22x12 inch (55x30 cm) rectangle. Spread poppyseed mixture over dough. Starting at one long side, roll up dough jelly-roll fashion. Cut roll lengthwise in half. Keeping cut sides up, twist strands together; place on cookie sheet. Cover, let rise 30 minutes until doubled. (You may twist the dough into a ring tucking the ends under to seal or you may leave it as a long bread.)

(Continued on next page)

SLOVAK POPPYSEED ROLL
Slovenský makový rožtek
(Continued)

Preheat oven to 350°F (180°C). Bake 30 minutes or until golden brown. Remove roll to wire rack set over waxed paper. In a cup, mix confectioners' sugar with water. Brush glaze over hot bread.

Filling: Stir poppyseed filling with orange peel, sugar, milk and raisins until well mixed.

Makes one loaf, 16 servings. Delicious!

This is a modern day one-loaf version of our mother's poppyseed roll. Several were made as a special treat at Christmas and Easter.

In memory of our mother:
Mary Martin McCoola

Joan M. Lacombe
Somers, Connecticut   U.S.A.

Esther M. Rish
Nanticoke, Pennsylvania
U.S.A.

TWO HOUR NUT ROLL
Dvoj hodinový-orechový koláč

6 cups (840 g) flour, sifted
2 yeast cakes (21 g)
1 teaspoon (5 mL) salt
3 tablespoons (45 mL) sugar
½ cup (1 dL) warm milk
½ pound (225 g) butter or margarine
3 eggs, beaten
1 cup (¼ L) sour cream or canned milk
1 egg, beaten for brushing
Powdered sugar for dusting

Dissolve yeast in warm milk and set aside. Combine flour, butter, salt, sugar, eggs and sour cream.

Add yeast and milk mixture. Blend well. Divide dough into four parts and roll out each part thin as for jelly roll. Spread with nut or poppy seed filling. Roll up and place on greased baking pan and allow to rise for one hour, or until doubled in bulk. Bake in preheated moderate oven 350°F (180°C) for 35 to 40 minutes. When removing from oven, brush with beaten egg. Sprinkle cooled koláč with powdered sugar.

My mother's recipe, Emma Yaros.

Emma S. Pella
Land O Lakes, Florida   U.S.A.

SWEET BREAD WITH CHEESE FILLING
Tvarohové koláče

Dough:
1 package (¼ ounce) (7g) dry yeast
¼ cup (½ dL) warm water
¼ cup (½ dL) milk
¼ cup (50g) sugar
¼ cup (50g) soft butter
½ teaspoon (2.5 mL) salt
2 eggs, beaten
2½ - 3 cups (350-420 g) flour
1 egg for brushing

Filling:
2 cups (½ L) ricotta cheese
2 egg yolks
¼ cup (50 g) sugar
¼ teaspoon (1.25 mL) almond extract

Dough: Soften yeast in warm water. Combine all ingredients and knead as usual for yeast dough. Place in greased bowl and let rise until doubled. Roll out on floured board to 18x16 inches (45x40 cm) and spread with cheese filling. Roll up, wet edges to seal. Let rise 1 hour. Place on greased baking pan. Brush with whole beaten egg. Bake at 350°F (180°C) for 35-45 minutes.

Filling: Combine all ingredients and mix well.

Note: Dough can be made the night before. Refrigerate; then continue without rising.

Viola Lastala
Enumclaw, Washington U.S.A.

WALNUT ROLLS - POPPYSEED ROLLS
Orechové - Makové koláče

Dough:
5 cups (700 g) all purpose flour
½ pound (225 g) butter or margarine
Small cream cheese
½ cup (1 dL) sour cream
3 whole eggs
1 envelope (¼ ounce) (7g) yeast
½ cup (1dL) warm milk
1 teaspoon (5 mL) sugar

Filling:
½ pound (225 g) nuts, finely chopped
1 cup (200 g) sugar
½ teaspoon (2.5 mL) nutmeg
1 can poppyseed filling
1 teaspoon (5 mL) lemon juice
¼ cup (50 g) sugar

Dough: Dissolve yeast and sugar in warm milk. Let set until foamy. Mix all ingredients together first with a wooden spoon and then with your hand. Mix dough until your hand comes out clean. Sprinkle dough lightly with flour and keep wrapped in cotton towel or cloth in refrigerator over night. Next morning keep dough in warm place for about one hour. Divide into 4 pieces. Let rest for a while. In the meantime prepare filling.

Filling: Mix chopped nuts with sugar and nutmeg. Mix poppyseed with lemon juice and sugar.

To roll: Roll out each piece. Fill 2 rolls with nuts mixture and roll like jelly roll. Fill the other 2 rolls with poppyseed filling and roll. Bake on cookie sheet at 350°F (180°C) about 30 minutes or until golden brown.

Betty Bull
Woodland Hills, California U.S.A.

APPLE, RAISIN, NUT BREAD
Jablkový, hrozienkový, orechový chlebíček

2 cups (280 g) flour
1 teaspoon (5 mL) baking powder
½ teaspoon (2.5 mL) baking soda
½ teaspoon (2.5 mL) salt
1 cup (200 g) sugar
½ cup (1 dL) butter
1 egg, beaten
½ teaspoon (2.5 mL) vanilla
¼ teaspoon (1.25 mL) lemon juice
¾ cup (1¾ dL) buttermilk, or: 1 tablespoon (15 mL) vinegar added to ¾ cup (1¾ dL) regular milk
1½ cups (3½ dL) apples, peeled and chopped (McIntosh are very good)
½ - ¾ cup (1 dL - 1¾ dL) nuts, chopped
1 cup (¼ L) raisins, (optional)
1 cup (¼ L) hot water (needed for soaking raisins)

Heat oven to 350°F (180°C). Grease a 9x5 inch 23x13 cm) loaf pan or 3 small loaf pans.
In a large bowl, combine flour, baking powder, baking soda, salt and sugar. Cut in butter until mixture resembles coarse cornmeal.
Stir together egg, vanilla, lemon juice and buttermilk. Add to dry mixture, stirring until just moistened. Do not over mix.
Fold in apples and nuts. Before adding raisins, place them in a small bowl, rinse raisins in 1 cup (¼ L) hot water; drain, and add to mixture.
Spread in pan. Bake 70 minutes for large loaf, or 40-45 minutes for 3 small loaves. Test with wooden toothpick. Cool in pan for 15 minutes. Turn out onto a rack and cool before slicing. Enjoy!

Helen Konvalinka
Turtle Creek, Pennsylvania
U.S.A.

APRICOT NUT BREAD
Marhuľový orechový chlebíček

1 cup (¼ L) dried apricots
½ - 1 cup (1 dL-¼ L) brandy, peach or apricot
1 cup (200 g) sugar
2 tablespoons (30 mL) butter, softened
1 egg, beaten lightly
Rind of 1 lemon, grated
½ cup (1 dL) orange juice
2 cups (280 g) flour
2½ teaspoons (12.5 mL) baking powder
½ teaspoon (2.5 mL) baking soda
½ teaspoon (2.5 mL) salt
½ - 1 cup (1 dL-¼ L) chopped nuts

Warm brandy, do not boil, and pour over apricots and let soak 2-3 hours, or even overnight. Drain. Reserve ¼ cup (½ dL) brandy, set aside.
Cut each apricot into 6 pieces, set aside.
Cream sugar and butter until light and fluffy. Add egg and lemon rind and beat till smooth and well-blended. Add brandy and orange juice. Add flour, baking powder, soda and salt gradually, stirring well between additions. Fold in nuts and apricots. Pour into 9x5 inch (23x13 cm) loaf pan or 3 small loaf pans that have been greased and floured.
Preheat oven to 350°F (180°C). Let dough mixture stand in pan for 20 minutes before putting in oven. Bake large loaf pan for 1 hour or bake small loaves for 35-40 minutes or until toothpick comes out clean as you are testing for doneness.
Turn out of pan and cool on rack. Mellow 24 hours before cutting. Enjoy!

Helen Konvalinka
Turtle Creek, Pennsylvania
U.S.A.

POPPYSEED BANANA BREAD
Makový-banánový chlebík

1 cup (200 g) sugar
½ cup (115 g) butter or oleo, softened
2 eggs
1 teaspoon (5 mL) grated lemon peel
2 very ripe bananas
2 cups (280 g) flour
2 teaspoons (10 mL) baking powder
½ teaspoon (2.5 mL) salt
½ teaspoon (2.5 mL) cinnamon
¼ - ½ cup (50-125 mL) poppyseed
1 cup (¼ L) walnuts, chopped (optional)

Preheat oven to 350°F (180°C). Beat butter and sugar until light and fluffy. Beat in eggs and lemon peel. Alternate mashed bananas with dry ingredients, ending with dry ingredients. Stir in poppyseed. Spoon into greased 9x5 inch (22 x 12 cm) loaf pan or 3 small loaf pans. Bake in preheated oven 60 to 70 minutes for larger pan; 35 to 45 minutes for small loaves, OR until wooden toothpick inserted in center comes out clean. Cool slightly in loaf pan before turning out onto wire rack to cool completely.

Helen Konvalinka
Turtle Creek, Pennsylvania U.S.A.

TO KNEAD DOUGH
Postup - ako miesiť cesto

To properly knead dough, fold opposite side over toward you. Using heel of hands, gently push dough away. Give it a quarter turn. Repeat process rhythmically until dough is soft and elastic, 5 to 8 minutes, using as little additional flour as possible. Always turn the dough in the same direction.

-Editor

NO KNEAD RAISIN BREAD
Hrozienkový chlebík

1 envelope (7 g) dry yeast
2 cups (1/2 L) warm milk
7 cups (980 g) Bisquick
¼ cup (½ dL) sugar
4 large eggs
¼ teaspoon (1.25 mL) cream of tartar
1 cup (½ dL) raisins

Sprinkle yeast over warm milk in saucepan. Let stand at room temperature for about 10 minutes.
In a large bowl, add Bisquick and sugar. In a small bowl whisk eggs and cream of tartar.
Add milk mixture and egg mixture to dry ingredients, stir until blended. Add raisins, mixing evenly into dough. Cover with plastic wrap. Let rise in warm draft-free area until doubled in bulk, about 1 hour. Lightly oil two 9x5x3 inch (23x13x8 cm) loaf pans. Divide dough evenly between prepared pans. Cover with plastic wrap. Let dough rise in warm area again about 1 hour.
Preheat oven to 350°F (180°C). Bake bread until golden brown, about 45 minutes.

Makes 2 loaves.

Dorothy Kabat
New Port Richey, Florida U.S.A.

ZUCCHINI BREAD
Tekvicový chlieb

3 eggs
1 cup (¼ L) oil
2 cups (400 g) sugar
2 teaspoons (10 mL) vanilla

2 cups (½ L) shredded zucchini, peeled or unpeeled
1 cup (¼ L) pineapple, crushed, unsweetened and drained
½ cup (1 dL) raisins
½ cup (1 dL) chopped nuts, or more
Dates (optional)

3 cups (420 g) flour
1 teaspoon (5 mL) salt
2 teaspoons (10 mL) baking soda
½ teaspoon (2.5 mL) cinnamon
¼ teaspoon (1.25 mL) baking powder

Beat in mixer until thick, 3 eggs, oil, sugar and vanilla. Set aside. Mix together zucchini, drained pineapple, raisins, chopped nuts, and/or dates. Set aside.
In another bowl mix all dry ingredients.
Add egg mixture to flour mixture, then add zucchini mixture and mix by hand. Grease and flour lightly four small 3x5 inch (8x13 cm) or 2 large bread pans. Bake in preheated oven 350°F (180°C) for 50-60 minutes or until loaves test done.

Irene Paluga Zvara
Poland, Ohio U.S.A.

SUBSTITUTION FOR CAKE FLOUR
Nahradenie - ľahká múka

Use 1 cup (140 g) minus 2 tablespoons (20 g) of all-purpose flour for 1 cup (140 g) cake flour

NOTE: All-purpose flour may be substituted for variety textures of European flour. Some cooks prefer 'Wondra' flour.

-Editor

PASTAS

Cestovina

BAKED POTATO PANCAKE CASSEROLE
Zemiaková pagáčová bábovka

7 large potatoes, grated
1 small onion, grated
½ cup (1 dL) carrots, grated
¾ cup (1¾ dL) cheese, grated (use round hole on grater)
¾ cup (1¾ dL) soda crackers, rolled very fine
4 eggs, beaten
Salt and pepper, to taste

Mix all ingredients together. Pour batter into a buttered square baking dish. Bake one hour at 350° (180°C).

Ann I. Sninsky
St. Clair, Pennsylvania U.S.A.

FRIED HOT CAKES
Langoše

5⅔ cups (800 g) light or cake flour
½ cup (1 dL) sour cream
1 cup (¼ L) water
1 cake (¼ ounce) (7 g) yeast
2 whole eggs, slightly beaten
1 teaspoon (5 mL) salt
Pinch of caraway seed
Oil for frying
Minced garlic, (optional)

Dissolve crumbled yeast in water. Add the rest of the ingredients and knead well. Place dough in greased bowl and let rise till doubled. Roll out dough and cut out round langoše. Fry in hot oil. May be served with minced garlic.

Marta Kováčiková
Zvolenská Slatina, Slovakia

CABBAGE CAKES
Kapustníky

Dough:
3/4 ounce (20 g) yeast
1 1/4 cups (3 dL) milk, lukewarm
3 1/2 cups (500 g hladkej) flour
1 egg
1 tablespoon (15 mL) sugar
2 1/2 - 3 tablespoons (40 g) butter, melted
Powdered sugar for dusting

Filling:
1/2 head of cabbage, shredded
Sweet cream
Vanilla sugar

Dough: In a small bowl, or cup, crumble yeast, add 1/4 cup (1/2 dL) lukewarm milk and let ferment, (rise).
Combine flour, egg, sugar and yeast mixture working well into a medium firm dough. Cover, and let stand for at least one hour.
On a board, roll out dough 1/4-1/2 inch (3/4-1 1/2 cm) thick. Cut into squares. In the center of each square place a small amount of filling. Wrap dough around filling as for "buchty." Place "kapustníky" on a greased baking pan. Drizzle with melted butter and bake in preheated 350°F (180°C) oven until golden brown. When cooled, sprinkle with powdered sugar.

Filling: Shred cabbage, add cream and vanilla sugar forming a thick consistency. Simmer until cabbage is softened and lightly golden.

A Slovak dessert snack.
Dobrú Chuť!

PhDr. Zora Mintalová
Slovenské Národné Múzeum
Martin, Slovakia

CABBAGE CAKES
Kapustníky

3 cups (420 g) flour
1 cup (¼ L) milk
¾ ounce (20 g) yeast
2 tablespoons (30 g) sugar
¼ cup (50 g) fat, melted
1 teaspoon (5 mL) salt
1 tablespoon (15 g) bacon fat, for brushing

Filling:
3 tablespoons (45 mL) bacon fat
1 pound (450 g) head of cabbage
Salt, pepper, sugar, to taste

Dough: Into lukewarm milk, add sugar and crumbled yeast. Let stand to foam. Sift flour, add melted fat, salt and yeast mixture. Knead into a thinner dough. Place in greased bowl, cover, and let rise until doubled. Divide dough in half. Roll each half into a thin layer. Place one rolled piece on a greased baking sheet. Spread cabbage filling, cover with other half of dough. Brush with melted bacon fat and bake in preheated oven 350°F. (180°C) until golden brown.

Filling: Shred cabbage and cook in 1 tablespoon (15 mL) melted fat, adding salt and pepper, and a little water. Cook until tender. Add sugar to taste.

Vincent Bruner
Hubbard, Ohio   U.S.A.

CABBAGE FILLED PATTY
Pagáč

¾ cup (1¾ dL) scalded milk
1 teaspoon (5 mL) salt
4 tablespoons (60 mL) sugar
3 tablespoons (45 mL) vegetable shortening
3 cups (420 g) flour
1 egg, slightly beaten
½ cake (21 g) yeast
1 tablespoon (15 mL) sugar
¼ cup (½ dL) lukewarm water

Filling:
1 medium cabbage
5 tablespoons (75 mL) butter
Salt, to taste

Dough: Dissolve yeast in lukewarm water and 1 tablespoon (15 mL) sugar. Pour scalded milk over salt, sugar and shortening. Add egg to yeast mixture. Stir in about half the flour, beating well. Add remainder of flour and mix well. Turn out on floured board and knead about 5 minutes. Place in greased bowl and let rise until doubled. Divide dough into two portions. Flatten out one piece. Roll in a rectangle to about ½ inch (1¼ cm) thickness. Spread filling over top of dough to about ½ inch (1¼ cm) from edge. Roll other piece of dough same size and place on top. Pinch edges together and roll lightly. With a fork, prick top and place on greased cookie sheet. Bake at 350°F (180°C) for about 25-30 minutes, until brown. Remove from oven and brush with melted, browned butter. Cut into squares when cool.

Filling: Shred cabbage and fry in butter until cabbage is soft and slightly brown. Salt to taste. Cool.

Note: For today's busy Slovak cooks who do not have time to make their own dough, two loaves of thawed, frozen bread dough may be substituted.

Anna Marie Popernack
Bobtown, Pennsylvania U.S.A.

CRACKLING CAKE
Trokšar

Our parents wasted nothing and could make the most appetizing, "unheard of" things for us from "extras" or "leftovers" - anything on hand (po ruky). They had six years of schooling in Slovakia where the official languages were German and Hungarian. They learned and preserved the Slovak language in the home and in their churches. With that knowledge and a generous amount of common sense, and dedicated to hard work, they gave us the best nurturing, parenting, education, and care - physically, mentally and spiritually, that anyone could give a child. They were strict, but that was so because they loved us and knew what was good for us. I thank God each time I think of them, and that is quite often.

After the hog was butchered, Mom rendered the fat (sadlo) into lard. There were many škvarky, the lard cracklings, which we ate with a little salt on them, but the quantity was limited since too much fat was not good for us.

Mom would make a "trokšar" or "pagač" using her ordinary plain daily bread recipe. This bread was made with flour, yeast, salt and lard and a little water. It was rolled out to pagač size, and the škvarky were stuck all over this trokšar at intervals of about an inch (2.5 cm) or less. When Mom had raisins around, she stuck a raisin here and there (tu i tam) to give it a sweet bite. We loved this. The trokšar was baked for about 20-25 minutes in a medium heat oven until golden brown. It was not too thick, about $3/8$-$1/2$ inch ($1 1/2$ cm), when baked. The trokšar was spread with melted butter after it was baked and we enjoyed it with hot tea with honey.

Mary Sterbinsky
Kingston, Pennsylvania
U.S.A.

Note: Cracklings often may be found in grocery stores today in the pork meat section along with pig's feet or smoked ham hocks.

- Editor

LEKVAR - FILLED STEAMED CAKES
Buchty na pare

3 1/2 cups (500 g) flour, sifted
3/4 ounce (21 g) yeast
1 1/2 cups - 1 3/4 cups (3.5 - 4 dL) milk, lukewarm
1/2 cup (40 g) powdered sugar
1 egg
Salt
Prune lekvar
Melted butter
Powdered sugar

Dissolve yeast in 1/2 cup (1 dL) of the lukewarm milk. Into sifted flour add the yeast mixture, remaining milk, powdered sugar, dash of salt, and egg. Work out dough to medium texture. Cover and let rise in warm place. On a floured board, roll out dough to 1/4 inch (.75 cm) square pieces. Into each piece place a heap of lekvar and wrap over with dough. Let dough rest and rise for a short time.

Place a strainer over top of pot and add just enough hot water to come below the strainer. Place dough into strainer, cover and steam for 15 minutes. Remove prepared buchty. To serve, add melted butter and sprinkled powdered sugar.

Optional: Dough can be cut into thicker, larger squares (4 pieces). Place a heaping amount of lekvar, wrap dough over, and steam as above.

Mary F. Kopsic
Youngstown, Ohio U.S.A.

GARLIC AND POTATO CAKE
Zemiaková baba s cesnakom

2¼ pounds (1000 g) potatoes, grated
1 egg
1 tablespoon (15 mL) milk
Salt, pinch
2 tablespoon (30 mL) marjoram
3 cloves garlic, pressed
⅔ cup (100 g hladkej) flour
Fat, shortening for greasing

Peel potatoes and grate finely. Add egg, milk, pinch of salt, marjoram, and garlic; mix well. Add flour to potato mixture and mix until well blended. Grease a baking pan or cookie sheet with unmelted shortening or lard. Spread potato mixture ⅜ inch (1 cm) thick. In preheated oven, 375°F (190°C) bake until rosy in color. Cut into squares or wedges. Serve with buttermilk.

Dobrú chuť!

4-6 servings, evening meal, or vegetable side dish.

PhDr. Zora Mintalová
Slovenské Narodné Múzeum
Martin, Slovakia

POTATO CAKE
Stará baba-bábovka

5 pounds (2.25 kg) potatoes, peeled
2 medium onions, peeled
6 eggs, beaten
1½ cups (215 g) white flour
1 teaspoon (5 mL) baking powder
3 teaspoons (15 mL) salt
1 teaspoon (5 mL) ground black pepper
½ pound (225 g) bacon, cut in pieces and fried

Grate potatoes and onion. Add beaten eggs and remaining ingredients including bacon fat. Mix well. Pour into greased 13x9 inch (33x23 cm) pan. Bake at 350°F (180°C) for 1 hour or more. Insert knife blade to check if done. Top should be golden brown.

In memory of Irma Vrbancic, a noted fraternalist, active in local and national Slovak fraternalism.

Marian Vrbancic Krumhansl
Cleveland, Ohio U.S.A.

POTATO CAKE WITH BACON
*Zemiaková haruľa
s údenou slaninou*

2¼ pounds (1000 g)
  potatoes, peeled
Salt, pepper, season to taste
1 egg
3 cloves garlic, pressed
¼ pound (100 g) smoked
  bacon, chopped
¼ cup (50 g) onion,
  chopped
⅔ - ¾ cup (100 g hladkej)
  flour
Fat for greasing

Peel potatoes and grate. Add garlic mixed with salt and pepper and egg. Chop bacon, fry, adding chopped onion and frying till golden. Mix bacon, onions and potato mixture. Add flour and mix well. Grease baking sheet generously. Spread potato mixture ⅜ inch (1 cm) thick and bake in preheated hot oven 375°F (190°C) until rosy in color. Serve with buttermilk as a potato side dish or an evening meal.

4-6 servings.

PhDr. Zora Mintalová
Slovenské Narodné Múzeum
Martin, Slovakia

POTATO CAKES
Zemiakové nálečníky

6 raw potatoes, peeled and
  shredded
2 eggs, beaten
1 onion, minced
1 clove garlic, minced
Salt, pepper, to taste
Oil

Mix all ingredients. In a large, heavy frying pan, heat oil. Using a tablespoon, form three patties. Fry each on both sides. Serve hot.

Klára Ivanková
Topoľovka, Slovakia

POTATO - POPPYSEED PIE WEDGES
Burašky

2½ cups (550 g) cooked potatoes
1½ cups (210 g) flour
Salt
1 egg, beaten
1 tablespoon (15 mL) fat (butter or margarine, melted)
1 cup (¼ L) milk
3 tablespoons (45 mL) poppyseed
3 tablespoons (45 mL) sugar
4 tablespoons (60 g) butter, melted and browned

Cook potatoes in jackets. Peel and shred. Add flour, salt and egg; mix into a potato dough. Divide dough evenly into small sections. Roll out each piece ¼ inch (½ cm) thick and 5 inches (12 cm) long. Place on greased cookie sheet. Score each roll or strip into 6 or 7 pie-shaped pieces, but do not cut completely through the dough. Brush with butter or margarine. Bake in preheated 350°F (180°C) oven until lightly golden. When done, place on platter and pour hot milk, melted browned butter, and sprinkle with poppyseed and sugar.

A. Lakota
Teplická, Bratislava
Slovakia

PRESS CAKE - POTATO OR CABBAGE FILLING
Pagáč

Dough:
1 cup (¼ L) milk
½ cup (1 dL) butter
1 yeast package (7 g)
½ cup (1 dL) warm milk
1 teaspoon (5 mL) sugar
4½ cups (630 g) flour
1 teaspoon (5 mL) salt
4 tablespoons (½ dL) sugar
2 egg yolks
Melted butter, for brushing

Potato filling:
4 medium potatoes
Salt, to taste
½ stick (56 g) butter
2 tablespoons (30 mL) sugar
1 teaspoon (5 mL) dried mint (kurtoška)

Cabbage filling:
½ head cabbage, small head
1 medium onion
1 small can sauerkraut, rinsed and squeezed
½ stick (56 g) butter
Salt, to taste

Dough: Put 1 cup (¼ L) milk in sauce pan and add butter; heat until butter is melted. Cool. Sprinkle yeast into warm milk with sugar and let dissolve. Measure flour, salt, sugar and mix in a bowl. Make well in center; add yeast mixture, beaten egg yolks, and cooled milk. Mix with hand until smooth and dough leaves hand. Let rise in buttered bowl until dough doubles, covered with a towel. Divide into 2 pieces and roll one piece to fit a large cookie sheet (11x16 inches) (28x40 cm). Fill with potatoes or cabbage filling. Roll out second dough and put on top. Seal all sides and brush with melted butter. Bake at 350°F (180°C) for 30 minutes, or until browned. Cut in squares and serve warm.
Potato filling: Cube and boil potatoes. Drain, salt to taste and add butter and sugar. Mash. Sprinkle with 1 teaspoon (5 mL) or more of dried mint (kurtoška). Mix well.
Cabbage filling: Cut cabbage fine. Dice onion. Melt butter in fry pan, add cabbage, onion and sauerkraut; fry. Add salt to taste.

On days when kolače were made, two doughs were set aside to make the pagač that was eaten for supper.

Mary Hric
Detroit, Michigan U.S.A.

ROMANIAN POTATO PLACINTA
Zemiakový koláč - Rumunský

Dough:
1 package (¼ ounce) (7 g) dry yeast
1 tablespoon (15 mL) corn oil
2½ cups (350 g) flour
1 cup (¼ L) water, warm
1 teaspoon (5 mL) salt
Oil for frying

Filling:
1 cup (¼ L) chopped onion
2 tablespoons (30 mL) corn oil
6 medium potatoes, peeled and diced
1 teaspoon (5 mL) salt
3 tablespoons (45 mL) corn oil

Oil for frying

Dough: Combine yeast, oil, water and salt, stirring until yeast is saturated. Add about half of the flour, stirring until moistened. Slowly add the remaining flour. Place dough on floured surface and knead for about 2 minutes. Cover dough with a bowl and let rest for 2 minutes. Continue to knead until dough is soft and smooth, about 10 minutes. Add additional flour as needed to keep from sticking during the kneading process. Place dough in a large bowl, covered with damp cloth and set in warm area for about 45 minutes or until doubled in bulk. Divide into 8 balls, cover with damp cloth and allow to rise an additional 45 minutes.

Filling: Boil peeled and diced potatoes; drain and mash. Sauté onion in 2 tablespoons (30 mL) oil until tender but not browned; add to potatoes. Add salt and 3 tablespoons (45 mL) oil, mix well. Flatten each ball of dough by hand to about 4 inches (10 cm) diameter and place about ⅓ cup (¾ dL) potato filling in center. Fold the dough over; pinch to enclose the filling. Keep dough covered with damp cloth at all times.

To fry: Flatten one potato filled dough at a time with hand, then complete with rolling pin to about a 6 inch (15 cm) diameter. Fry in 2 tablespoons (30 mL) hot oil until browned on both sides. Add additional oil as needed.

Makes 8 cakes.

Bradley J. Stanciu
Chicago, Illinois U.S.A.

SHEEP CHEESE FLAT CAKES - PIZZA
Posúch bryndzový

Dough:
2¼ cups (300 g polohrubej) flour
¾ ounce (20 g) yeast
½ teaspoon (2.5 mL) salt
3 tablespoons (50 g) lard or shortening
1 egg yolk, beaten
Milk, lukewarm

Topping:
2¼ cups (300 g) sheep cheese
1 egg
2 tablespoons (30 g) butter
Salt
½ cup (1 dL) sour cream
Dill, finely chopped

Dough: In a larger bowl, crumble yeast in flour, add salt and lard, work as for pie. Add egg yolk and enough warm milk to make a soft consistency dough. Work dough well. Cover with cloth, set in warm place and let rise until doubled in bulk.

On a greased pan, similar to pizza pan, place dough and press evenly across pan. Spread topping and bake in moderate oven 350°F (180°C) until lightly browned. When baked, cut into serving size pieces.

Topping: Combine all ingredients and mix well.

This posúch is classified as a pastry snack served either with buttermilk or tea; or as an evening meal.

Serves 4.

PhDr. Zora Mintalová
Slovenské Narodné Múzeum
Martin, Slovakia

SLOVAK UNSWEETENED FILLED CAKE
Pagáč

4 cups (560 g) flour
¼ pound (115 g) butter
1½ cups (3½ dL) warm milk
1 cake (2 ounce) (56 g) yeast
3 egg yolks
¼ cup (50 mL) sugar
1 teaspoon (5 mL) salt
Egg and milk (beat together for brushing)
Melted butter for brushing

Filling:
Fried cabbage, or mashed potatoes, or fried sauerkraut

Dissolve yeast in lukewarm milk. Cream butter, add sugar and egg yolks. Mix well. Add yeast/milk mixture, salt and flour. Knead until smooth. Let rise until doubled in size. Punch down. Cut dough into four pieces. Work each piece into a ball. Let rest for 15 minutes. Roll out each piece to about 9x14 inch (22x35 cm) size. Spread filling over half of dough. Fold the other half over and pinch edges together. Place on greased cookie sheet and let rise. Prick surface with a fork. Brush with egg and milk mixture and bake at 350°F (180°C) for 30 minutes or until golden brown. While hot, brush with melted butter.

In memory of
Mary Zvara Cverna
Lorain, Ohio   U.S.A.

SMALL UNSWEETENED CAKES
Pagáč

Dough:
- ¾ cup (1¾ dL) scalded milk
- 1 teaspoon (5 mL) salt
- 4 tablespoons (½ dL) sugar
- 3 tablespoons (45 mL) shortening
- 3 cups (420 g) flour
- 1 egg, slightly beaten
- 1 cake (21 g) yeast
- ¼ cup (½ dL) lukewarm water

Cabbage filling:
- 1 medium head cabbage, chopped
- Butter

Potato filling:
- 3 medium potatoes
- 1 egg, beaten
- Chives

Sauerkraut filling:
- ½ pound (225 g) sauerkraut, drained
- Butter

Dough: Pour milk over salt, sugar and shortening. Cool to lukewarm. Add egg. Add yeast which has been dissolved in water. Add about half the flour. Beat well. Add remainder of flour. Beat well. Turn out on floured board and knead about 5 minutes. Place in greased bowl and let rise until doubled in bulk. Divide dough into two portions. Flatten out one piece to about 2 inch (5 cm) thickness. Place desired filling in center. Draw up and pinch edges together to cover filling. Roll out lightly and carefully to pie shape, about ¾ inch (1.875 cm) thick. Follow same method for remaining half of dough. Place on greased cookie sheet. Let rise about ½ hour. Bake at 375°F (190°C) about 20-30 minutes. When done, brush both sides with browned butter.

Cabbage filling: Sauté cabbage in butter until soft.

Potato filling: Cook and mash potatoes. Combine mashed potatoes, egg, and chives.

Sauerkraut filling: Drain sauerkraut. Fry slowly in butter about 5 minutes.

Betty Williams
Youngstown, Ohio U.S.A.

TURKEY "LONGUSH" MEAT PIE
Moriaková paštéta

1 package frozen bread dough or "kysnute cesto"
1 pound (450 g) ground turkey
1½ onions, chopped
2 tablespoons (30 mL) oil
1 tablespoon (15 mL) parsley, chopped
Salt and pepper, to taste
8 ounces (227 g) tomato sauce
8 plum tomatoes, sliced thin
½ pound (225 g) mild cheese, grated

Prepare dough, either frozen (thaw according to package directions) or any basic raised dough, by rolling out to the size of a cookie sheet, and bake until done. Season tomato sauce with salt and pepper, and spread over baked dough. Sauté ½ onion in 1 tablespoon (15 mL) oil, add ground turkey and parsley, and fry until cooked. Season with salt and pepper. Spread meat mixture over sauce. Slice or chop plum tomatoes thin and spread evenly over cooked, crumbled turkey till completely covered. Sprinkle grated cheese over sliced tomatoes. Sauté 1 onion in 1 tablespoon (15 ml) oil until transparent and golden. Spread over cheese. Put "longush" back into a preheated moderate oven 350°F (180°C) and bake until cheese melts. Cut into squares and serve warm.

Edna Mae Valasek Bresnie
Peoria, Arizona U.S.A.

WHITE BREAD CAKE FOR CHRISTMAS / EASTER
Beluš

(With Rice or Cabbage Filling)

1 cup (¼ L) evaporated milk
2 tablespoons (30 mL) butter, lard, or oleo
4 tablespoons (½ dL) sugar
1 teaspoon (5 mL) salt
1 cake yeast (7 g)
½ cup (1 dL) lukewarm water
2 eggs
4¼ cups (595 g) flour

Rice filling:
⅓ cup (¾ dL) rice, or slightly more
⅓ teaspoon (1⅔ mL) salt
1 cup (¼ L) water, or less
½ cup (1 dL) milk
3 tablespoons (45 mL) sugar or 2 tablespoons (30 mL) honey
2-3 ounces (57-85 g) butter or oleo (butter taste is preferred)
½ teaspoon (2.5 mL) vanilla
3-4 light sprinkles of cinnamon
1 egg, beaten
½ stick (½ dL) butter, not oleo, melted, for brushing

Cabbage filling:
½ of a small head of cabbage, cut up very fine
Pinch of salt
3 tablespoons (45 mL) sugar, or less
6-7 teaspoons (30-35 mL) butter
Small onion, chopped very fine
Water, just enough to prevent scorching
½ stick (½ dL) butter, not oleo, melted, for brushing

Dough: Combine milk, butter, oleo, or lard, sugar and salt. Scald in a pan over low heat; do not boil. Let cool.

Place yeast into lukewarm water with sugar, to cause fermentation, for about 10 minutes.

In a large bowl, beat eggs well; add the cooled milk and butter mixture and the yeast. Stir in enough flour to make a good bread sponge, 4 cups (560 g) flour, not more than 4¼ cups (595 g). Do not knead, just mix it a little.

(Continued on next page)

WHITE BREAD CAKE
(Continued)

Let rise in draft-free place until double in bulk, about 1½ hours. When double in bulk, cut through dough with a blunt knife a good number of strokes; let rise again until double in bulk (2nd rising). The dough will then be ready to use for beluš, or for making rolls. Recipe will make 4 rolls or 4 beluš cakes. While dough is rising for second time, prepare filling.

Rice filling: Wash and drain rice; place in a small double boiler over medium heat with salt and water. Add more water if needed after cooking for 20 minutes. Stir rice with a wooden spoon so it cooks evenly. Add milk, sugar, butter, vanilla and cinnamon; mix well and cook about 5 minutes more, or until rice is done. Add beaten egg and mix in quickly to form a light custard, not watery, but just soft enough to be a filling. Cool the custard.

Cabbage filling: Fry onion in butter until golden brown; add cabbage and salt. Cook for 5-10 minutes; add sugar, keep stirring with wooden spoon. Cabbage will become light brown. Add very little water, if necessary, to keep cabbage from scorching. Watch closely; cabbage does not take much longer than 30-35 minutes to cook since it has been cut fine.

To fill beluš: Divide dough into 4 balls. Roll out each to a 7 inch (18 cm) diameter. Place a portion of the cooked rice mixture, or cabbage filling, in the middle of the rolled out dough. Bring up all "ends" and "sides" to the center, and knead dough with fingers into the middle of what becomes a rice or cabbage filled ball. Repeat with remaining 3 balls. Let rise for about 20 minutes. Roll out each filled ball ½-¾ inch (1½-2 cm) and place on a cookie sheet. Bake 20-25 minutes in 350°F (180°C) oven. If filling keeps coming out when rolling out, just cut away the excess filling. Also, prick the tops of the beluš with a fork before placing in the oven to bake. Top of beluš may be brushed with evaporated milk before baking for a softening and shiny dough top. Bake until golden brown, remove from oven.

Topping: Melt butter in a small saucepan over low heat, until it is bubbling and has that "buttery" smell. Do not let it get dark brown or burned. It must be golden brown. Spread quickly on the beluš while it is hot. Then sprinkle granulated sugar over the bubbling butter so that the sugar melts into the

(Continued)

WHITE BREAD CAKE
(Continued)

hot butter topping. Slice into strips or wedges and it is ready to eat. Beluš is better hot than cold; however, with hot tea, even cool beluš is a delicacy. It can also be frozen for future use, and then warmed in the oven. Please do not use oleo for the topping. Only butter will make it the spišský rice or cabbage beluš that it is supposed to be.

Beluš was made by our mother, Theresa Sterbinsky for us at Christmas and Easter. She learned to make beluš in Gelnica, Spišská Župa, Slovakia.

Rolls filled with nuts, poppyseed, cottage cheese and golden raisins, and prunes, were not eaten until the Vel'ký Deň or Great Day. Those days were Hod Boží Vianočný, Hod Boží Vel'konočný, and Hod Boží Svätodušný (Christmas, Easter, and Pentecost). At the Christmas Eve or Holy Saturday Holy Supper, we ate the less festive rice or cabbage-filled beluš. When made just right, beluš is really a "delicacy", better than any pizza or other "dough" specialties.

Mary Sterbinsky
Kingston, Pennsylvania, U.S.A.

ANNE'S CREPES
Aničkiné palacinky

1 cup (¼ L) cold water
1 cup (¼ L) cold milk
4 eggs, beaten
½ teaspoon (2.5 mL) salt
1 tablespoon (15 mL) sugar
1 teaspoon (5 mL) vanilla
2 cups (280 g) all-purpose flour
4 tablespoons (60 mL) butter, melted

Combine all ingredients, mixing for at least 2-3 minutes. Refrigerate batter for several hours. Heat a crepe pan or iron skillet over medium high heat until very hot. Pour in a scant ¼ cup (50 mL) of batter. Return pan to heat 1 minute. Turn palacinka when bottom is lightly browned. Cook 30 seconds on second side. Slide out of pan onto waxed paper. Repeat with remaining batter.

Palacinky can be refrigerated or frozen. To freeze, stack cooled crepes between waxed paper, or roll up and pack in freezer bags. Thaw wrapped crepes at room temperature about 1 hour. Very good with cottage cheese filling or lekvar filling.

Anne Zvara Sarosy
Slovak World Congress
Women's Committee, Chairperson
Campbell, Ohio U.S.A.

BROCCOLI CREPES WITH HAM / BACON
Palacinky s kelom a údeným mäsom

2 cups (½ L) milk
3 eggs, beaten
1 cup (150 g) flour
1⅓ cups (300 g) cooked, chopped broccoli
⅓ cup (75 g) cooked ham, fried bacon, or cooked sausage, or cooked weiners
¼ teaspoon (1.25 mL) pepper
½ teaspoon (2.5 mL) salt
5 tablespoons (75 g) oil for frying
Ketchup
Mustard
Sour cream for topping

Prepare dough by mixing milk, beaten eggs and flour. Add cooked broccoli and chopped, cooked ham, or fried bacon bits (preferably smoked meat) or cooked weiners cut into small pieces. Add salt and pepper to taste. Heat oil in fry pan, and with a small dipper pour small amount of mixture onto heated skillet. Brown on both sides. Season with ketchup or mustard, and roll up. Top with a spoonful of sour cream.
Very good with mashed potatoes, or potato kaša.

Anna Škovierová
Očova, Slovakia

CABBAGE CREPES
Kapustové palacinky

1¼-1½ pounds (600 g) head of cabbage
3 cups (¾ L) milk
3 eggs, beaten
1¾ cups (245 g) flour
½ teaspoon (2.5 mL) salt
1 teaspoon (5 mL) baking powder
2 tablespoons (30 g) melted butter
Oil for frying

Shred, very thinly, head of cabbage. Scald with boiling water, let set for 30 minutes. Drain, and cool.
Combine milk, eggs, flour, salt, baking powder and melted butter. Mix into a thin crepe batter. Adjust consistency of batter by adding either more flour or milk, since texture of European flour may differ. Add cooled, shredded cabbage into batter.
Heat oil in pan and pour small amount of batter, spreading by tilting pan; flip over to brown other side.

An European Recipe.

CONGRESSMAN JAMES A. TRAFICANT'S COTTAGE CHEESE CREPES
Tvarohové palacinky

3 large eggs, beaten
1 cup (140 g) sifted flour
1/4 teaspoon (1.25 mL) salt
2 tablespoons (30 mL) sugar
2 tablespoons (30 mL) melted margarine

Filling:
Carton of cottage cheese
Sugar to taste

Mix together the flour and salt. Beat eggs and add margarine and sugar. Gradually add dry ingredients to make a batter. Heat 1 teaspoon (5 mL) oil in frying pan, let pan get hot. Ladle the batter into pan, lift pan and let batter spread to form a large pancake, turn over when lightly browned. Cook opposite side the same. Remove from pan and continue frying until all batter is used. You can also use a crepe maker if you have one. Stack pancakes (crepes) on platter. Mix cottage cheese and sugar (to taste). Spread cottage cheese onto crepes and roll like jelly roll. Place on cookie sheet and warm in 350°F (180°C) oven for 30-35 minutes.

Serve with melted butter poured on top. You can also use jams, jellies, fresh fruit or sautéed vegetables as a filling. Serve for a meal or a dessert.

With my roots embedded in the Slovak culture, it pleasures me to pay recognition to Slovakia as a recent free nation. This book will highlight just one of the many threads that make up the fabric of our country. Cooking is one aspect that makes our country unique. It holds the ability to pass on to future generations the heritage that we have learned from our ancestors. I am excited to be a part of this cookbook that commemorates Slovakia as a free nation.

Do videnia!

James A. Traficant, Jr.
17th District, Ohio
House of Representatives
Washington, D.C. U.S.A.

CREPES
Palacinky

1³/₄ cups (245 g)
　all-purpose flour, sifted
3¹/₂ teaspoons (17.5 mL)
　baking powder
2 tablespoons (30 mL) sugar
1 teaspoon (5 mL) salt
1 egg, beaten
2 cups (¹/₂ L) milk
3 tablespoons (45 mL)
　cooking oil or
　melted butter
1 teaspoon (5 mL) vanilla

Fillings:
Cottage cheese,
　strawberries, blueberries,
　cherries, hot spiced apple
　slices,
　applesauce or lekvar

Crepes: Combine all ingredients, stirring until smooth. Cover and let stand for a few minutes. The batter should be thin, just thick enough to coat a spoon dipped in it. If the batter is too thick, stir in a little more milk. Heat a 6 inch (15 cm) frying pan and grease lightly. Pour in just enough batter to cover the pan with a very thin layer. Tilt the pan so the batter spreads evenly. Cook on one side, turn with a spatula and brown the other side. Cook the palacinky one by one. Roll up or fold in quarters. Keep warm in oven until ready to serve.

Anna Sosnicky
Union, New Jersey　U.S.A.

PANCAKES (SO LIGHT THEY FLY)
Palacinky (také ľahké, až lietajú)

1½ cups (3½ dL) any commercial pancake mix
1 cup (¼ L) milk
1 egg, beaten
½ teaspoon (2.5 mL) baking soda (level)
¼ teaspoon (1.25 mL) baking powder (level)
¼ teaspoon (1.25 mL) salt
1½ tablespoons (22.5 mL) bacon fat, or oil, hot
Blueberries (optional)

Stir egg, milk and pancake mix into a light batter then add salt, baking powder, and baking soda. Mix again and add hot bacon grease or oil. Let set for 5 minutes. Add more water or milk at this time. Griddle must be smoking hot, lightly greased. Spoon on batter. Batter must be thin so batter on skillet is not more than ⅛ - 3/16 inch (½ - ¾ cm) thick, no thicker. The baking powder will double the size. Blueberries may be sprinkled on one side (1 teaspoonful (5 mL) per pancake). Cook about ½ minute on one side then turn and cook the other side approximately 1 to 2 minutes.

Makes about 15 pancakes.

Steve Bacon
Poland, Ohio   U.S.A.

SLOVAK PANCAKES
Slovenské palacinky

6 eggs
3 cups (420 g) flour
½ cup (100 g) sugar
½ teaspoon (2.5 mL) salt
1½ quarts (1½ L) milk
Powdered sugar for sprinkling

Beat eggs well. Add sugar, salt and one cup (¼ L) milk. Beat very well. Gradually add flour and remaining milk. Beat until very smooth. Heat a greased skillet or crepe pan to hot, pour about two tablespoons (30 mL) of mixture and brown on both sides. Fill with jelly, jam, lekvar, cottage cheese, applesauce. Roll up, sprinkle with powdered sugar. This recipe makes about 30 pancakes.

My mother, Emma Yaros, frequently made these for Saturday lunch. They were a favorite of my father, Andrew and brother, Andy, Jr.

Emma S. Pella
Land O Lakes, Florida   U.S.A.

COTTAGE CHEESE DUMPLING BALLS
Tvarohové guľky

¼ cup (70 g) butter
2 eggs
Salt, pinch
1⅛ pounds (500 g) cottage cheese
4 tablespoons (60 g) bread crumbs
¼ cup (50 g) grits
⅔ cup (100 g) grits flour
½ teaspoon (½ balička) baking powder

Coating:
½ cup (100 g) bread crumbs
½ cup (100 g) butter
Powdered sugar for sprinkling

Press cottage cheese through a sieve. Set aside. Cream butter, add eggs, salt and continue to cream mixture well. Add cottage cheese, bread crumbs and grits. Sift baking powder into flour and add to cheese mixture forming a dough. Take small portions of dough and roll into small balls. Place cottage cheese balls (dumplings) into boiling salted water and cook for 10 minutes. Drain.

Coating: Melt butter, add bread crumbs and brown. Coat dumpling balls with bread crumb mixture. Sprinkle with powdered sugar and serve warm.

4-6 servings - luncheon meal.

PhDr. Zora Mintalová
Slovenské Narodné Múzeum
Martin, Slovakia

DUMPLINGS
Halušky

3 cups (420 g) flour
1/8 teaspoon (.6 mL) white pepper
3 eggs, slightly beaten
1 teaspoon (5 mL) salt
1 cup (1/4 L) water
1/4 cup (1/2 dL) butter

Combine flour, salt and pepper in a bowl. Make a well in the center. Add eggs and water into well. Mix thoroughly. In large pan, boil salted water. Scoop up dough on to a spatula. Cut off small pieces with a knife. Drop pieces into boiling water. As halušky rise to the top, remove with a slotted spoon. Put into bowl. Add butter to keep from sticking. Keep warm until all are cooked. Toss and serve.

Yields 6 servings.

Joan Jurishica
Milwaukee, Wisconsin   U.S.A.

DUMPLINGS
Halušky

4 cups (1 L) water
1 large potato, peeled and diced
1 1/2 cups (3 1/2 dL) elbow macaroni
1 stick (115 g) butter
1 medium onion, diced
Salt and pepper
3/4 cup (1 3/4 dL) creamed cottage cheese, large curd

Bring water to a boil and add potato and macaroni. Cook until tender and drain. Meanwhile, brown butter and onion in frying pan. Add to macaroni and heat. Salt and pepper to taste. Lower heat and add cottage cheese. Mix well. (Do not heat too long after adding cottage cheese as cheese may become stringy.)

Makes 4 large servings.

Ruth Williamson
Columbiana, Ohio   U.S.A.

LIVER DUMPLINGS
Pečienkové halušky

¼ pound (115 g) chicken livers
2 eggs
1 small onion, grated
1 clove garlic, finely minced
½ teaspoon (2.5 mL) salt
1 tablespoon (15 mL) parsley, finely chopped
Flour
Chicken broth

Wash chicken livers and chop very finely. Place in bowl and add remaining ingredients. Thoroughly mix together using enough flour to thicken lightly. Drop by ½ teaspoons (2.5 mL) into boiling chicken broth and cook about 20 minutes or until done. If batter becomes too stiff, water may be added.

Elsa Truba
Toronto, Ontario   Canada

NOODLE DUMPLINGS
Halušky

1½ cups (215 g) flour
1 teaspoon (5 mL) baking powder
½ teaspoon (2.5 mL) salt
1 teaspoon (5 mL) butter
2 eggs, well beaten
½ cup (1 dL) milk

Mix all ingredients into a thick batter. Fill a kettle with water and bring to a boil. Add salt. Put batter on a flat dish, and with teaspoon drop from side of dish into boiling, salted water. Cook for a few minutes after halušky rise to the top of water. Drain, rinse with warm water. Serve in a soup or with fried cabbage.

To prepare cabbage, shred and fry slowly in butter until cabbage is soft and slightly brown. Salt to taste. Mix with the halušky noodles.

Anna Marie Popernack
Bobtown, Pennsylvania   U.S.A.

POTATO DUMPLINGS
Halušky

1 potato, grated into bowl
1 egg
3 cups (420 g) flour
Salt to taste
Water

Cottage cheese filling:
2 small potatoes
1 pint ($^1/_2$ L) creamed large curd cottage cheese
$^1/_2$ stick (60 g) butter

Sweet cabbage filling:
1 head cabbage
$^1/_2$ stick (60 g) butter
Oil
Bacon (optional)

Dough: Mix all ingredients and put dough through halušky maker, or drop dough with teaspoon from plate, into large pot of boiling water. Boil until dumplings rise to the top. When cooked, run cold water directly over the dumplings in the cooking pot; drain half of the liquid, add more cold water. Drain.

Cottage cheese filling: Dice peeled potatoes into small cubes. Place in water and cook until soft. Drain. In a saucepan, place butter and cook until slightly browned. Combine the drained potatoes, cottage cheese and butter with the halušky. **Optional:** Cube bacon, cook until crisp, add to halušky.

Sweet cabbage filling: Shred cabbage. Place enough oil in pan to cover bottom. Fry cabbage, keep turning as it browns. Add butter and continue browning. Add to halušky. Season with salt, as needed. **Optional:** cube bacon, cook until crisp, add to halušky.

Steve Bacon
Poland, Ohio U.S.A.

POTATO DUMPLINGS
Zemiakové halušky

1 egg, beaten
3 potatoes, grated
2½ cups (350 g) flour
1½ teaspoons (7.5 mL) salt

Have all ingredients and utensils ready before grating potatoes. In a medium size bowl, mix together egg and potatoes. Add dry ingredients and mix thoroughly. If dough appears stiff, add a little lukewarm water. Place batter, a portion at a time, on a plate and with the end of a teaspoon, push a small piece of dough into the boiling water. Cook for a few minutes after the halušky come to the top. Remove from stove and drain in colander, rinsing with lukewarm water. Transfer to warmed serving bowl. Stir in choice of accompaniment, usually cooked cabbage or cottage cheese.

Anne Katanik
Etobicoke, Ontario Canada

POTATO DUMPLINGS WITH COTTAGE CHEESE
Zemiakové halušky s tvarohom

1¾ pounds (800 g) potatoes, grated
3 cups (400 g hladkej) flour
Salt
½ cup (100 g) smoked bacon, chopped, or 3 ounces (80 g) butter
14 ounces (400 g) dry cottage cheese

Peel and grate potatoes, add salt, to taste, and flour, and work into a stiff dough. If potatoes are too moist, add more flour.

Into a kettle of boiling salted water, drop bits of dough using a teaspoon or a spaetzle maker. Cooked dumplings will rise to top of boiling water. Boil a few minutes longer after they surface. Remove dumplings with a slotted spoon and drain. Drizzle with either fried, crisp bacon bits or melted, browned butter. Sprinkle with crumbled cottage cheese and mix. Serve with sour milk or whipped buttermilk.

Serves 4 for lunch.

PhDr. Zora Mintalová
Slovenské Národné Múzeum
Martin, Slovakia

SCRAPED DOUGH DUMPLINGS WITH SAUERKRAUT
Strapačky s kyslou kapustou

2¼ pounds (1000 g) potatoes, peeled
1 teaspoon (5 mL) salt
2¼ cups (300 g hladkej) flour
Sauerkraut
Cracklings

Chop sauerkraut into fine shredded pieces. Set aside. Peel potatoes, grate and add salt. Add flour, mixing to form dough. Place a small portion of dough on wooden platter and with a knife, section off small pieces into boiling salted water. When dumplings come to top, lift with a slotted ladle and place in a bowl. Add sauerkraut and mix. Sprinkle with chopped, melted down cracklings.

Serves 4-6 - lunch or dinner

Since this is an old European recipe, škvarky (cracklings) were always available. The recipe calls for homemade sauerkraut cured in a barrel. The amount used varies to each individual's preference.

PhDr. Zora Mintalová
Slovenské Národné Múzeum
Martin, Slovakia

SLOVAK DUMPLINGS
Slovenské halušky

1 medium potato, finely grated
1 egg
¼ cup (½ dL) water
2½ - 3 cups (350 g - 420 g) flour
1 teaspoon (5 mL) salt

Combine all ingredients in mixing bowl. Mix to form a soft dough. Place dough on a plate; with teaspoon push small bits of dough off edge of plate into kettle of boiling, salted water. Cook 20 minutes or more, stirring. Drain, and rinse with cool water.

Use in soup or mixed with cottage cheese or fried cabbage.

Mrs. Joseph F. Kopachko
Smock, Pennsylvania U.S.A.

DUMPLINGS TOSSED WITH SAUERKRAUT
Metané halušky

Dough:
2 medium potatoes, grated
2 eggs
2 cups (280 g) flour, approximately
Water
1 teaspoon (5 mL) salt

Sauerkraut:
¼ pound (115 g) butter or oleo
1 onion, minced
1 pound (450 g) sauerkraut

Dough: Combine grated potatoes, eggs and flour; adding more or less flour to make a soft dough. Fill a large enamel kettle with water; bring to a boil and add salt. Place dough on board or plate, and with a teaspoon scrape off small chunks of dough into boiling water. Cook about 15 minutes or until done. Drain; cool slightly.
Sauerkraut: Rinse sauerkraut, drain. Sauté onion in butter, add sauerkraut and fry until lightly golden. Mix with halušky.

Mary Roman
Youngstown, Ohio U.S.A.

SLOVAK SAUERKRAUT WITH POTATO DUMPLINGS

Slovenská kyslá kapusta so zemiakovými haluškami

- ¼ cup (½ dL) bacon drippings
- ½ cup (1 dL) chopped onions
- 1 large can (27 ounces) (766 g) sauerkraut, washed
- 2 tablespoons (1/4 dL) brown sugar
- 1 teaspoon (5 mL) caraway seeds
- 1 tablespoon (15 mL) vinegar

Potato Dumplings:
- 2 medium potatoes
- 1 egg
- 1 teaspoon (5 mL) salt
- 2 cups (280 g) flour
- ¼ cup (1/2 dL) water

Sauté onions in bacon drippings for about 5 minutes, then add washed sauerkraut, cover the pot and cook until sauerkraut is hot. Add remaining ingredients and cook for another 15-20 minutes.

Dumplings: Peel, cut into sections and liquify potatoes with the egg in a blender. Add to flour and salt, mix well. If dough is too stiff, add about ¼ cup (½ dL) water. Place dough on plate and using a spoon or fork, cut off small bits of dough and drop into boiling water, or use a halušky maker. Cook about 8 or 9 minutes. Drain and rinse with cold water.

Thomas Klimek Ward
Honorary Consul of the
Slovak Republic

Editor, Slovak American Newsletter
Chicago, Illinois U.S.A.

SMOKED MEATBALL DUMPLINGS
Revúcke guľky

4½ pounds (2000 g) potatoes
⅔ pound (300 g) smoked meat or cracklings (škvarky)
¼ pound (100 g) smoked bacon
2 tablespoons (20 mL) flour
Marjoram, pinch
3 cloves garlic, pressed
Salt and black pepper to taste
Flour for coating

Peel and grate potatoes and place into a sieve to drain off liquid. Press out water/liquid. In the meantime, grind smoked meat or cracklings (škvarky) and smoked bacon. Combine ground meat with grated potatoes, add 2 tablespoons (20 mL) flour, garlic and season with salt and pepper according to taste. Mix well. Form mixture into balls (meat ball size). Coat with flour. Cook in boiling salted water until done. Serve with sauerkraut soup as a lunch or supper dish.

PhDr. Zora Mintalová
Slovenské Narodné Múzeum
Martin, Slovakia

APPLE DUMPLINGS
Jablkové knedle

1¾ cups (4 dL) water
¼ cup (40 g) margarine
2¼ cups (300 g) flour
Salt
2 eggs
1½ pounds (¾ kg) apples, peeled and cut into quarters
⅓ cup (80 g) butter
⅓ cup (80 g) nuts
1 cup (100 g) powdered sugar

Place salt and margarine into boiling water. Add flour, cooking mixture into thick dough. Let cool. Add eggs into cooled mixture. Roll out dough on floured board and cut into squares. Into each square, stuff a quarter piece of apple and cover well. Cook knedl'e in salted water (like for pirohy). Drain, and sprinkle with ground nuts and powdered sugar.

L'udmila Šandorfi
St. Catherine's, Ontario, Canada

APRICOT DUMPLINGS
Marhuľové knedle

3 cups (600 g) mashed potatoes
1½ cups (200 g) flour
1 egg
Salt
1½ pounds (600 g) small, ripe apricots, pitted
¼ cup (50 g) sugar cubes
⅓ cup (80 g) butter, melted
1 cup (200 g) cottage cheese
¾ cup (80 g) powdered sugar

Cook potatoes in skins, peel, and mash. Add flour, salt, egg, and work dough well. Roll out on floured board and cut dough into squares. Stuff ¼ cube sugar into apricot and insert into each piece of dough. Cook in salted water (like for pirohy). Drain. When serving, brush with melted butter, spread cottage cheese and dust with powdered sugar.

L'udmila Šandorfi
St. Catherine's, Ontario, Canada

CHERRY POTATO DUMPLINGS
Zemiakové knedle s čerešňami

1 pound (450 g) potatoes
⅓ cup (75 g) butter
Salt
4 tablespoons (60 g) grits
4 tablespoons (60 g) heavy flour
1 egg

Filling:
Sweet cherries, pitted, or other fresh fruit for filling
½ cup (100 g) walnuts, ground
Powdered sugar for sprinkling

Cook potatoes in skins, peel and mash. Mix butter, salt, egg, grits and flour. Add potatoes and mix. Form small balls (walnut size). Fill with pitted cherries or other fresh fruit. Cook in boiling, salted water. Drain, sprinkle with nuts and powdered sugar. If desired, pour a little melted butter over knedle.

Vincent Bruner
Hubbard, Ohio U.S.A.

FRESH FRUIT DUMPLINGS
Čerstvé ovocné knedlíky

2 cups (280 g) flour
4 tablespoons (60mL) melted butter
1 teaspoon (5 mL) salt
1 egg, slightly beaten
¼ cup (½ dL) milk
Fresh fruit
Sugar for sprinkling

Fruit filling: Use pitted, fresh fruit. Cut plums and apricots in halves; peaches, apples, or pears in quarters; blueberries or cherries (sweet or sour), may also be used. Beat egg, add milk, half of the melted butter, and mix. Add flour, salt, and knead until smooth. Cut or pinch off dough into small pieces. Roll flat and wrap evenly around the fruit. Moisten dough edges and seal well all around. In a large kettle bring salted water to a boil; drop dumplings into water and cook for 8-10 minutes. Do not overcook. Remove from water immediately and drain in a colander. Pour remaining half of the melted butter over dumplings. Place colander over hot water until ready to serve. Arrange on a platter and drizzle with more butter, if desired. Sprinkle with granulated or powdered sugar. For other toppings, use crumbled pot cheese, ground poppyseed, or bread crumbs fried lightly in butter. Recipe makes approximately 20 apricot-sized dumplings.

Louise Hartz
Pasadena, Maryland   U.S.A.

PEACH DUMPLINGS
Broskyňové knedle

2 cups (280 g) flour
1 egg
¾ cup (1¾ dL) milk
½ teaspoon (2.5 mL) salt
4 ripe peaches, pitted or unpitted

Mix flour, egg, milk, and salt in bowl. Divide dough in four equal parts and wrap around peaches. Place dough covered peaches in large pot of boiling water. Cook, covered, 15-20 minutes. Serve with melted butter, cinnamon and sugar, or cottage cheese.

In memory of my grandmother, Carolyn Vlack.

Gretchen Vlack
Santa Cruz, California U.S.A.

PLUM DUMPLINGS
Slivkové gule

Dough:
2½ cups (6 dL) cooked, cold, mashed potatoes
2 eggs
1 teaspoon (5 mL) salt
2 cups (280 g) flour (approximately)

Filling:
1½ dozen ripe freestone Italian plums, pitted
½ cup (100 g) sugar
Cinnamon, as desired

Topping:
2 cups (½ L) bread crumbs
⅔ cup (130 g) sugar
½ cup (1 dL) butter

Add eggs and salt to the potatoes. Add enough flour to make a smooth dough, not too stiff. On floured board roll dough to ¼ inch (¾ cm) thickness. Cut into 3 inch (8 cm) squares.
Fill plum cavities with the sugar, cinnamon mixture. Place a plum on each 3 inch (8 cm) square. Press dough around plums to form balls. Cook 10 minutes in boiling water, in covered pot. Drain well. Roll in bread crumbs which have been browned in the butter with sugar added.

Rene Dorsett
San Francisco, California, U.S.A.

PLUM DUMPLINGS
Slivkové gule

18 fresh plums, unpitted
1 cup (¼ L) milk
2½ (37.5 mL) tablespoons butter
½ cup (1 dL) farina
3 whole eggs
2 cups (280 g) all-purpose flour
Poppyseed or farmer's cheese for sprinkling
Sugar for sprinkling

Bring milk and butter to boil. Stirring constantly, slowly pour in farina. Continue cooking until thickened and boiling. Cool slightly. Add eggs, one at a time, beating well after each addition. Beat in flour until easy to work with. Divide dough in half. Shape each piece into a 9x9 inch (23x23 cm) square. Dough can be rolled out thinner to make smaller dumpling balls. Press plums evenly into bottom layer. Cover, cut, or shape with hand to form individual balls. Seal well. Cook in salted, boiling water. Loosen with spatula. Boil 15 minutes. Drain. Place in buttered sauce pan or plate. Serve with ground poppyseed and sugar (good with plum filling) or farmer's cheese and sugar (good with apricot filling). Or dumplings may be served with cream.

Fresh apricots may be substituted for plums. Pitted plums may be used, however, the juice of the fruit has a tendency to run into dough. Or, replace fruit pit with a sugar cube.

Dough balls may be frozen. To freeze: place dumplings on a sheet and freeze. When frozen, package and seal. To cook frozen dumplings, drop in boiling, salted water and boil for 20-25 minutes or until soft.

Maria Krupa
Rockaway, New Jersey   U.S.A.

STEAMED DUMPLINGS
Parené buchty

4¹/₃ cups (610 g) flour
2 tablespoons (30 g) powdered sugar
¹/₄ teaspoon (1¹/₄ mL) salt
²/₃ cup (1¹/₂ dL) milk
2 egg yolks, beaten
2 tablespoons (30 g) softened butter

Prune lekvar
¹/₂ cup (100 g) ground poppyseed, or ¹/₂ cup (100 g) ground nuts for sprinkling
¹/₂ cup (115 g) lightly browned butter, for drizzle
1 cup (3 dL) powdered sugar for dusting

Yeast fermentation (kvasok):
¹/₄ cup (¹/₂ dL) milk
¹/₂ large cake (30 g) yeast
1 tablespoon (15 g) powdered sugar

Dough: Crumble yeast into ¹/₄ cup (¹/₂ dL) milk, add 1 tablespoon (15 g) powdered sugar; set aside to rise. Sift flour, salt and 2 tablespoons (30 g) powdered sugar; add 2 egg yolks, beaten, remaining milk and 2 tablespoons (30 g) softened butter. Add yeast mixture, knead dough well. Set aside in warm place to rise and double in bulk.

On a floured board, roll out dough to ³/₈ inch (1 cm) thick. With a round pastry cutter, or a glass, cut out circles of dough. Place a dab of lekvar, about a heaping teaspoon (5 mL) in center of cut out dough pieces. Cover with another round piece of dough, press edges completely around to seal and set aside to rise.

In a large pot, fill half full with water. Across top of pot, tie a napkin or white cloth. When water comes to a boil, place filled dough (buchty) on cloth; cover with a bowl that fits tightly across top of pot so as not to permit steam to escape. Steam buchty for 8-10 minutes. To test for doneness, insert a wooden tooth pick. Buchty are cooked when tooth pick is clean, not sticky with dough. Remove dumplings from steam and place on serving dish. Brown butter and drizzle over dumplings. Sprinkle with either poppyseed or nuts; sprinkle with powdered sugar. Serve warm.

Filling: Lekvár may be substituted with any type of fruit filling. Cottage cheese and cinnamon can be substituted for sprinkling.

Ján Lakota
Teplická, Bratislava
Slovakia

TORN DOUGH DUMPLINGS WITH MILK
Trhance s mliekom

2 large potatoes
1 cup (2 dL) water
Salt
3 1/2 cups (8 dL) milk
Butter
4 tablespoons (35 g) wheat flour (best bread dough flour)
Water

Torn dough is prepared as follows:

Mix flour and very small amount of water to make a stiff dough. On a wooden platter, or board, tear dough into small pieces (trhance). Peel potatoes, cut into small cubes and cook in 1 cup (2 dL) water, salted, until soft. Add milk and small amount of butter to the cooked potatoes, then add the trhance and let come to a full boil. Remove from heat and let set 5-10 minutes. Serve for lunch or supper.

Serves 4.

Mučné jedlo!

PhDr. Zora Mintalová
Slovenské Národné Múzeum
Martin, Slovakia

WILMETTE LASAGNA
"Vilmetové" rezance

4 cups (1 L) spaghetti sauce
8 ounces (225 g) lasagna noodles, cooked according to package directions
¼ pound (115 g) cream cheese
¾ pound (336 g) Ricotta or farmer's cheese
¾ pound (336 g) Mozzarella cheese, shredded
20 ounces (560 g) frozen chopped spinach, cooked and cooled
1 can (approximately 400 g) artichokes, sliced
½ pound (225 g) Italian sausage, sliced
1 cup (¼ L) fresh mushrooms, sliced
3 tablespoons (45 mL) Parmesan cheese, grated

Arrange ⅓ of the noodles on bottom of a 13x9 inch (33x23 cm) baking dish. Spoon over ⅓ of sauce and dot with ⅓ of all ingredients. Repeat layering ingredients twice more, ending with Mozzarella cheese. Sprinkle top with Parmesan cheese.
Cover loosely with foil. Bake in 375°F (190°C) oven for 30 minutes. Remove foil. Bake about 10 minutes longer, until filling is bubbly and cheese is melted. Remove from oven. Let stand 10-15 minutes before serving.

Serves 8.

Martha Mistina Kona
Slovak World Congress
Slovak Heritage, Culture Commission, Chairperson
Wilmette, Illinois U.S.A.

COTTAGE CHEESE NOODLES
Tvarohové šúľance

Dough:
- 14 ounces (400 g) cottage cheese
- 1 egg
- 3 tablespoons (40 g) bread crumbs, finely ground
- 2-3 tablespoons (30-40 g) grits
- Pinch of salt
- 2 tablespoons (20 g) powdered sugar

Topping:
- 2-3 tablespoons (35-40 g) grits (krupice)
- 1/4 cup (60 g) butter
- 1 cup (2 dL) milk

Dusting:
Powdered sugar

Dough: Press cottage cheese through sieve. Add egg, bread crumbs, grits, pinch of salt, and powdered sugar. Mix.
On bread board, roll dough to thickness of finger. Cut into small strips. Press or roll each piece with hand into a noodle rope or roll.
Cook in boiling, salted water. Drain.

Topping: In an empty, dry fry pan, fry grits dry till rosy. Add butter and milk. Cook until grits swell and are dissolved. Pour over noodles. Dust with powdered sugar. Serve as a side dish, or, a luncheon - dinner main dish.

4 servings.

PhDr. Zora Mintalová
Slovenské Národné Múzeum
Martin, Slovakia

FRIED NOODLES
Čir

2 cups (280 g) sifted flour
2 eggs
½ teaspoon (2½ mL) salt
4 tablespoons (½ dL) butter
3 cups (¾ L) chicken soup or stock
Salt and pepper to taste
Cooked chicken giblets (optional)

Mix flour, eggs and salt together. Add water, if necessary to make a stiff dough. Knead into a ball and grate on medium side of grater. Spread out to dry overnight. Melt butter. Add dried noodles and brown 5-10 minutes, stirring frequently to prevent burning. Add soup, ½ cup (1 dL)) at a time. Cook covered until liquid is absorbed. Season to taste. Cooked chicken giblets may be chopped and added when done.

In memory of
Dorothy Sarvaš Zvara

SLOVAK EGG NOODLES
Vajíčkové rezance

3 eggs, slightly beaten
Flour

Mix eggs and enough flour to make a stiff dough. Knead very well on floured board until very smooth and elastic. Put under bowl for about 10 minutes to rest. Roll out on lightly floured board until very thin. Let dry for a few minutes. Roll up dough and cut very fine; or cut rolled out dough into 2½ inch (6½ cm) wide strips, stack strips in one pile, and cut through all strips very fine; or cut small squares with a fancy cutter. Spread out cut noodles across board to prevent from sticking if being used immediately. Dry spread out noodles thoroughly if noodles are to be stored for future use.

In memory of
Dorothy Sarvaš Zvara

MIXED NOODLE CASSEROLE
Prekladané rezance

1 pound (400-450 g) dry noodles
⅓ cup (80 g) butter, melted
4 tablespoons (60 g) nuts, ground
4 tablespoons (60 g) poppy seed
½ cup (100 g) lekvar
¼ cup (1/2 dL) milk
1 egg
Salt
1 cup (100 g) powdered sugar
Powdered sugar for sprinkling

Cook noodles in salted water. Drain, and add butter. Mix well. Divide noodles into three portions. Mix ⅓ noodles with lekvar. Mix another third with ground poppyseed which has been mixed with half of the sugar. Grease a casserole and layer the bottom with poppyseed noodles. Place the lekvar noodles over the layer of poppyseed noodles. Sprinkle this second layer with ground nuts and remaining sugar. Place the remaining ⅓ noodles on top for the third layer. Combine beaten egg with milk and pour over top layer. (Add more milk if mixture seems too dry.) Cover, place in moderate oven 350°F (180°C) and bake 15-20 minutes or until heated through. To serve, sprinkle with additional powdered sugar.

L'udmila Šandorfi
St. Catherine's, Ontario Canada

POTATO AND NOODLE FLAKES CASSEROLE
Granadírmarš

1 1/3 - 1 1/2 cups (200 g hrubej) flour
1 egg
Water
Pinch of salt
2 tablespoons (30 g) fat, butter or margarine
1 3/4 pounds (800 g) potatoes
1/4 cup (60 g) onion
1/3 cup (70 g) bacon
Paprika

Combine flour, egg, pinch of salt and just enough water to form a stiff, firm noodle dough. Roll out dough thin and let partially dry. Cut noodles into thin flake shape. Cook in boiling, salted water. When done, drain well, place in bowl and drizzle with melted fat.
Potatoes may be cooked peeled or in skins. Cube peeled and cooked potatoes.
Mix noodle flakes with potatoes. Chop bacon and fry. Add chopped onion and fry until golden. Add paprika, mix well and add to potato-noodle mixture. Mix and serve for either lunch or dinner.

Serves 4.

PhDr. Zora Mintalová
Slovenské Národné Múzeum
Martin, Slovakia

POURED DOUGH NOODLES
Liate cesto

Egg
Flour
Salt
Water, few drops

Liat' means to pour. This quick dough can be used in any liquid soups. In the older days, mothers that just had a baby cooked (zapraženú rascovú polievku) broth and dropped in the "liate cesto."

It is very nourishing. It can also be stretched, depending on how much you use of the above ingredients. This thin dough is excellent in lentil soup, chicken or beef soup or any favorite broth.

Popsun is hard dough and is grated. Besides flavoring the soup, it also acts as a thickening. Use it in barley, potato or combined soups.

Margaret A. Kluka
Barberton, Ohio   U.S.A.

CABBAGE AND NOODLES
Kapusta a rezance

- 1 pound (450 g) homemade noodles or 1 package of broad noodles
- 3 pounds (1$^{1}/_{3}$ kg) cabbage, shredded
- 2 pounds (900 g) fresh sauerkraut
- 2 large onions, chopped
- $^{1}/_{2}$ pound (115 g) bacon fat or margarine
- 4 whole bay leaves
- 6 whole allspice
- Salt and pepper, to taste

Boil noodles, drain, set aside. Steam cabbage till tender. Cook sauerkraut till tender. Drain cabbage and sauerkraut and mix together. Sauté onion in bacon fat and add to cabbage/sauerkraut mixture. Add bay leaves and allspice. Fry on low heat till well mixed and sautéed. Add noodles to sautéed mixture. Salt and pepper to taste.

Dorothy Rygiel
New Jersey   U.S.A.

SAUERKRAUT AND NOODLES
Rezance s kyslou kapustou

1/4 pound (115 g) butter or oleo
1 medium onion, sliced
28 ounces (794 g) sauerkraut
1/2 pound (225 g) noodles
Sugar
Salt, pepper
Bread crumbs

Sauté onion in melted butter until transparent. Add drained sauerkraut, sugar, salt and pepper to taste. Simmer for about 20 minutes. Prepare noodles according to directions. Drain well and add to sauerkraut. Place cooked kraut and noodles into casserole. Sprinkle with buttered bread crumbs and heat in oven.

Note: This was my grandma's recipe, only she used home made noodles or halušky. I use spiral noodles or bows. Also, sauerkraut may be drained and rinsed in hot water to remove tartness. Casserole is delicious with any meat entrée.

Margaret Mowery
Akron, Ohio   U.S.A.

WHITE NOODLES
Biele rezance

2 cups (280 g) flour
1 egg
Pinch of salt
1/2 cup (1 dL) farina
1 tablespoon (15 mL) butter, margarine or oleo
Milk

Mix flour, egg, salt, and add just enough water to knead. Roll thin. Cut rolled out dough into strips. Cut noodles medium thick. Fry farina in butter or shortening until light brown. Add a little milk. Turn off heat. Mix and spoon over noodles.
Option: May mix in a little jam or prune butter (lekvar).

Julia Kunchak Compan
Akron, Ohio   U.S.A.

COUSIN RITA'S BAKED DUMPLINGS
Pečené pirohy

Dough:
2½ cups (350 g) flour
2 eggs, slightly beaten
1 pint (½ L) sour cream
1 teaspoon (5 mL) oil

Filling:
2-3 potatoes, peeled and cubed
1 quart (1 L) salted water
1 teaspoon (5 mL) salt

Topping:
2 tablespoons (30 mL) butter
1 onion, chopped finely
¼-½ cup (½ dL-1 dL) milk

Dough: Mix all ingredients and set dough aside for ½ hour. If dough is too sticky, add flour, 1 tablespoon (15 mL) at a time until dough is manageable to work with. Roll dough on floured board. Cut with knife into 3 inch (7.5 cm) squares. Fill with 1 teaspoon (5 mL) mashed potatoes. Fold dough over, pinch edges together to seal potato filling. Bake at 350°F (180°C) on greased cookie sheet 12-15 minutes, or until light golden. Turn over, bake till done on both sides.

Filling: Cube potatoes and cook in salted water. Drain, mash, and add salt. This should make 1 cup (¼ L) mashed potatoes.

Topping: In a skillet melt butter. Add onion and sauté until lightly browned. Add milk and simmer. Add pirohy and coat with milk sauce mixture. Serve warm.

Edna Valašek Bresnie
Peoria, Arizona U.S.A.

DUMPLINGS
Knedle

4 medium potatoes
2 tablespoons (30 g) butter or oleo
¼ cup (½ dL) milk
2½ cups (350 g) flour (or more)
Lekvar, prune filling

Topping:
1 medium onion, chopped
2 sticks (225 g) butter or oleo
½ cup (1 dL) bread crumbs

Peel and cube potatoes, boil until tender and drain. Add butter and milk, mash, and let cool. Add flour to make a smooth dough. Roll out and cut into squares (like for pirohy). Place lekvar or prune filling in center. Fold over into triangle, and pinch edges together. Roll in palm of hand to form a ball. Drop dumplings into boiling water. When dumplings rise to surface, continue to cook 5 minutes longer. Drain.

Topping: In a fry pan, sauté onion in ½ stick (¼ dL) oleo or butter until browned and crisp. Add remaining 1½ (1¾ dL) sticks of butter or oleo, and bread crumbs. Mix well. Pour over cooked dumplings. (Use a pot with lid and gently shake dumplings until topping is evenly distributed around dough.)

Serves 4-6.

Mrs. Robert Hnat
Youngstown, Ohio U.S.A.

PIROHY

2 eggs
1 cup (¼ L) water
1 teaspoon (5 mL) salt
4 cups (560 g) flour, approximately
1 stick (115 g) butter
Boiling salted water

Cheese filling:
1 cup (¼ dL) dry cottage cheese
1 egg
Pinch of salt

Cabbage filling:
1 cup (¼ dL) cabbage, grated
½ teaspoon (2.5 mL) salt
2 tablespoons (30 mL) butter
1 small onion, chopped

Potato filling:
5 medium potatoes, cooked and mashed
1 teaspoon (5 mL) salt
4 slices mild yellow cheese

Prune filling:
Use prepared lekvar/prune butter out of jar

Dough: Mix water, eggs, and salt. Add enough flour to make a medium soft dough. Knead until air bubbles appear. Dough should be soft but not sticky. Divide dough into two parts. Roll out thin and cut with round glass or cookie cutter. Place desired filling in center of each circle. Fold over and pinch edges to seal. Set aside on well floured board till all pirohy are completed.

Drop in boiling salted water till pirohy come to the top. Continue to boil about 10 minutes. When cooked, drain and rinse in cool water.

Melt 1 stick (115 g) butter and pour over cooked pirohy.

Cheese filling: Combine dry cottage cheese, egg, pinch of salt and mix well.

Cabbage filling: Sauté grated cabbage, salt, chopped onion in butter. Stir often.

Potato filling: Cook and mash potatoes. Add salt and four slices mild yellow cheese. Stir well.

Prune filling: Use prepared prune butter/lekvar.

In memory of
Mrs. Katherine Sarosy Machuga

Helen Machuga Livesay
Struthers, Ohio   U.S.A.

POTATO AND CHEESE DUMPLINGS
Pirohy

3 cups (¾ L) mashed potatoes
1 cup (¼ L) cottage cheese
1 tablespoon (15 mL) vegetable shortening
1 onion, chopped
1 teaspoon (5 mL) salt
Pepper to taste
3½ cups (490 g) sifted flour
1 egg, beaten
1 cup (¼ L) water
½ teaspoon (2.5 mL) salt

Filling: Combine mashed potatoes with cottage cheese. Sauté onions in shortening, add salt and pepper, and mix with potatoes and cheese.

Dough: Combine flour, egg, water and salt. Roll thin on floured board. Use about ⅓ of the dough at a time, and cut into circles about 3 inches (7.5 cm) in diameter. In center of each circle, place 1 tablespoon (15 mL) of potato mixture and form into dumplings, folding over and pinching ends to seal. Place dumplings into 3 quarts (3 L) of boiling, salted water and continue to boil them 4 minutes after they float. Remove carefully with slotted spoon into a colander and spray with a little cold water to set them. These are delicious served with sour cream. May be frozen and then defrosted and reheated.

Makes 3 dozen.

Anna Sosnicky
Union, New Jersey U.S.A.

SHEEP CHEESE DUMPLINGS-PIROHY
Bryndzové pirohy

Dough:
2¼ pounds (1000 g) potatoes
⅞ cup (120 g hrubej) coarse flour
Salt
Egg
¼ pound (120 g) grits

Filling:
1 cup (200 g) sheep cheese
1 potato, cooked and mashed
2 tablespoons (30 mL) milk
Salt

Topping:
¼ pound (100 g) bacon, cut into bits and fried
½ cup (100 g) sheep cheese
Dill or parsley

Dough: Peel potatoes, cube, and cook until tender. Drain, and while warm press through a sieve. Add flour, mix and let dough cool. Into the cool dough add egg, grits, and pinch of salt. Mix, and roll out dough to $1/16$ inch (3-4 mm). Divide into two parts. Place small mounds of cheese mixture filling evenly across on one section of dough. Cover with other half of rolled out dough. With fingers, press dough around mounds and using a small glass, cut around circular edge; or merely cut out squares. Press down edges well around filled dumplings. Cook in boiling salted water. Drain, and drizzle with fried bacon bits. Sprinkle with cheese mixed with either dill or parsley.

Filling: Into fresh sheep cheese, add cooked potato that has been mashed or pressed through a sieve. Add milk and season with salt.

Serve with buttermilk as a luncheon meal.

Dobrú chuť!

4-6 servings.

PhDr. Zora Mintalová
Slovenské Národné Múzeum
Martin, Slovakia

POTATO PANCAKES
Zemiakove palacinky

3 cups (¾ L) raw potatoes, grated
1½ tablespoons (15 g) flour
2 eggs, well beaten
1 teaspoon (5 mL) salt
1 teaspoon (5 mL) onion, minced
⅛ teaspoon (.6 mL) baking powder

Grate potatoes, pouring off liquid and draining well. Lightly stir in well beaten eggs. Add flour, salt, onion and baking powder. Drop from spoon onto a well-greased pan and brown on both sides.

Dolores Paunicka Callahan
Lowell, Indiana   U.S.A.

POTATO PANCAKES
Nalesníky

1 pound (450 g) potatoes
¾ cup (105 g) flour
1 egg, beaten
1 teaspoon (5 mL) salt
1 teaspoon (5 mL) baking powder
2 tablespoons (30 mL) shortening

Peel and grate potatoes. Add egg, salt and baking powder. Gradually add flour until mixture becomes thick. Mix thoroughly. Drop one teaspoonful (5 mL) at a time onto hot, greased skillet. Brown lightly on both sides.

In memory of Dad,
Matthew Duke.

Anna Marie Popernack
Bobtown, Pennsylvania   U.S.A.

POTATO PANCAKES - BAKED
Nalesníky

6 large potatoes
½ cup (70 g) flour
1 teaspoon (5 mL) salt
1 tablespoon (15 mL) butter

Peel and grate potatoes. Mix potatoes with flour and salt. Spread on greased 12x18 inch (30x45 cm) cookie sheet. In a preheated oven, bake at 375°F (190°C) for 1 hour or until golden brown. Spread with melted butter and cut into pieces, 4 square inches (10x10 cm).

In memory of
Mrs. Katherine Sarosy Machuga

Helen Machuga Livesay
Struthers, Ohio U.S.A.

POTATO PANCAKES WITH APPLESAUCE
Zemiakové palacinky s jablčnicou

1 onion, grated
¼ teaspoon (1.25 mL) pepper
3 cups (¾ L) potatoes, grated
1½ cups (210 g) flour
½ teaspoon (2.5 mL) garlic powder
1 tablespoon (15 mL) salt
1 egg, slightly beaten
¼ cup (½ dL) oil
Applesauce

Heat oil in frying pan. In a bowl, mix remaining ingredients, except applesauce, and ladle some batter into pan. Fry on both sides until golden brown. Serve with applesauce.

POTATO PANCAKES WITH BRATISLAVA BUTTER SAUCE
Lokša

2 pounds (900 g) potatoes
3 tablespoons (45 mL) butter
2 cups (½ L) milk
1½ teaspoons (7.5 mL) salt
3 cups (420 g) flour

Butter Sauce:
¼ pound (115 g) butter, melted
1 tablespoon (10 g) flour
1 teaspoon (5 mL) water

Peel and cube potatoes, cook until done. Drain and mash. Add butter, milk and salt. Mix thoroughly. Store in refrigerator for several hours until firm and well chilled.

Remove from refrigerator. Add 3 cups (420 g) flour and knead well on floured breadboard. Divide dough into 3-4 pieces and roll each thin. Cut out circles and fry lokša on heated, ungreased griddle until browned. When cooked, spread with Bratislava Butter Sauce, roll loosely and serve.

Bratislava Butter Sauce: Melt butter, add flour and fry over medium high heat until browned. Add water. Lower heat and cook a minute longer. Serve over pancakes.

Marge Koscak
Parma, Ohio U.S.A.

POTATO PANCAKES WITH SAUERKRAUT FILLING
Lokše

Dough:
1½ pounds (700 g) potatoes
2-2¼ cups (300 g) flour
1 tablespoon (15 mL) salt
Fat (oil or margarine) for frying

Filling:
2 onions (medium sized,) minced
¼ pound (100 g) smoked bacon, chopped
3 cups (400 g) sauerkraut, drained
Caraway seed, crushed
2 tablespoons (30 g) butter

Dough: Cook potatoes in skins, peel and mash. Add salt, flour, and mix into smooth dough. On floured board, shape dough into roll. Cut into small circles. Flatten and roll out thin to make a 7 inch (17.5 cm) circle. Fry, on both sides, in hot fat. Brush with melted butter.

Filling: Fry chopped bacon bits, add minced onion and sauté until golden in color. Add drained sauerkraut and caraway seed and continue cooking until softened. Place filling on each fried lokša and roll up.

Anna Škovierová
Očova, Slovakia

MASHED POTATO PANCAKES
Zemiakové palacinky

2 cups (½ L) mashed potatoes
1 cup (250 mL) milk
3 eggs
1 teaspoon (5 mL) baking powder
¼ teaspoon (1.25 mL) salt
2 teaspoons (10 mL) sugar
2 tablespoons (20 mL) corn starch or 4 tablespoons (40 mL) flour
3 tablespoons (45 mL) oil

Cook 3 potatoes, cubed. Drain and mash. Beat eggs, add remaining ingredients and mix well. Add mixture to mashed potatoes. In a skillet or frying pan, spread batter, pancake size, and fry in hot oil until brown. Turn, and brown the other side.

POTATO PATTIES
Gruľovníky

10 potatoes, medium to large
2 eggs
Salt
4½ cups (630 g) flour
Shortening or lard
Sugar
Melted butter

Boil potatoes until tender. Mash or rice. Salt to taste. Cool. Add two eggs and mix well. Add flour, more if dough is too sticky. Cut dough in half and roll each half with hands into long ropes, approximately 2 inches (5 cm) in diameter. Cut ropes into 2 inch (5 cm) sections, about 22 pieces.

On a floured board, with rolling pin, roll out each individual piece into an 8 inch (20 cm) circle, approximately ¼ inch (¾ cm) thick. Keep board well floured.

In electric fry pan, at 425°F (220°C), melt 1 tablespoon (15 mL) shortening. Fry one circle at a time on each side, until browned. Add small amounts of shortening when necessary. After removing pancake from skillet, brush with melted butter and sprinkle with sugar. Stack on a platter and cut into wedges to serve.

Gruľovníky is one of my husband's favorites. He remembers it as a child in the village of Viťaz, Okres Prešov, Župa Šariš, Slovakia. His mother made this recipe from left over cold mashed potatoes. She dry fried them with no fat on top of an old country stove. I ruined a fry pan without using fat, so I use a little Crisco and fry them in my electric fry pan. This is a simple, poor man's fare but thoroughly enjoyed.

Mary Hric
Detroit, Michigan U.S.A.

POTATO THIN PANCAKES
Zemiaková lokša

5 medium sized potatoes
2-2½ cups (280 g-350 g) flour
1 egg
1 teaspoon (5 mL) salt, if desired
Butter, melted and browned

To make mashed potatoes: peel and cut into cubes. Cover with water and boil until done. Drain. Whip potatoes to make them smooth and lump free. Add salt and egg. Slowly work in flour to get a consistency similar to pie crust.

Divide the dough into pieces that will stretch 6-8 inches (15-20 cm) when rolled as thin as possible on a floured board. Preheat fry pan to hot. Do not grease pan. Place rolled out dough in pan or griddle and fry until dark blisters form (takes about 1 minute). Flip and cook the other side. When done, brush both sides with melted butter that has been browned. Serve warm. Makes about 10 lokše.

Barbara Kowalski
Jermyn, Pennsylvania U.S.A.

POTATO CAKES
Haruľa-zemiaková baba

3½ pounds (1500 g) potatoes
½ cup plus 1 tablespoon (80 g) flour
⅓ cup (75 mL) smoked bacon, chopped
3 tablespoons (45 mL) melted butter
1 egg, beaten
1 teaspoon (5 mL) salt
¼ teaspoon (1.25 mL) pepper
2 cloves garlic, minced
1 onion, minced
Marjoram, pinch

Fry bacon bits; remove bacon and sauté onion in bacon fat until transparent. Add garlic to onion. Peel potatoes and grate. Add flour, salt, pepper, pinch of marjoram and beaten egg. Mix well. Add bacon bits and onion to potato mixture and mix. Spread potato dough evenly on greased baking sheet and brush top with melted butter. Bake in preheated moderate oven 350°F (180°C) about 45 minutes or until lightly golden. Cut into square pieces and serve.

Optional: Place a heaping tablespoon of apple sauce on top of each piece of baba.

Anne Zvara Sarosy
Campbell, Ohio   U.S.A.

SLOVAK POTATO PANCAKES
Slovenské zemiakové placky

4 large potatoes, liquified
1 teaspoon (5 mL) salt
1 teaspoon (5 mL) black pepper
½ cup (70 g) flour
1 medium onion, chopped
1 egg, beaten
Garlic powder, to taste
Marjoram, to taste

Peel and grate or liquify potatoes in blender with onion and combine with other ingredients, mixing into a smooth batter. Place by tablespoonsful into a well oiled frying pan. Fry until both sides are golden brown.

Thomas Klimek Ward
Honorary Consul
Slovak Republic
Chicago, Illinois   U.S.A.

PASTRIES AND DESSERTS

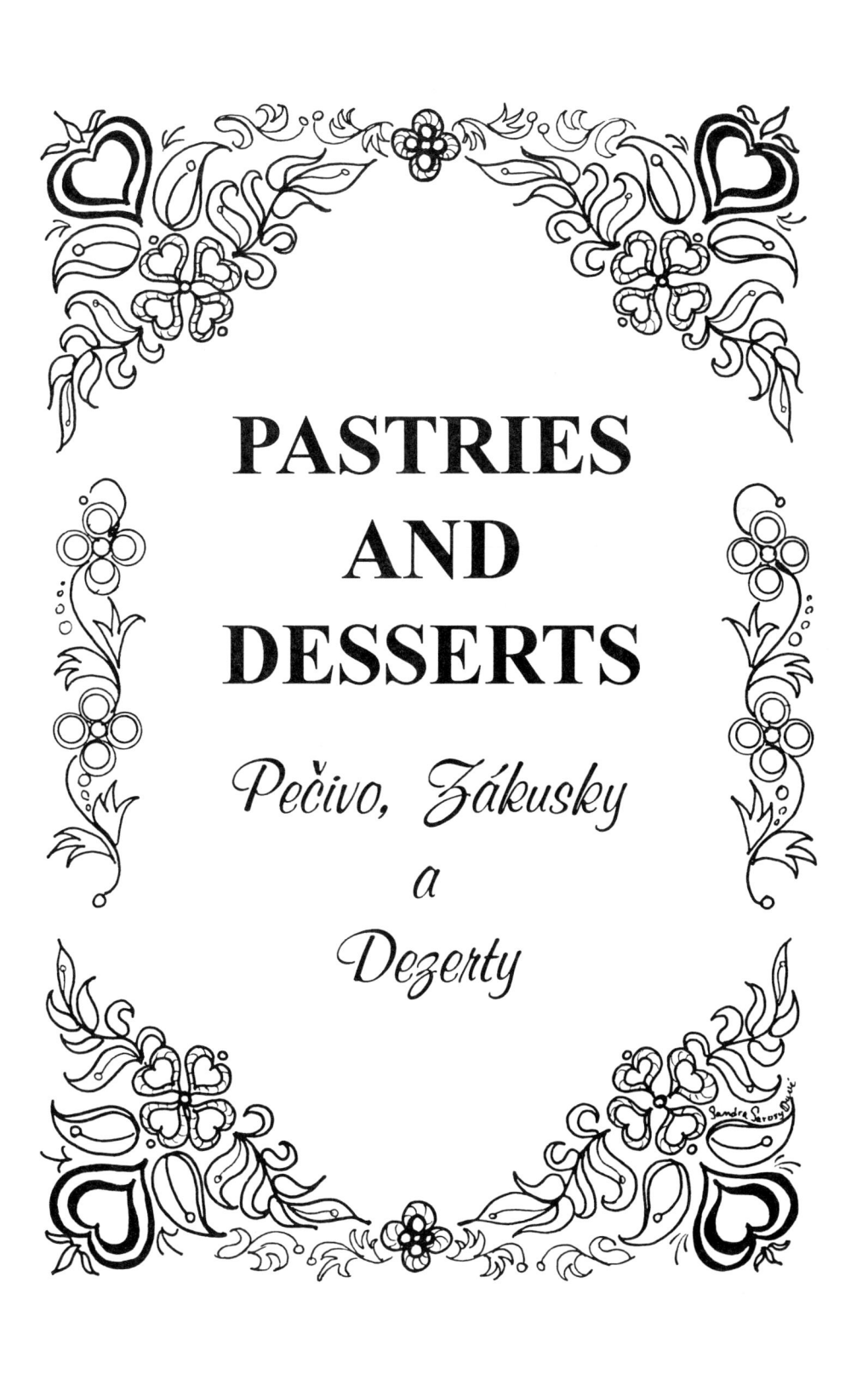

Pečivo, Zákusky

a

Dezerty

APPLE CAKE
Jablčník

4 cups (1 L) diced apples
2 cups (280 g) flour
1½ cups (300 g) sugar
2 teaspoons (10 mL) soda
1 teaspoon (5 mL) vanilla
2 teaspoons (10 mL) cinnamon
¾ teaspoon (3.75 mL) salt
½ cup (1 dL) oil
1 cup (¼ L) chopped nuts
2 eggs

In a large bowl, break eggs over apples. Mix with fork. Add sugar, nuts, cinnamon and oil. Sift flour, salt, and soda and add to apple mixture. Add vanilla. Mix well. Put in oblong cake pan and bake in preheated oven at 325°F (160°C) for 45 minutes to 1 hour.

Betty Williams
Youngstown, Ohio U.S.A.

APPLE PRUNE CAKE
Jablková, slivková bábovka

2 cups (400 g) sugar
1½ cups (3½ dL) vegetable oil
3 eggs
2 cups (½ L) apples, peeled and shredded
3 cups (420 g) flour
2 teaspoons (10 mL) baking soda
1 teaspoon (5 mL) salt
1 teaspoon (5 mL) cinnamon
½ teaspoon (2.5 mL) cloves
12 ounces (340 g) dried pitted prunes, chopped (2 cups) (400 g)
1 cup (200 g) chopped nuts
Confectioners' sugar

In a large mixing bowl, beat sugar, oil and eggs for about 2 minutes; blend in apples. Combine dry ingredients; gradually beat into egg mixture. Stir in prunes and nuts. Spoon into a greased and floured 10 inch (25 cm) tube pan; bake at 325°F (165°C) for 1 hour and 20 minutes or until a toothpick inserted near the center comes out clean. Cool in pan for 15-20 minutes; invert and cool completely. Dust cake with powdered sugar before serving.

Yields 12-14 servings.

Julianne Elizabeth Zetts
Canfield, Ohio U.S.A.

RAW APPLE CAKE
Jablková bábovka

1³/₄ cups (4 dL) brown sugar
1 cup (¼ L) vegetable oil
3 large eggs
1 teaspoon (5 mL) salt
2 cups (280 g) flour
1 teaspoon (5 mL) baking soda
1 teaspoon (5 mL) cinnamon
1 teaspoon (5 mL) vanilla
4 cups (1 L) diced apples (about 6)
1 cup (¼ L) chopped nuts

Icing:
1 - 8 ounce (225 g) package cream cheese
1 cup (225 g) butter
1 cup (¼ L) icing sugar (powdered sugar)
Milk

In a large bowl combine brown sugar, oil and eggs. Mix well. Add salt, flour, soda, cinnamon and vanilla. Mix well. Fold in apples and nuts. Pour into greased and floured 9x13 inch (23x33 cm) pan. Bake at 350°F (180°C) for 45 minutes.

Icing: Combine all ingredients and beat well. Add enough milk to make a spreadable consistency. Mix well until fluffy.

Betty Kominar
Windsor, Ontario, Canada

OLD FASHIONED APPLESAUCE CAKE
Starodávna jablková bábovka

2½ cups (350 g) flour
1¾ cups (275 g) sugar
¼ teaspoon (1.25 mL) baking powder
1½ teaspoons (7.5 mL) baking soda
1½ teaspoons (7.5 mL) salt
1 teaspoon (5 mL) cinnamon
½ teaspoon (2.5 mL) cloves
½ teaspoon (2.5 mL) allspice
½ teaspoon (2.5 mL) nutmeg
½ cup (115 g) shortening
15 ounces (420 g) applesauce
3 eggs (⅔ cup) (1½ dL)
1 cup (¼ L) seedless raisins
1 cup (¼ L) chopped nuts

Preheat oven to 350°F (180°C). Grease well and flour baking pan, size 13x9x2 inches (33x23x5 cm). Sift flour, sugar, baking powder, baking soda, salt and spices into a large bowl of an electric mixer. Add shortening and applesauce and beat one minute at low speed to combine. At medium speed, beat 2 minutes. Continually clean the sides of the bowl with a scraper. Add eggs and beat 2 minutes. Combine walnuts and raisins, fold into the batter. Turn batter into prepared pan, bake 45 minutes until a toothpick comes out clean. Let cake cool completely in the pan on a wire rack. Cut in 16 rectangles. Frost if desired.

Recipe of Mrs. Ruth Norton
Submitted by:
Joseph M. Biros
Middletown, Pennsylvania U.S.A.

BANANA SPLIT CAKE
Banánová torta

1 can (19 ounces) (530 g) crushed unsweetened pineapple
2 cups (½ L) crushed graham crackers
¼ pound (115 g) margarine, melted
2 eggs
1 teaspoon (5 mL) vanilla
2 cups (½ L) powdered sugar
½ pound (225 g) margarine
4-5 bananas, sliced
2 packages frozen strawberries
2 packages (envelopes) whipped topping mix
Crushed nuts
Maraschino cherries

Drain pineapple well. Combine graham crackers and ¼ pound (115 g) melted margarine; press into 9x15 inch (23x38 cm) pan and chill. Beat together eggs, vanilla, powdered sugar, and ½ pound (225 g) soft margarine at least 10 minutes. Spread over graham cracker crumb crust and chill. Spread pineapple over mixture. Spread sliced bananas over pineapple. Spread slightly thawed sliced frozen strawberries over bananas.

Beat 2 envelopes whipped topping mix according to package directions and spread over fruit. Sprinkle crushed nuts over whipped topping and decorate with cherries. Chill well before serving.

Makes 15-18 servings.

Michelle Marcuz
Slovak Domovina Dancers
Windsor, Ontario, Canada

BLACK RUSSIAN KAHLUA CAKE
Čierna ruská liehová torta

Cake:
1 yellow cake mix, regular
1/2 cup (100 g) sugar
6 1/2 ounces (195 g) large box chocolate instant pudding mix
1 cup (1/4 L) vegetable oil
4 eggs
1/4 cup (1/2 dL) Kahlua (coffee liqueur)
3/4 cup (1 3/4 dL) water
1/4 cup (1/2 dL) vodka (optional)
Note: if vodka is omitted, add 1/8 cup (1/4 dL) additional water and 1/8 cup (1/4 dL) additional Kahlua

Glaze:
1/2 cup (1 dL) powdered sugar
1/4 cup (1/2 dL) Kahlua

Whipped cream or ice cream

Preheat oven to 350°F (180°C). Spray or grease standard size (12 cups) (2 3/4 L) bundt pan.

Cake: Mix all liquid ingredients with dry ingredients and beat for 4 minutes. Pour mixture into bundt pan; bake for 50 minutes. (Cake will rise high in pan).
Cool 10 minutes; invert pan onto serving dish, remove cake.
Poke holes on top of cake for glazing.

Glaze: Mix sugar with liqueur and let stand while cake is baking. Pour glaze over cake (into holes) after cake is cooled. Serve with whipped cream or ice cream.

Kay Sarosy
Seven Hills, Ohio U.S.A.

BLUEBERRY CAKE
Modrinková torta

1¹/₂ cups (3¹/₂ dL) blueberries, fresh or drained well, if frozen
¹/₂ cup (115 g) butter
1 cup (200 g) sugar
2 eggs, separated
1¹/₂ cups (215 g) all-purpose flour
1 teaspoon (5 mL) baking powder
1 teaspoon (5 mL) vanilla
¹/₄ teaspoon (1.25 mL) salt
¹/₃ cup (³/₄ dL) milk

Cream butter and sugar until light and fluffy. Add egg yolks and vanilla, beat well. Sift dry ingredients. Add to butter mixture, alternating with milk. Beat well after each addition. Fold in stiffly beaten egg whites. Spread half the batter into a greased and floured 9 inch (23 cm) square cake pan. Sprinkle berries across top of batter, cover with remaining batter. Bake in preheated oven at 350°F (180°C) for 35 minutes.

Note: This makes one large square layer cake. Recipe can also be used to make blueberry cupcakes.

Dolores Paunicka Callahan
Lowell, Indiana U.S.A.

CARROT WALNUT CAKE
Mrkvičková-orechová bábovka

4 eggs, separated
2 cups (400 g) sugar
3 cups (¾ L) grated carrots
1 cup (¼ L) vegetable oil
½ cup (1 dL) lemon juice
3 tablespoons (45 mL) milk
½ cup (100 g) finely ground walnuts
1 cup (¼ L) chopped raisins
Powdered sugar for dusting

Mix and sift together:
3 cups (420 g) all purpose flour
2 teaspoons (10 mL) baking soda
2 teaspoons (10 mL) baking powder
½ teaspoon (2.5 mL) salt
1½ teaspoons (7.5 mL) cinnamon
1 teaspoon (5 mL) nutmeg

Preheat oven to 350°F (180°C). Grease well and flour a 12 cup (3 L) tube pan. In a large bowl, sift dry ingredients and set aside. In another bowl, beat egg yolks and sugar. Add oil, lemon juice and milk. Add the carrots and mix well. Combine mixture with dry ingredients. Add walnuts and raisins. Beat egg whites until stiff and fold into cake mixture. Pour into pan and bake in 350°F (180°C) oven for 55-60 minutes or until toothpick inserted in center comes out clean. Remove from oven and let stand for 10 minutes or more. Turn onto plate and cool completely. To serve, sprinkle with confectioners' sugar or frost with cream cheese frosting.

Mary Skyba
Murray Hill, New Jersey U.S.A.

ANN'S CHEESECAKE
Aničkin syrovník
(originálny)

An original recipe

Crust:
1¼ cups (175 g) flour
½ cup + 1 tablespoon (130 g) butter, softened
⅛ cup (30 g) white sugar
⅛ cup (30 g) brown sugar
¼ cup (½ dL) chopped nuts, (optional)

Filling:
6 eggs, separated
3 packages (8 ounces) (224 g) cream cheese, softened
1½ cups (300 g) sugar
½ teaspoon (2.5 mL) vanilla
½ teaspoon (2.5 mL) almond extract

Topping:
½ pint (¼ L) whipping cream, whipped

Crust: Combine flour, butter, sugar (and nuts) in a bowl. Mix well with a fork. Press into bottom of a well-greased 9x13 inch (23x33 cm) glass baking dish. Bake at 350°F (180°C) for 10-12 minutes until very lightly golden. Cool for about 15 minutes.

Filling: Beat egg whites until stiff, gradually adding half of the sugar (¾ cup) (150 g). Set aside.
Combine cream cheese, remaining sugar, egg yolks, vanilla and almond extract. Beat until smooth. Fold in egg whites. Pour on top of crust. Bake at 350°F (180°C) for about 30 minutes, or until top starts to crack slightly and is tinged with golden brown. Cool. When cold, cover with whipped cream.

Ann Melek
Boardman, Ohio   U.S.A.

CHEESE CAKE
Syrová torta

1 package (3 ounces) (85 g) lemon gelatin
¾ cup (1¾ dL) boiling water
1 package (8 ounces) (227 g) cream cheese, softened
1 cup (200 g) sugar
1 teaspoon (5 mL) vanilla
1 large can (12 fluid ounces) (340 g) evaporated milk, cold
Juice from ½ lemon (optional)
1 package whipped topping mix prepared according to package directions

Crust:
28 graham crackers
¼ cup (50 g) sugar
½ cup (1 dL) margarine, melted

Mix lemon gelatin with boiling water; let cool. In another bowl, mix cream cheese, sugar and vanilla.

Whip evaporated milk with lemon juice until very stiff. Set aside. Combine gelatin with the cream cheese mixture and mix well. Fold in beaten evaporated milk.

Mix graham cracker crumbs with sugar and melted margarine. Line bottom of 9x13 inch (23x33 cm) pan with mixture, patting down firmly. Retain approximately ¼ cup (½ dL) of crumb mixture. Pour gelatin/cheese mixture into cracker crust. Refrigerate.

Before serving, mix and beat whipped topping mix according to directions. Spread on top of cream cheese mixture and sprinkle the remaining graham cracker crumbs over top of whipped topping.

Makes approximately 20 servings.

Marcy Pekarcik-Butorac
Fountain Valley, California
U.S.A.

CHERRY CHEESE CAKE
Čerešnový syrovník

1 cup (¼ L) graham crackers, or vanilla wafers, crushed
¼ cup (½ dL) margarine, melted
1 package (8 ounces) (224 g) cream cheese, softened
⅓ cup (¾ dL) sugar
1 can (19 ounces) (532 g) cherry pie filling
1 envelope dessert topping mix

Combine crumbs and margarine and press into bottom of 8 inch (20 cm) square pan and chill. Prepare whipped dessert topping as to package directions. Blend cream cheese with sugar. Blend prepared topping into cheese mixture at lowest speed on mixer. Pour into crust. Chill thoroughly (can be put in freezer about one hour to set). Top with cherry pie filling. Chill several hours before serving.

Irene Timko
Slovak Domovina Dancers
Slovak World Congress
Heritage, Culture Commission, Sec.
Windsor, Ontario, Canada

CINNAMON COFFEE CAKE
Škoricová bábovka

Dough:
- 1/4 pound (115 g) butter or oleo
- 1 cup (200 g) sugar
- 2 eggs
- 1/2 pint (1/4 L) sour cream
- 1 teaspoon (5 mL) vanilla
- 2 cups (280 g) flour, sifted
- 1 1/2 teaspoons (7.5 mL) baking powder
- 1 teaspoon (5 mL) baking soda

Topping:
- 1/2 cup (100 g) sugar
- 2-3 tablespoons (30-45 mL) cinnamon

Fruit Topping:
Blueberries or apples

Dough: With electric mixer, cream butter, add sugar and beat well. Add eggs and continue beating well. Add sour cream and vanilla. Mix well with spoon. Sift and measure flour, sift together with baking powder and baking soda. Add flour to cake mixture, and blend till smooth.

Pour half of batter in greased square pan and sprinkle half of topping. Spread other half of batter and sprinkle with remaining topping. Dot with blueberries or sliced apples. Bake at 375°F (190°C) in preheated oven for about 30-35 minutes. Test with toothpick for doneness.

Serves 9.

Marge Orsulak
Pocono Summit, Pennsylvania
U.S.A.

CINNAMON - RAISIN COFFEE CAKE
Škoricová - hrozienková bábovka

½ cup (1dL) butter, melt and cool
1½ cups (210 g) flour
1 teaspoon (5 mL) baking soda
¼ teaspoon (1.25 mL) salt
⅔ cup (130 g) sugar
2 eggs
1 cup (¼ L) sour cream or yogurt
1 teaspoon (5 mL) vanilla
¾ cup (1¾ dL) raisins

Topping:
½ cup (1 dL) chopped nuts
⅓ cup (¾ dL) brown sugar
1 tablespoon (15 mL) cinnamon

Batter: Add sugar and eggs to butter, whisking to blend well. Whisk in yogurt and vanilla. Stir in raisins. Sift flour, baking soda, and salt and add to butter mixture. Stir just until well mixed. Spread half of batter into greased 9 inch (23 cm) square pan. Sprinkle with half of topping. Cover with remaining batter and topping. Bake at 350°F (180°C) for 35-40 minutes or until toothpick comes out clean.
Topping: Combine all ingredients. Mix well.

Serves 8-10.

Anna Marie Janicek
Oak Creek, Wisconsin   U.S.A.

MOM'S CHOCOLATE CAKE
Mamičkiná čokoládová torta

2 cups (280 g) cake flour
2 cups (400 g) sugar
1 level tablespoon (15 mL) baking soda
1 tablespoon (15 mL) baking powder
1 tablespoon (15 mL) vanilla
1 cup (¼ L) milk
2 eggs, beaten
¾ cup (105 g) cocoa
1 cup (¼ L) boiling coffee
½ cup (1 dL) oil

Sift flour, sugar, soda and baking powder together. Add milk and eggs, mixing well. Add vanilla. Mix cocoa and coffee and blend gently into the flour mixture. Lastly, add oil and blend well into cake mixture. Grease and flour a 9x13 inch (23x33 cm) pan or 2 round 9 inch (23 cm) cake pans. Pour mixture into pans and bake at 350° F (180°C) for 40 minutes or until done.

Marcella Straka
Hellertown, Pennsylvania   U.S.A.

EARTHQUAKE CAKE
Bábovka zemetrasenia

1 cup (250 mL) nuts, ground
1 cup (250 mL) coconut
1 German Chocolate Cake mix

Icing:
1 pound (450 g) powdered sugar
¼ pound (115 g) margarine
1 package (8 ounces) (224 g) cream cheese, softened
1 teaspoon (5 mL) vanilla

Spread nuts and coconut on bottom of a 9x13 inch (23x33 cm) greased cake pan. Mix cake according to package directions and pour over nut/coconut mixture.
Icing: Combine all ingredients for icing, mixing completely, and spread over batter. Bake at 350°F (180°C) for 45 minutes.

Marge Offinitz
Parma Heights, Ohio   U.S.A.

OUR TRADITIONAL HOLIDAY LAMB CAKE
Vel'konočná ovečka - torta

2 cups (280 g) sifted flour
2 ½ teaspoons (12.5 mL) baking powder
¾ teaspoon (3.75 mL) salt (optional)
1 cup (200 g) sugar
3 egg whites, beaten
½ cup (1 dL) margarine or butter
¾ cup (1¾ dL) milk
2 teaspoons (10 mL) vanilla

Sift all dry ingredients. Mix sifted dry ingredients with softened butter or margarine. Add milk and vanilla. Beat with mixer for 2 minutes. Beat egg whites. Fold in beaten egg whites into the first mixture. Beat together for one minute. Grease lamb mold well with oil, dust with flour.
Bake in moderate oven 350°F (180°C) 25-30 minutes or until done.

Martha Mistina Kona
Slovak World Congress
Heritage, Culture Commission, Chairperson
Wilmette, Illinois   U.S.A.

LATTUS CAKE
Mramorová bábovka

- 2 sticks (225 g) oleo or butter
- 2 cups (400 g) sugar
- 4 eggs
- 1 pint (½ L) sour cream
- 3 ½ cups (490 g) flour
- 2 teaspoons (10 mL) baking powder
- 2 teaspoons (10 mL) baking soda
- ½ teaspoon (2½ mL) salt
- 2 teaspoons (10 mL) vanilla

Topping:
- ½ cup (100 g) sugar
- 2 teaspoons (10 mL) cinnamon
- 2 tablespoons (30 mL) coconut
- ½ cup (1 dL) chopped walnuts

Topping: Mix together and set aside.

Cake: Cream butter and sugar. Add eggs and sour cream. Mix dry ingredients and add gradually to the butter, sugar, eggs and sour cream. Add vanilla. Grease a 9x13 inch (23x33 cm) pan and sprinkle half the topping on it. Pour in half the batter. Cut several times through batter with a knife to make a swirl (as for marble cake). Add remaining batter; spread remaining topping over and cut through with knife again.

Bake at 350°F (180°C) for 40-50 minutes.

This cake is sometimes called Sour Cream Coffee Cake or Jewish Coffee Cake. It is very good and moist.

Elizabeth Mindzal
Mt. Pleasant, Pennsylvania U.S.A.

LINDY'S TROPICAL DELIGHT
Tropický rozkoš

- 1 can (20 ounces) (560 g) crushed pineapple with juice
- 2 cups (280 g) flour
- 2 cups (400 g) sugar
- 2 eggs
- 2 teaspoons (10 mL) baking soda
- 1 cup (200 g) chopped nuts
- 2 teaspoons (10 mL) vanilla
- 1 banana, cut up in small pieces

Frosting:
- 8 ounces (225 g) cream cheese, softened
- 1 stick (115 g) margarine, softened
- 1½ cups (3½ dL) powdered sugar
- 1 teaspoon (5 mL) vanilla
- 1 teaspoon (5 mL) lemon juice

Cake: Place all ingredients in large mixing bowl and stir until moistened. Pour into 9x13 inch (23x33 cm) pan. Bake at 350°F (180°C) for 35-40 minutes.

Frosting: Place all ingredients in medium mixing bowl and blend until smooth. Frost the cooled cake. Keep cake refrigerated. Serve cake at room temperature.

Delicious! You're sure to enjoy this one.

Dr. Lindy Kona
Chicago, Illinois U.S.A.

LUNCH BOX CAKE
Ovocné pečivo

2¼ cups (315 g) flour
2 teaspoons (10 mL) baking soda
1 teaspoon (5 mL) salt
1 cup (¼ L) brown sugar
2 eggs
¼ cup (½ dL) soft butter or margarine
1 can (19 ounces) (532 g) fruit cocktail, drained and reserve liquid
½ cup (1 dL) semi-sweet chocolate chips
½ cup (1 dL) chopped nuts
½ cup (1 dL) raisins (optional)

Grease and flour 13x9x2 inch (33x23x5 cm) pan. Combine all ingredients and reserved fruit liquid, but not fruit, chocolate chips and nuts. Beat for 2 minutes at medium speed. Stir in drained fruit cocktail. Mix thoroughly. Pour batter into pan. Sprinkle nuts and chocolate chips and/or raisins on top. Bake at 350°F (180°C) for 35-40 minutes.

Irene Timko
Slovak Domovina Dancers
Slovak World Congress
Heritage, Culture Commission, Sec.
Windsor, Ontario, Canada

EXCELLENT BUNDT NUT CAKE
Výborná orechová bábovka

½ cup (12 dkg) sweet butter
1¼ cups (25 dkg) sugar
4 egg yolks
1¾ cups (25 dkg) semolina flour ("Wondra")
⅓ cup (8 dkg) ground nuts
½ teaspoon (2.5 mL) vanilla extract
1 teaspoon (5 mL) baking powder (1 prašok do pečiva "Oetker")
⅔ cup (1½ dL) milk
Rind from 1 lemon
4 egg whites, stiffly beaten

Cream butter, add sugar and egg yolks; cream until light and fluffy. Add nuts, vanilla, lemon rind and milk. Mix well. Add stiffly beaten egg whites and flour which was sifted with baking powder.
Pour dough into a well greased and floured bundt pan and bake in preheated oven 350°F (180°C) for ½ hour or until done.

Antonia Kralik
Berwyn, Illinois U.S.A.

CHEESE AND POPPYSEED CAKE
Syrový a makový dort

Dough:
1 cup (140 g) flour
4 tablespoons (60 g) water
¼ cup (60 g) granulated sugar
¼ cup (60 g) butter
2 egg yolks, slightly beaten

Filling:
3 packages (8 ounces each) (675 g) cream cheese, softened
1 teaspoon (5 mL) vanilla
1 cup (200 g) granulated sugar
4 eggs

Topping:
1 tablespoon (15 mL) lemon juice
1 can (12 ounces) (336 g) poppyseed filling

Dough: Stir together flour and ¼ cup (60 g) granulated sugar. Cut in the butter, till pieces are the size of small peas. Combine egg yolks and water, sprinkle over flour mixture. Gently toss with a fork till dough forms a ball. Shape dough into a ball. Pat dough evenly over the bottom and 1½ inches (3.75 cm) up sides of a springform pan. Bake in a 350°F (180°C) oven for 20 minutes or till golden brown. Cool on wire rack.

Filling: In a large mixing bowl, beat cream cheese and vanilla till smooth. Beat in the 1 cup (200 g) sugar till fluffy. Add eggs. Beat at low speed until just blended. Turn into crust-lined pan. Bake in a 350°F (180°C) oven for about 1 hour or till filling is set. Cool 5 minutes.

Topping: Stir lemon juice into poppyseed filling. Carefully spread filling over baked cheesecake. Bake in a 450°F (230°C) oven 5 to 8 minutes more or till topping is set. Cool completely on wire rack. Remove sides from springform pan. Serve cake at room temperature but store leftover cake in refrigerator.

Serves 12 to 16.

Ilonka Martinka-Torres
Castro Valley, California, U.S.A.

LEMON POPPYSEED POUND CAKE
Citronová maková bábovka

3 cups (420 g) flour
2 cups (400 g) sugar
1/4 cup (50 g) poppyseed
1 cup (225 g) butter, softened
1 cup (1/4 L) buttermilk
4 eggs
1/2 teaspoon (2 1/2 mL) baking soda
1/2 teaspoon (2 1/2 mL) baking powder
1/2 teaspoon (2 1/2 mL) salt
4 teaspoons (20 mL) lemon peel, grated
1/2 teaspoon (2 1/2 mL) vanilla

Glaze:
1 cup (140 g) powdered sugar
1-2 tablespoons (15-30 mL) lemon juice

Mix all dry ingredients, flour, sugar, poppyseed, soda, baking powder and salt; set aside. Heat oven to 325°F (165°C). Grease and flour a 12 cup (3 L) bundt pan, or 10 inch (25 cm) tube pan. Cream butter, add eggs, beating well. Add flour mixture alternating with buttermilk to creamed butter/egg mixture. Add lemon peel and vanilla. Pour into cake pan. Bake in preheated oven for 55-65 minutes, or until wooden pick inserted in center comes out clean. Cool 10 minutes; remove from pan. Cool completely.

Glaze: Mix powdered sugar and lemon juice in a small bowl; drizzle over cake.

Julianne Elizabeth Zetts
Canfield, Ohio   U.S.A.

POPPYSEED CAKE
Maková bábovka

3 cups (420 g) all-purpose flour
2 cups (400 g) sugar
1½ cups (3½ dL) salad oil
4 eggs
1 teaspoon (5 mL) vanilla
½ teaspoon (2.5 mL) salt
1½ teaspoons (7.5 mL) baking soda
14 ounces (392 g) evaporated milk
½ cup (1 dL) poppyseed or 1 jar poppyseed filling
1 cup (¼ L) chopped nuts (optional)

Combine all ingredients except for poppyseed and chopped nuts. Mix until smooth.
Add poppyseed and chopped nuts. Beat well (if using mixer, on medium speed) for 2 minutes.
Bake at 350°F (180°C) for 1 hour and 10 minutes in 10 inch (25 cm) tube pan. Do not grease pan. Cool cake before removing from pan.

Kay Krajewski
Garfield Heights, Ohio U.S.A.

POPPYSEED CAKE
Makovník

3 eggs, beaten
2 cups (400 g) sugar
1½ cups (3½ dL) oil
1 teaspoon (5 mL) vanilla
1½ teaspoons (7.5 mL) soda
3 cups (420 g) flour
1 teaspoon (5 mL) salt
1 tablespoon (15 mL) grated lemon or orange rind
1 can (12 ounces) (354 mL) canned milk
1 can poppyseed filling
1 cup (¼ L) finely chopped nuts

Sift flour, soda and salt. Beat eggs till thick and lemon color. Mix sugar, oil and vanilla with egg mixture. Add flour and rind and mix well. Add poppyseed, milk and nuts. Bake in lightly greased tube pan at 350°F (180°C) for 1 hour and 10 minutes.

Betty Williams
Youngstown, Ohio U.S.A.

POPPYSEED CAKE
Maková bábovka

3/4 cup (1 3/4 dL) ground poppyseed
3/4 cup (1 3/4 dL) milk
3/4 cup (1 3/4 dL) butter
1 1/2 cups (300 g) sugar
3/4 cup (1 3/4 dL) milk
2 teaspoons (10 mL) baking powder
2 cups (280 g) flour, sifted three times
4 egg whites, beaten
Powdered sugar, dusting

Cook poppyseed in scalded milk mixture; bring to boil then cool. Cream sugar and butter; add poppyseed and milk mixture. Add additional milk, flour, baking powder. Mix. Fold in well beaten egg whites.
Turn into a well greased and floured 10 inch (25 cm) tube pan. Bake in a 375°F (195°C) oven for 50-55 minutes.
Let cool and ice top or sprinkle with powdered sugar.

Tessie Oros
Reading, Pennsylvania U.S.A.

SOUR CREAM CAKE
Bábovka z kyslej smotany

1/4 pound (115 g) butter
2 eggs
1 cup (200 g) sugar
1/2 pint (1/4 L) sour cream
1 teaspoon (5 mL) vanilla
1 1/2 cups (210 g) flour, sifted
1 teaspoon (5 mL) baking powder
1/2 teaspoon (2.5 mL) baking soda
1/2 cup (1 dL) walnuts, chopped

Cream butter, add eggs and sugar and cream well. Add sour cream and vanilla. Sift dry ingredients and add to butter mixture. Continue mixing until well blended. Fold in ground nuts. Bake in a greased and floured 9x5 inch (23x13 cm) loaf pan for 50-60 minutes at 350°F (180°C).
Recipe can be doubled and baked in a tube pan at 350°F (180°C) for 1 1/2 hours or until done. Cake is not too sweet, but sweet enough to enjoy with coffee.
May be frozen for future use.

Agnes Virostek
Boonton, New Jersey U.S.A.

MOM'S SOUR CREAM COFFEE CAKE
Bábovka z kyslej smotany (Mamičkina)

1 cup (200 g) sugar
½ cup (1 dL) butter
2 eggs
1 cup (¼ L) sour cream
1 teaspoon (5 mL) vanilla
2 cups (280 g) flour
1 teaspoon (5 mL) baking powder
1 teaspoon (5 mL) baking soda
¼ teaspoon (1.25 mL) salt

Filling:
½ cup (1 dL) chopped walnuts
2 teaspoons (10 mL) cinnamon
½ cup (100 g) sugar

Cream butter and sugar; add eggs, sour cream, vanilla. Add flour, baking powder, baking soda, and salt to the butter mixture, blending lightly. Pour half the batter into a lightly greased 9 inch (23 cm) square pan. Sprinkle with half of the filling mixture. Add remaining batter and finish with filling mixture on top. Bake in 350°F (180°C) oven for 40 minutes.

This was an old recipe that my mother used to make. We were on a farm and always had lots of fresh butter, eggs, and cream.

Mary Marsh
Niagara Falls, New York   U.S.A.

POUND CAKE
Bábovka

½ pound (225 g) butter
½ pound (225 g) cream cheese
2 cups (½ L) sugar
6 eggs
2 cups plus 2 tablespoons (280 g plus 20 mL) Presto flour
1 teaspoon (5 mL) vanilla

Cream together butter and cream cheese. Add sugar, eggs, one at a time beating after each addition, flour and vanilla; mix well. In a greased and floured tube pan, or 2 bread pans, greased and floured, bake at 350°F (180°C) for 1 hour.

Ellen Gregus
Palisades, New York   U.S.A.

SOUR CREAM COFFEE CAKE
Bábovka z kyslej smotany

2½ cups (350 g) sifted flour
2 teaspoons (10 mL) baking powder
1 teaspoon (5 mL) baking soda
½ teaspoon (2.5 mL) salt
1 cup (230 g) butter or margarine
1 cup (200 g) sugar
3 eggs
1 teaspoon (5 mL) vanilla
1 cup (¼ L) sour cream

Filling and Topping:
2 teaspoons (10 mL) cinnamon
¾ cup (1¾ dL) brown sugar, firmly packed
½ cup (1 dL) chopped nuts

Sift flour once, measure, add baking powder, baking soda, and salt and sift again. Cream butter and sugar until light and fluffy. Add eggs, one at a time, beating well after each addition. Add vanilla and blend. Alternate dry ingredients with sour cream, beating until smooth after each addition. Pour half the batter into a 9x13 inch (23x33 cm) well-greased loaf pan.

Filling and Topping:
Mix cinnamon, brown sugar and nuts and sprinkle half of it on the batter. Top with remaining batter and sprinkle remaining nut mixture. Bake in 375°F (195°C) oven about 25 minutes, or until a cake tester inserted in center comes out clean.

Margaret Siska
Chicago, Illinois U.S.A.

SOUR CREAM POUND CAKE
Bábovka s kyslej smotany

3 cups (420 g) sifted all-purpose flour
¼ teaspoon (1.25 mL) baking soda
½ cup (115 g) butter or margarine
½ cup (115 g) shortening
3 cups (600 g) sugar
6 eggs
½ pint (¼ L) sour cream
1 tablespoon (15 mL) vanilla

Miracle Frosting:
2 egg whites
2½ cups (6 dL) sifted confectioners' sugar
4 tablespoons (60 mL) butter or margarine
½ teaspoon (2.5 mL) vanilla

Cake: Sift together flour and baking soda; set aside. In large bowl, cream butter, shortening and sugar; beat until light and fluffy. Add the eggs one at a time, beating each addition well. Add sour cream alternately with sifted dry ingredients to cream mixture. Blend in vanilla. Bake at 350°F (180°C) for 70 minutes; reduce temperature to 300°F (150°C) and bake an additional 10 minutes or until cake tests done.

Frosting: Beat egg whites until stiff and gradually add 1½ cups (300 g) powdered sugar. Cream butter or margarine and add 1 cup (200 g) powdered sugar slowly, beating constantly. Combine mixtures and add vanilla.

Olga C. Kozlowski
Philadelphia, Pennsylvania U.S.A.

ZUCCHINI CAKE
Tekvicová bábovka

1 cup (¼ L) oil
2 cups (400 g) sugar
2 cups (½ L) grated zucchini
3 eggs
3 cups (420 g) flour
1 teaspoon (5 mL) salt
½ teaspoon (2.5 mL) baking powder
1 teaspoon (5 mL) baking soda
1 cup (¼ L) raisins
3 teaspoons (15 mL) cinnamon
½ cup (1 dL) walnuts, chopped

Mix oil, sugar and eggs. Beat well. Add zucchini and vanilla. Mix well. To above mixture, add remainder of dry ingredients. Bake in a greased and floured tube pan at 325°F (160°C) for 65 minutes or until cake tests done.

Betty Kominar
Slovak Domovina Dancers
Windsor, Ontario, Canada

ZUCCHINI CHOCOLATE CAKE
Tekvicový čokoládový koláčik

2½ cups (350 g) sifted flour
¼ cup (35 g) cocoa
1 teaspoon (5 mL) baking soda
1 teaspoon (5 mL) salt
½ cup (115 g) margarine
½ cup (1 dL) cooking oil
1¾ cups (350 g) sugar
2 eggs
1 teaspoon (5 mL) vanilla
½ cup (1 dL) buttermilk
2 cups (½ L) grated zucchini
1 cup ¼ L) chocolate chips
1 cup (¼ L) chopped nuts

Cream butter, oil and sugar. Add eggs, one at a time, mixing well after each addition. Alternate dry ingredients, which have been sifted together, with buttermilk. Mix well. Add vanilla. Stir in grated zucchini. Pour into a greased and floured 9x13 inch (23x33 cm) pan. Top with chocolate chips and nuts. Bake at 325°F (165°C) for 55 minutes.

Margaret Siska
Chicago, Illinois U.S.A.

ALMOND WAFERS
Mandľové oplátky

½ cup (1 dL) butter
1 cup (200 g) sugar
1 egg
½ cup (1 dL) almonds, finely ground
Rind of 1 lemon, grated
½ teaspoon (2½ mL) cinnamon
½ teaspoon (2½ mL) ground cloves
½ teaspoon (2½ mL) nutmeg
2 cups (280 g) flour
1 teaspoon (5 mL) almond extract

Cream butter, add sugar gradually; add egg and beat until frothy. Add lemon rind and finely ground almonds. (Grind almonds with skins on until they resemble coarse corn meal.) Sift flour once and measure. Add spices to flour and sift again. Add to butter and sugar mixture. Mix well. Form into a roll and chill at least 12 hours or overnight. Cut very thin slices and bake on slightly greased cookie sheet in slow oven, 325°F (165°C) for 15-20 minutes or until faintly browned.

Kathy Ruszczyk Malone
Colorado Springs, Colorado
U.S.A.

FRIED DOUGHNUT STRIPS
Čeregi (Krapne)

3 cups (420 g) flour
½ cup (115 g) butter
4 tablespoons (60 mL) sugar
Pinch of salt
½ cup (1 dL) sour cream
3 egg yolks
3 egg whites
1 teaspoon (5 mL) vanilla
Powdered sugar for dusting
Hot oil for frying

Beat egg yolks and egg whites separately until foamy. In a bowl mix flour, salt, sugar and butter until crumbly, like for pie dough. Add sour cream and egg yolks, mix well. Add egg whites and vanilla, mixing thoroughly. On a lightly floured board, roll dough out thin. Using a pastry wheel, cut into strips 1x3 inches (2.5x7.5 cm). Make slit lengthwise in center and pull one end through. Fry in hot fat until lightly browned. Drain. (A diamond shaped cookie cutter may be used for cutting čeregi). Sprinkle with powdered sugar before serving.

MARDI GRAS ANGEL WINGS
Božie milosti na Fašiangy

1³/₄ cups (250 g hladkej) flour
½ teaspoon (2.5 mL) salt
3½ tablespoons (50 g) margarine
⅓ cup (50 g) powdered sugar
2 egg yolks, beaten
3 tablespoons (45 mL) wine
4 tablespoons (60 mL) sour cream
Powdered sugar and vanilla sugar for dusting*
Oil or lard for frying

Note: If vanilla sugar is not available, add ½ teaspoon (2.5 mL) vanilla to dough and sprinkle only with powdered sugar.

- Editor

Sift flour once, measure, add salt and sift again. Crumble margarine into flour and work as for pie crust. Add sugar, beaten egg yolks, wine and sour cream. Mix well. Place dough on floured board and roll out thin. With a cookie cutter, or wine glass, press out pieces. Roll out each piece into an oblong or square shape. With a knife or sharp object, make 2 parallel cuts in dough. DO NOT CUT THROUGH THE EDGE. Intertwine each end into nearest slit. Fry in hot fat. When both sides are pinkish in color, lift out with slotted spoon. Drain off fat. When cooled, sprinkle with mixtures of powdered and vanilla sugars.

These cookies were baked for the closing of the Mardi Gras celebration and the last of sweets to be enjoyed before the Lenten fast.

PhDr. Zora Mintalová
Slovenské Národné Múzeum
Martin, Slovakia

OVEN BAKED ANGEL WINGS (FLANCATE)
Anjelské krídla

½ pound (1 cup) (225 g) margarine
2 cups (280 g) flour
2 egg yolks, unbeaten
½ cup (1 dL) sour cream
1 teaspoon (5 mL) vanilla
Powdered sugar

Crumble margarine into flour as for pie dough. In a small bowl, with a fork, mix together the egg yolks, sour cream and vanilla. Add to flour mixture and continue mixing with fork, and then with hands, to form a firm dough. Cover and refrigerate overnight.

Divide dough into 4 equal parts. Working with one piece at a time, roll out very thin on a floured bread board. Cut into 2 inch (5 cm) squares and cut a slot in center.

Bake in a 350°F (180°C) oven on an ungreased cookie sheet for 10-15 minutes, until just very light brown. When cooled, sprinkle with powdered sugar.

Marge Koscak
Parma, Ohio   U.S.A.

ANISE HORNS
Anizové trubičky

Baked in Slovakia especially for New Year's celebration

3 eggs, separated
1½ cups (150 g) powdered sugar
¾ cup (100 g) flour
Anise powder

Beat egg yolks and sugar until light and fluffy. Beat egg whites, stiff. Alternately add egg whites and flour into the egg yolk mixture.

Drop by spoonfuls onto greased cookie sheet. Dust with anise powder.
Bake in preheated oven 375°F (190°C) until light golden. Immediately after removing baking sheet from oven, wrap each cookie, while still hot, around a ladle to form a cone or horn. Serve with eggnog.

Lučenec, Slovakia

BARBARA BUSH'S OATMEAL LACE COOKIES
Barbary Bušovej čipkavé ovseníky

½ cup (70 g) flour
¼ teaspoon (1.25 mL) baking powder
½ cup (100 g) sugar
½ cup (100 g) quick cooking oats
2 tablespoons (30 mL) whipping cream
2 tablespoons (30 mL) white corn syrup
⅓ cup (¾ dL) melted butter
1 tablespoon (15 mL) vanilla

Sift flour and baking powder together. Mix all ingredients together until well blended. Drop by slightly heaped ¼ teaspoonful (1.25 mL) 4 inches (10 cm) apart onto ungreased cookie sheet. Only bake about 6-8 cookies at a time. Bake at 375°F (190°C) for 4-6 minutes, until lightly browned. Let stand a few seconds, then remove from pan. Yields 4 dozen.

Barbara Bush, Wife of George Bush
Former U.S. President
Texas, U.S.A.

BEAR CLAWS
Medvedie labky

9 ounces (25 dkg) butter
  (1 cup plus 2 tablespoons)
2½ cups (36 dkg) flour
1 cup (21 dkg) nuts, ground
1 cup (20 dkg) sugar
1 lemon rind
1 teaspoon (5 mL) cinnamon

Crumble butter into flour, then combine all other ingredients and mix well. Bake in molds in moderate preheated oven 350°F (180°C) until golden.

Marta Kovačiková
Zvolenská Slatina, Slovakia

BRATISLAVA BARS
Bratislavské tyčinky

Dough:
¾ cup (15 dkg) nuts, ground
¼ cup (5 dkg) almonds, ground
1½ ounces (3 tablespoons) (4 dkg) chocolate, grated
1 ounce (2 tablespoons) (3 dkg) butter, crumbled
1¼ cups (3 dL) powdered sugar
1 teaspoon (5 mL) vanilla sugar (vanilkového cukru)
1 egg

Glaze:
2 cups (½ L) powdered sugar
1 egg white
1 tablespoon (15 mL) lemon juice
½ teaspoon (2.5 mL) hot water

Dough: Combine all ingredients and mix well. Lightly roll dough in oblong 4 inches (10 cm) wide and ½ inch (1 cm) thick. Pour lemon glaze over top, cut into ½ inch (1 cm) strip bars and arrange on greased baking sheet. Bake in preheated oven 350°F (180°C) until lightly golden.

Lemon Glaze: Beat egg white, add the rest of the ingredients and mix into a heavier, thicker glaze.

Veľmi dobré!

Ľudmila Šandorfi
St. Catherine's, Ontario, Canada

BUTTER COOKIES
Maslové koláčky

1 cup (200 g) sugar
1 pound (450 g) butter
2 egg yolks, slightly beaten
½ lemon, rind and juice
1 teaspoon (5 mL) baking powder
6 cups (840 g) flour
1 cup (¼ L) walnuts, ground fine
2 egg whites
1 cup (200 g) sugar

Cream butter, add 1 cup (200 g) sugar, then slightly beaten egg yolks. Add rind of lemon and lemon juice. Add flour mixed with baking powder. Mix together, kneading well. Chill dough several hours or overnight.
Roll dough on slightly floured board ¼ inch (½ cm) thick. Using a cookie cutter, cut cookies, brush with slightly beaten egg whites, sprinkle with sugar and chopped nuts. Bake in moderate oven at 350°F (180°C) for 10 to 15 minutes or until slightly golden.

Martina Kovačiková
Zvolenská Slatina, Slovakia

BUTTER WEDGES
Maslové cviky

2½ cups (28 dkg) powdered sugar
1¼ cups (28 dkg) butter
5 egg yolks
1 lemon rind
1¾ cups (24 dkg) flour
1 teaspoon (5 mL) baking powder
5 egg whites, beaten stiff
Blueberries
Red food coloring
Powdered sugar for dusting

Cream butter, add powdered sugar, mixing well. Add egg yolks, lemon rind. Sift together flour and baking powder and add to mixture. Beat egg whites until stiff and fold into batter. Pour batter dough into baking pan. Bake at 350°F (180°C) until sides loosen from pan. To serve, dust with powdered sugar.
Variation: Top with blueberries before baking, or divide dough in half, and to one portion add red food coloring.

Ellen Gregus
Palisades, New York U.S.A.

CHRISTMAS HONEY COOKIES
Medovníky

2 cups (280 g hladkej) flour, sifted
1 teaspoon (5 mL) baking soda
1¼ cups (180 g) powdered sugar
1 teaspoon (5 mL) cinnamon
3 cloves, pressed
1 tablespoon (15 mL) honey
2 eggs, beaten
Egg yolk for brushing
Ground nuts for topping

Sift flour, add baking soda and sift again. Combine sugar, cinnamon, pressed cloves and mix into flour. Add honey and beaten eggs and mix well. Let dough rest for 2 hours.
Roll out dough on bread board to ⅜ inch (1 cm) thickness. Using a cookie cutter or a wine glass, cut out round cookies. Place on greased/floured cookie sheet. Brush each cookie with beaten egg yolk. Sprinkle with ground nuts and bake in preheated moderate oven 350°F (180°C) until lightly golden.

Medovníky are baked most frequently for the Christmas holidays.

PhDr. Zora Mintalová
Slovenské Národné Múzeum
Martin, Slovakia

CHRISTMAS STARS
Vianočné hviezdičky

1¼ cups (28 dkg) butter
1¼ cups (14 dkg) powdered sugar
¾ cup (14 dkg) nuts, ground
3 cups (42 dkg) flour (hladka)
1 egg
½ teaspoon (2.5 mL) lemon rind

Cream butter, add egg and sugar; mix until light. Add flour, mix well. Add nuts and lemon rind. Roll out dough and cut out with star-shaped cookie cutter. Bake on cookie sheet in a preheated moderate oven 325°F (160°C) 10-15 minutes or until lightly golden.

Martina Kováčiková
Zvolenská Slatina, Slovakia

Eva Škovierová
Očova, Slovakia

MOM'S CHRISTMAS COOKIES
Mamičkiné vianočné rožky (originálne)

- 3 cups (420 g) flour
- ¼ cup (½ dL) butter
- ¼ cup (½ dL) Crisco, not oleo or margarine
- ½ cup (100 g) sugar
- 3 teaspoons (15 mL) baking powder
- 3 eggs, beaten
- ½ cup (1 dL) whole milk
- 1 teaspoon (5 mL) vanilla
- ½ teaspoon (2.5 mL) salt

Blend sugar, butter, Crisco; add eggs, milk, vanilla, salt, baking powder and flour. The batter should be fairly soft. Divide dough into balls about ¾ pound (340 g) each and refrigerate for not less than 6 hours or overnight.

Roll out on board in mixture of half flour and half sugar to about ⅛ inch (½ cm) thick. Cut into 3 inch (8 cm) squares. Fill with either nut, apricot, poppyseed, or lekvar prepared filling. Roll up from one corner to the opposite corner to form a crescent. Place on cookie sheets and bake in moderate oven 350°F (180°C) until lightly golden.

Sister M. Annette
Vincentian Sisters of Charity
Pittsburgh, Pennsylvania
U.S.A.

NO BAKE CHOCOLATE COOKIES
Čokoládové zákusky (nepečené)

2 cups (400 g) sugar
4 tablespoons (60 g) cocoa
1 stick (115 g) oleo
½ cup (1 dL) milk
1 cup (¼ L) peanut butter
1 teaspoon (5 mL) vanilla
1½ cups (3½ dL) rolled oats, uncooked
1½ cups (3½ dL) coconut
½ cup (1 dL) nuts, chopped

In a saucepan, combine sugar, cocoa, oleo and milk; bring to rolling boil and cook for 1 minute. Add peanut butter, stirring until peanut butter melts. Remove from heat. Add vanilla, rolled oats, and coconut. Set in a warm place for a few minutes until oats swell. Add nuts; blend well. Drop by teaspoonful onto waxed paper and let set until cool.

Marge Orsulak
Pocono Summit, Pennsylvania
U.S.A.

DEVIL EYES COCOA BALLS
Diablové oči

½ cup (10 dkg) nuts, ground
1 cup (10 dkg) powdered sugar
½ cup (10 dkg) raisins
1 teaspoon (1 ks vanilka) vanilla
6½ tablespoons (1 dL) rum
½ cup (10 dkg) chocolate, melted
Cocoa
Candied cherries

In a jar with a cover, put raisins, rum and vanilla and tighten lid. Let stand overnight, or about 12 hours. Pour raisin mixture in a bowl. Mix nuts with sugar and add to raisins. Melt chocolate and add to raisin/nut mixture. Shape mixture into small balls (any size preferred) and roll in cocoa. Place cherry in center of each ball. Refrigerate before serving.

Dobrú chuť!

Milka Rešovská
Kuchyňa, Slovakia

Submitted by cousin
Martha Alexander Smith
Reynoldsburg, Ohio U.S.A.

CREAM CHEESE CRESCENTS
Syrové rožky

Dough:
1/2 pound (225 g) butter
1/2 pound (227 g) cream cheese
1/2 pound (227 g) sifted flour

Filling:
1/2 pound (227 g) walnuts, ground fine
1 1/2 cups (3 1/2 dL) sugar
5 egg whites, beaten stiff
1 teaspoon (15 mL) vanilla
Powdered sugar

Dough: Cream ingredients until smooth and creamy. Place dough in refrigerator overnight. Roll out on floured board to 1/8 inch (1/2 cm) thick. Cut into 2 inch (5 cm) squares. Fill with nut or apricot filling. Roll into crescents. Bake at 400°F (205°C) until light brown. Sprinkle with powdered sugar when cool.

Filling: Beat egg whites, stiff. Gradually add vanilla and sugar. Fold in ground walnuts.

Kathryn Compell
Chicago, Illinois   U.S.A.

DATE STICKS
Datľové paličky

1 cup (200 g) sugar
1/4 cup (1/2 dL) oleo or butter
2 eggs
4 tablespoons (60 mL) hot water
1 1/2 cups (3 1/2 dL) dates, chopped
1 teaspoon (5 mL) vanilla
Pinch of salt
1 cup (140 g) flour
1 teaspoon (5 mL) baking powder
1 cup (1/4 L) nuts, chopped
Powdered sugar

Pour hot water over dates and let stand for 10 minutes. Cream sugar and oleo. Add eggs and beat well. Mix in vanilla and salt; add dates and nuts. Mix flour and baking powder; add to batter and mix well. Pour into greased 9x9 inch (23x23 cm) pan. Bake 45-50 minutes in preheated oven 325°F (165°C). When cool, cut in small squares. Fill a plastic bag with powdered sugar and add a few date squares at a time. Shake bag until all pieces are coated.

Mary Kronen
Rossford, Ohio   U.S.A.

FIG ROLLS
Figové rožky

1 pound (.50 kg) figs, ground
2 cups (.20 kg) powdered sugar
1½ cups (.30 kg) nuts, ground
1 orange, rind and juice
2-3 tablespoons (.05 L) rum

Glaze:
3 ounces (.08 kg) chocolate
⅓ cup (.08 kg) margarine

Grind figs in a meat grinder. Mix figs with ground nuts, add powdered sugar, orange rind, and juice. Add rum, according to taste, and mix well. Take small pieces of mixture and form into small rolls. Melt chocolate and margarine and mix into a glaze. Coat rolls with glaze.

Lučenec, Slovakia

GYPSY COOKIES
Cigánské rezy

1¾ cups (250 g) flour
½ cup (60 g) powdered sugar
¼ pound (100 g) margarine
1 teaspoon (5 g) baking powder
½ cup (100 g) lekvar
¾ cup (180 g) sugar
⅓ cup (80 g) nuts, ground
1 tablespoon (20 g) cocoa
1 egg yolk
3 egg whites

Mix flour with powdered sugar and baking powder. Add margarine, mix well. Add egg yolk and work dough well. Roll dough into a thick layer and place on ungreased baking sheet. Place in oven and slightly bake, until dough forms a light crust. Remove and spread lekvar over partially baked dough. Beat egg whites, add sugar, and continue beating until very stiff. Add ground nuts and cocoa to egg whites and spread over top of lekvar. Complete baking in moderate oven 350°F (180°C) until done.

Ľudmila Šandorfi
St. Catherine's, Ontario, Canada

HONEY CAKES
Medovníky

3 cups plus 2 tablespoons (40 dkg) cake flour
1¹/₃ cups (14 dkg) powdered sugar
2 eggs, beaten
½ cup (10 dkg) butter
3 tablespoons (45 mL) honey
Pinch of cinnamon
1 teaspoon (5 mL) baking soda

Cream butter, add powdered sugar, eggs, and mix well. Add remaining ingredients, mixing dough well. Roll out to ³/₈ inch (1 cm) thick. Cut into various shapes. Bake on greased cookie sheet in preheated hot oven 375°F (190°C) until lightly golden.

Martina Kovačiková
Zvolenská Slatina, Slovakia

PECAN FINGERS
Pikanové prstičky

1 cup (¼ L) butter
2 cups (280 g) flour
2 cups (1/2 L) pecans, ground fine
½ cup (1 dL) powdered sugar
2 teaspoons (10 mL) vanilla
¼ cup (60 mL) powdered sugar, for sprinkling

Cream butter and sugar. Add flour and mix like pie dough. Add vanilla and pecans. Mix well. Roll into the shape of small fingers. Bake at 350°F (180°C) for about 20 minutes. Do not burn. Put powdered sugar in paper bag. Place cookies in bag and gently turn until coated.

Joan Jurishica
Milwaukee, Wisconsin U.S.A.

LORRY'S GRANDMOTHER'S JAM COOKIES
Marhuľové-broskyňové koláčky
(Starej mamičky Lorusky)

4 cups (570 g) flour
1½ cups (3½ dL) sugar
1 teaspoon (5 mL) baking powder (scant)
1 pound (450 g) shortening
2 tablespoons (30 g) butter
7 egg yolks, beaten
1 whole egg, beaten
1 egg white, beaten
½ cup (1 dL) finely chopped walnuts
½ cup (1 dL) peach or apricot jam

Place the flour, baking powder and sugar in a large mixing bowl. Cut in the shortening and butter with a pastry blender until crumbly. (As you would if making pie crust.) Stir in 7 egg yolks and one whole egg, a little at a time, using a fork until dough begins to stick together. Knead until well mixed, adding a little more flour if dough is sticky. Chilling dough at this time will make it easier to handle. Roll out on lightly floured surface to about ⅛ inch (.3 cm) thickness. Using a 2 inch (5 cm) round, scallop-edged, cookie cutter, cut out cookies. With a thimble, cut out centers of half the cookies. Brush the cookies that have the cut out centers with the beaten egg white and sprinkle with chopped walnuts. Place cookies on an ungreased cookie sheet. Bake in a 350°F (180°C) oven for about 10 minutes. Do not allow to brown. When all are baked, put together by placing a dab of jam on the bottom half whole cookie. Top with the nut sprinkled half.

Recipe from my late grandmother's collection,
Mrs. Annie Belas

Lorry Katanik
Mississauga, Ontario, Canada

LEKVAR, NUT OR APRICOT COOKIES
Lekvárové, orechové, marhuľové koláčky

1/2 ounce (14 g) yeast
  (2 packages dry yeast)
5 cups (700 g) flour
2 cups (450 g) margarine
3 egg yolks, beaten
1 cup (1/4 L) sour cream
Powdered sugar
Granulated sugar

Crumble yeast into flour, cut in margarine, add eggs and sour cream and mix or knead until smooth. Divide into five rolls and refrigerate until dough is completely chilled. (Dough may be refrigerated overnight).

Roll each piece out on surface dusted with powdered sugar. Cut into 3 inch (7.5 cm) squares. Drop a teaspoon of favorite filling in middle and fold two of the four corners to center so points touch. Roll in granulated sugar. On a greased cookie sheet, bake in preheated oven at 375°F (190°C) for 8-10 minutes. Remove from cookie sheet and dust with powdered sugar.

Makes five to six dozen cookies.

Kathy Ruszczyk Malone
Colorado Springs, Colorado
U.S.A.

DELUXE LEMON BARS
Nadherné citronové obdĺžníčky

Dough:
2 sticks (½ L) butter, melted
½ cup (1 dL) powdered sugar
2 cups (280 g) flour
¼ teaspoon (1.25 mL) salt

Topping:
4 eggs
2 cups (400 g) granulated sugar
¼ cup (35 g) flour
⅓ cup (¾ dL) fresh lemon juice
Rind of 1 lemon, grated
½ teaspoon (2.5 mL) baking powder

Dough: Stir together with a wooden spoon, melted butter, powdered sugar, flour and salt. Press into 9x13 inch (23x33 cm) pan with your fingers until even. Bake at 350°F (180°C) for 20 minutes or until lightly browned.
Topping: Mix eggs, granulated sugar, flour, fresh lemon juice, grated lemon rind and baking powder. Beat 1 minute. Pour on top of dough. Return to the oven and bake for an additional 20-25 minutes. Let cool. Sprinkle with powdered sugar. Cut into small squares as cookies are very rich.
Cookies freeze well.

Agnes Virostek
Boonton, New Jersey U.S.A.

SLOVAKIAN COOKIES
Soley-koley

½ pound (225 g) butter
1 cup (200 g) sugar
2 egg yolks
2 cups (280 g) flour
1 cup (1/4 L) chopped nuts
½ cup (1 dL) strawberry jam

Preheat oven to 350°F (180°C). Butter the bottom of a 9 inch (23 cm) square baking pan.
Cream butter and add sugar; mix until fluffy. Add egg yolks. Beat well. Add flour; fold in nuts. Spoon half of the batter into pan and spread. Top with jam. Cover with remaining batter.
Bake 40 minutes or until light brown. Cut into squares.

Mary H. Gyomber
Denver, Pennsylvania U.S.A.

MARBLE PIZZELLES
Mramorované pečené krapne

6 eggs, beaten
1¼ cups (250 g) sugar
1 cup (¼ L) oil
2 tablespoons (30 mL) anise extract or 1 drop anise oil
3 cups (420 g) flour
¼ teaspoon (1.25 mL) salt
1 teaspoon (5 mL) vanilla or 1 teaspoon (5 mL) lemon extract
3 teaspoons (15 mL) baking powder
¼ cup (50 g) cocoa

Beat eggs well, add sugar, oil and extracts. Sift flour with salt and baking powder.
Add flour slowly to egg mixture. Beat well.
Take ⅓ of dough and add the ¼ cup (50 g) cocoa. Mix well.
Drop by teaspoonful on hot pizzelle iron, some white dough, some chocolate dough.

Agnes Puhalla
Youngstown, Ohio   U.S.A.

RAISIN BARS
Koláč s hrozienkami

6 egg whites, beaten stiff
½ cup (90 g) sugar
6 egg yolks, beaten
½ cup (10 dkg) ground nuts
½ cup (10 dkg) raisins
1 tablespoon (15 g) cocoa
¼ teaspoon (1.25 mL) baking powder
⅓ cup (5 dkg) flour (polohrubej)

Filling:
2 eggs
2 tablespoons (30 mL) black coffee
⅔ cup (12 dkg) granulated sugar
2 tablespoons (30 g) butter

Beat 6 egg whites stiff; add 6 tablespoons (90 g) sugar. Continue beating and add 6 egg yolks. Add ground nuts, raisins and flour, sifted with cocoa and baking powder. Bake in greased baking pan in preheated oven 350°F (180°C) until done when tested with a toothpick. Cool, top with cream filling and cut into desired size bars.
Filling: Mix all ingredients together and cook in a double boiler until mixture thickens. Let cool before spreading on cake.

Martina Kováčiková
Zvolenská Slatina, Slovakia

RAISIN PUFF COOKIES
AN ORIGINAL RECIPE
Hrozienkové chumáčiky - originálne

2 cups (½ L) raisins
1 cup (¼ L) water
1 cup (¼ L) oil
1 cup (200 g) sugar
2 eggs, beaten
1 teaspoon (5 mL) vanilla
3 cups (420 g) flour
1 teaspoon (5 mL) soda
½ teaspoon (2.5 mL) salt
Granulated sugar for coating

To prepare raisins, cook in 1 cup (¼ L) water until all water has evaporated and been absorbed; or let raisins stand in hot water over night.

Mix oil and sugar and beat well. Add beaten eggs and vanilla. Sift flour, soda and salt and add to egg mixture, mixing well. Add cooled, drained raisins. Mixture will be fairly stiff. You may need to use your hands for the last mixing. Form dough into walnut-size balls. Dip in granulated sugar. Place on ungreased cookie sheet, 2 inches (5 cm) apart. Bake at 350°F (180°C) for 15 minutes or until nice and brown.

Yields 4½ - 5 dozen cookies.

Sister M. Annette
Vincentian Sisters of Charity
Pittsburgh, Pennsylvania
U.S.A.

RUM BARS
Opitý František

Dough:
6 egg yolks, beaten
6 egg whites, beaten stiff
2 cups (22 dkg) powdered sugar
1/2 pound (22 dkg) butter
7/8 cup (12 dkg) flour
1 1/2 tablespoons (22 mL) cocoa
1 teaspoon (5 mL) baking powder
Spicy lekvar
Chopped apricots (or other fruit)
1/2 pound (22 dkg) nuts, ground or chopped
3/4 cup (15 dkg) sugar
4 tablespoons (1/2 dL) rum

Glaze:
2 ounces (5 dkg) chocolate
3 tablespoons (5 dkg) butter

Cream butter, add beaten egg yolks and powdered sugar; beat until light and creamy. Add flour, cocoa and baking powder. Mix well; fold in beaten egg whites. Pour batter into greased baking sheet and bake in preheated moderate oven 350°F (180°C) until golden or done. Remove from baking sheet and let cool. Spread spicy lekvar over cooled cake. (To make a spicy lekvar, add allspice or cinnamon, cloves and nutmeg to taste). Next, place chopped apricots, or other fruit, over lekvar. Sprinkle ground nuts, sugar and rum. Drizzle with chocolate glaze.

Marta Kovačiková
Zvolenská Slatina, Slovakia

SLOVAKIAN BARS
Slovenské štvorčeky

1/2 cup (115 g) butter
1 cup (200 g) sugar
2 egg yolks
2 cups (280 g) flour
1 cup (1/4 L) walnuts, ground
1/2 cup (1 dL) apricot jam

Cream butter and sugar, add egg yolks and beat well. Add flour and nuts. Press half the dough into 8 inch (20 cm) square pan. Spread apricot jam; press remainder of dough on top of jam. Bake in preheated oven 325°F (160°C) for 45-60 minutes or until done. Cool; cut into small square pieces.

SECRET KISSES
Tajné božteky

1 cup (¼ L) butter
1 cup (¼ L) finely chopped walnuts
½ cup (100 g) sugar
1 teaspoon (5 mL) vanilla
2 cups (280 g) sifted flour
1 package Hershey Kisses
Powdered sugar

Beat butter, sugar, and vanilla until light and fluffy. Add walnuts and flour; blend well. Chill dough for one hour. Shape one teaspoon (5 mL) of dough around each Kiss. Bake at 375°F (190°C) for 10-12 minutes. Roll in powdered sugar while still warm. Cool completely.
Note: Recipe only uses one half of Hershey Kisses, so double recipe for a full bag of chocolate candies.

Irene Las
Joliet, Illinois U.S.A.

SLOVAK SPRITZ
Slovenské šišky

½ quart (½ L) milk
8 tablespoons (80 g) flour
1 teaspoon (5 mL) salt
1½ teaspoons (7.5 mL) baking powder
4 eggs, slightly beaten
Fat, for frying

Sift flour, salt and baking powder; add half of the flour mixture into milk. Mix well. Add remaining flour and cook until mixture thickens and lifts from sides and bottom of pan. Cool. Add eggs and mix well. Fill spritz and deep fat fry.

Julia Kunchak Compan
Akron, Ohio U.S.A.

SOUR CREAM CRESCENTS
Kyslé smotanové kifle

Dough:
1 pound (450 g) margarine
5 cups (700 g) flour
6 egg yolks
8 ounces (224 g) sour cream
Granulated sugar

Filling:
6 egg whites, beaten stiff
Sugar to taste
1 pound (450 g) ground nuts (or enough for spreading consistency)

Dough: Mix margarine and flour like pie dough. Add egg yolks and sour cream. Mix well with hands. Roll dough into balls a little smaller than a walnut. Refrigerate overnight.

Next day, roll each ball in granulated sugar to a flat circle. Spread nut filling or other filling such as apricot butter or lekvar.

Roll up as little nut rolls. Bake on ungreased cookie sheet, 350°F (180°C) for 20 minutes.

Filling: Beat egg whites stiff. Gradually add sugar, to taste. Fold in ground nuts.

Yields about 75 crescents.

Agnes Puhalla
Youngstown, Ohio   U.S.A.

MA POLAKOVIC'S SUGAR COOKIES
Cukrové koláčky
(Mamky Polakovičovej)

1 cup (¼ L) shortening, butter or oleo
1 cup (200 g) sugar
3 eggs
3 cups (420 g) flour
1 teaspoon (5 mL) baking powder
1 teaspoon (5 mL) vanilla or lemon extract

Mix shortening and sugar; add eggs and mix well. Add flour, baking powder and flavoring; mix well. Chill before rolling out on floured board. Cut out cookies and bake in a preheated oven 375°F (190°C) for 10-12 minutes. Dip cookies in a saucer of sugar. These can be frosted or decorated.

Millie Heban
Rossford, Ohio   U.S.A.

WALNUT CRESCENTS
Orechovníky

2½ cups (350 g) flour
½ pound (225 g) butter
½ cup (1 dL) whipping cream
4 eggs, separated
1 egg, whole
1 pound (450 g) walnuts
1 cup (200 g) sugar
1 teaspoon (5 mL) vanilla

Dough: Mix flour and butter as for pie crust. Mix whipping cream, 4 egg yolks, one whole egg, and whip. Slowly add whipped mixture to flour and butter and mix with wooden spoon. Knead dough thoroughly. Mix and blend with fingers. On wax paper on large plate make 70-100 1 inch (2.5 cm) balls. Cover with cloth and refrigerate over night.

Filling: Crush walnuts. Beat 4 egg whites. Add sugar gradually to whites and beat until stiff; add walnuts and vanilla. Roll out each ball of dough until very flat, add filling, roll into crescent and bake at 400°F (200°C) until light brown. Make sure seam is on bottom.

Joe Timko
Windsor, Ontario, Canada

VANILLA HORNS
Vanilkové rožky

2½ cups (350 g) flour
½ pound (225 g) sweet butter
⅓ cup (¾ dL) sugar
2 egg yolks
1¾ cups (3¾ dL) almonds, ground
Powdered sugar for dusting
Vanilla sugar

(See notes on making vanilla sugar)

Crumble butter into flour. Add sugar and egg yolks, mix. Add almonds and mix well. Pinch pieces of dough and form cylinder horns. Place on greased cookie sheet and bake at 350°F (180°C) about 20 minutes or until lightly golden. Mix vanilla sugar with powdered sugar. Roll, or dust horns with powdered sugar.

Ellen Gregus
Palisades, New York U.S.A.

APPLE DUMPLING PUDDING
Jablčný knedlikový nákyp

1 cup (200 g) sugar
1 egg, beaten
1 cup (140 g) flour
2 teaspoons (10 mL) baking powder
Pinch of salt
1 teaspoon (5 mL) vanilla
2 tablespoons (30 mL) butter
2/3 cup (1 1/2 dL) milk
5-6 apples

Sauce:
2 cups (1/2 L) brown sugar
2 tablespoons (30 mL) corn starch
2 cups (1/2 L) boiling water
1 teaspoon (5 mL) vanilla
5 tablespoons (75 g) butter

Line bottom of pan with diced apples. Beat egg and sugar well. Add remaining ingredients and mix well. Pour over diced apples. Bake at 350°F (180°C) for 30 minutes.

Sauce: Cook all ingredients until bubbly. Pour over pieces of cake at serving time. Serve sauce warm.

Sandra Joyce
Slovak Domovina Dancers
Windsor, Ontario, Canada

APPLE CREAM PARFAIT
Jablkový krém

1 cup (20 dkg) apples, cooked and mashed
1 cup (10 dkg) powdered sugar
3 egg whites, stiffly beaten
Almonds
Cream, whipped

Prepare apples, cook and mash. Add sugar and mix well. Beat egg whites until very stiff. Lightly fold in egg whites. Place sauce in dessert dishes, top with sliced almonds and whipped cream.

Antonia Kralik
Berwyn, Illinois U.S.A.

APPLE PUDDING
Jemná žemľovka s jablkami

- ¼ cup (60 g) butter
- ⅓ cup (40 g) powdered sugar
- 2 eggs, separated
- 2 tablespoons (30 g) hazel nuts, chopped and toasted
- 3 tablespoons (40 g) raisins
- 5 slices bread or buns (žemľe)
- 1 pint (2 cups) (½ L) sweet cream (half and half)
- 1 pound (400 g) apples, grated
- Butter
- Bread crumbs for dusting

Cream butter, add sugar and mix well. Add egg yolks and beat until light and fluffy. Chop nuts and toast in pan, dry. Pour hot water over raisins, drain and pat dry. Cut bread in pieces and moisten in cream; add butter mixture, nuts and raisins. Beat egg whites until stiff; fold into bread mixture. Grease pudding pan or casserole with butter, dust with bread crumbs. Pour half of bread mixture into baking dish. Add grated apples over mixture. Lastly, pour bread mixture over apples. In preheated oven 350°F (180°C) bake for 30 minutes.

Anna Škovierová
Očova, Slovakia

BAKED CHRISTMAS APPLES
Pečené vianočné jablká

10-12 red apples
1/3 cup (3/4 dL) melted butter
1 cup (200 g) sugar
3 teaspoons (15 mL) cinnamon
1 cup (1/4 L) ground nuts
2 egg whites, beaten stiff
2 tablespoons (30 mL) sugar

Core out the center of apple, removing all seeds. Mix sugar with cinnamon, add butter and groundnuts. Stuff apples with mixture; arrange on baking pan and bake in moderately hot oven 400°F (200°C) for 25-30 minutes. In the meantime, beat egg whites stiff; add sugar and beat well. Remove baked apples from oven, place a dab of egg white on each and bake a few minutes longer. Serve warm.

Eva Škovierová
Očova, Slovakia

STEWED DRIED FRUIT COMPOTE FOR CHRISTMAS EVE
Kompót zo sušeného ovocia

9 ounces (250 g) prunes
9 ounces (250 g) dried pears
Dried apples, varied amount
Water
Cinnamon
Cloves
Sugar

In a bowl, combine dried fruits, cover with water and let stand until fruit becomes soft and puffy. Add cinnamon, cloves and sugar to taste.

Transfer fruit and liquid to cooking pot, bring to boil and simmer, covered, until cooked.

This dessert was served at the Christmas Eve supper. It was also a popular dish served at many spinning sessions where women and young maidens gathered during winter evenings to spin flax and hemp.

PhDr. Zora Mintalová
Slovenské Národné Múzeum
Martin, Slovakia

BREADED CREPES WITH APPLE FILLING
Palacinky - jablkové plnené
(v strúhanke vyprážené)

1 cup (140 g) flour
2 tablespoons (30 mL) sugar
1/2 teaspoon (2 1/2 mL) salt
1 cup (1/4 L) milk
3 eggs
Butter for frying
Powdered sugar for sprinkling

Filling:
1/2 cup (1 dL) chopped nuts
Dash of cinnamon
Dash of nutmeg
8 tart apples
1/2 cup (100 g) sugar

Breading:
2 eggs, beaten
Bread crumbs or cracker crumbs
Butter

Crepes: Beat eggs in mixer; add half of milk and mix slowly; add flour, sugar, salt and remainder of milk; mix until smooth. Fry in small frying pan using about 1/2 tablespoonful (7.5 mL) butter for each crepe. Pour just enough batter into pan to cover bottom. (To make batter spread more easily, use a little more milk as pancakes should be very thin.) Brown pancakes on both sides using either a spatula or a knife for turning. Pancakes have a tendency to brown very quickly.

Filling: Peel apples, slice and cook with sugar, stewing until tender. Cool; add chopped nuts, cinnamon and nutmeg. Fill each crepe and roll.

Dip each rolled pancake in beaten eggs and then in bread or cracker crumbs; brown in butter. Serve warm, sprinkled with powdered sugar.

Kathy Ruszczyk Malone
Colorado Springs, Colorado
U.S.A.

PLUM PUDDING
Slivkový nákyp

1³/₄ cups (250 g) flour
¹/₂ cup (100 g) butter
2¹/₂ cups (6 dL) milk, warm
2¹/₄ cups (250 g) powdered sugar
Lemon rind
¹/₂ teaspoon (2.5 mL) salt
6 eggs, separated
¹/₂ cup (100 g) nuts
1¹/₂ pounds (700 g) plums, pitted
Cinnamon
Butter or margarine
Bread crumbs

In a large skillet, brown flour slightly, add butter and make a light roux (zápražka). Add warm milk, mix until smooth (omačka). While mixing, add sugar, lemon rind, salt, egg yolks, one at a time, and lastly add stiffly beaten egg whites. In a pudding pan which has been greased with butter and coated with sifted bread crumbs and half of the ground nuts, pour half of the pudding mixture. On top of the mixture, layer pitted plums, add remaining nuts, sprinkle with cinnamon. Finally, pour remaining pudding mixture. Cover and set pan into a larger pot filled with hot water. Place in hot oven and steam for 45 minutes. Remove from pan by gently tapping out.

Hlavné mučne jedlo!

Maria Sarvaš Kováčiková
Pod Krivan, Slovakia

RICE PUDDING
Ryžový nákyp

1 quart (1 L) milk
3 cups (³/₄ L) water
1 cup (¹/₄ L) rice (Carolina)
¹/₂ cup (100 g) sugar
2 cups (¹/₂ L) milk
3 eggs, beaten
3 tablespoons (45 mL) vanilla
Cinnamon

Combine first four ingredients. Cook 45 minutes or until rice is soft. Add 2 cups (¹/₂ L) milk, 3 beaten eggs. Bring to a boil, add vanilla. Let mixture cool. Top with cinnamon.

Judge Joseph J. Talafous, Sr.
Jersey City, New Jersey U.S.A.

DOUGHNUTS
Fánky

3 eggs, beaten
1 teaspoon (5 mL) sugar
Pinch of salt
1 teaspoon (5 mL) melted butter, shortening or oil
2 tablespoons (30 mL) wine
1½ cups (210 g) flour, sifted
Powdered sugar
Oil for frying

Beat eggs until light and fluffy; add pinch of salt, sugar and melted butter, and beat well. Continue beating, add wine and beat all ingredients. Add sifted flour and mix until dough is of medium stiffness and can be rolled out. Separate into 3 parts. Knead as for noodles.
Roll out very thin and cut into strips. Cut strip into pieces about 1½ inches (3.75 cm) wide, 3-4 inches (7.5-10 cm) long. Make a slit in each piece, turning one end through.
Fry in hot fat. Do not fry too long, only until a light brown on each side. Watch carefully. Drain on paper toweling. When cool, dust with sifted powdered sugar and serve. An old Slovak recipe.

Anna Sosnicky
Union, New Jersey   U.S.A.

DOUGHNUTS
Fánky

2 cups (280 g) flour
2 eggs
⅓ cup (¾ dL) sugar
Pinch of salt
½ cup (1 dL) butter, lard, or oleo
Water
Shortening, for frying
Powdered sugar, for dusting

Mix all ingredients together. Use enough water to make a dough like noodles. Roll out as for a large pie crust and cut into pie slices. Make slits and pull one end of dough through. Fry in deep, hot shortening. Drain. Sprinkle with powdered sugar.

Joan Jurishica
Milwaukee, Wisconsin   U.S.A.

DOUGHNUTS
Fánky

3/4 ounce (20 g) yeast
2 tablespoons (30 g) sugar
2 1/4 cups (300 g polohrubej) flour
2 egg yolks
1/2 teaspoon (2.5 mL) salt
1 tablespoon (15 mL) rum
1/4 cup (1/2 stick) (50 g) margarine
1/2 cup (1 dL) sour cream or milk
1 1/2 cups (300 g) fat, lard for frying
Vanilla sugar for dusting*

Note: If vanilla sugar is not available, add 1 teaspoon (5 mL) vanilla to dough, and dust with powdered sugar.   -Editor

Crumble yeast mixed with sugar and add to flour. Add egg yolks, salt, rum, margarine. Add more or less sour cream or milk, to form a medium stiff dough. Work dough well. Place dough in a larger bowl, cover with cloth and let rest for about 30 minutes. Roll dough on a floured board to 1/8 inch (1/2 cm) thickness. With a cookie cutter, or wine glass, cut out rectangular or oblong pieces, and crosswise make a cut in the center. Fry in hot fat. Drain. When cooled, sprinkle with powdered sugar.

Fánky were a favorite pastry during the Mardi Gras celebration.

PhDr. Zora Mintalová
Slovenské Národné Múzeum
Martin, Slovakia

DOUGHNUTS
Fánky

1 3/4 cups (25 dg) flour
Pinch of salt
1/4 cup (5 dg) butter, melted
1/2 cup (5 dg) powdered sugar
2 egg yolks
2 tablespoons (30 mL) rum or wine
5 tablespoons (75 mL) sour cream
1 lemon rind, grated
Oil, for frying
Powdered sugar for dusting

Mix flour with salt and melted butter. Add powdered sugar, egg yolks, rum, sour cream and grated lemon rind. Mix well. Place mixture on floured board and roll out thin. With cookie cutter wheel, cut into squares. Make 2 slits in center of each square and braid edge through slit. Drop into hot oil and fry. Dust with powdered sugar.

L'udmila Šandorfi
St. Catherine's, Ontario
Canada

APPLE SQUARES
Jablkové zákusky

Dough:
2/3 cup (1 1/2 dL) milk
1 teaspoon (5 mL) sugar
1 package (7 g) yeast
1/4 cup (1/2 dL) water, very warm
4 egg yolks
1 cup (1/4 L) margarine
4 cups (570 g) flour

Filling:
Sliced apples
Sugar
Cinnamon

Dough: Scald milk, add sugar and cool to lukewarm. Dissolve yeast in water, then add to milk. Beat egg yolks into milk/yeast mixture. With pastry blender cut margarine into sifted flour, add the liquid mixture and work well. Divide dough in half. On floured board, roll out one half of dough to fit and overlap edges of jelly roll pan, about 16 x 10 inches (40 x 25 cm). Spread with apple filling. Roll out remaining dough to cover. Seal edges. Slash dough surface to let steam escape. Cover, let rise in warm place, free from draft, until doubled, about 1 hour. Bake at 375°F (190°C) about 35 minutes.

Filling: Peel and slice apples. Mix with sugar and cinnamon to taste. Use enough apples for a generous filling.

Helen Semyan
Youngstown, Ohio   U.S.A.

APRICOT AND LEKVAR SQUARES
Marhuľové a lekvárové zákusky

4 cups (570 g) flour
3½ teaspoons (17.5 mL) baking powder
1 teaspoon (5 mL) salt
1 cup (200 g) sugar
1 cup (225 g) shortening
3 egg yolks
1 cup (¼ L) sour cream or canned milk
2 teaspoons (10 mL) lemon juice
1 teaspoon (5 mL) vanilla
2 jars (2 cups) (500 mL) apricot filling
1 jar (1 cup) (250 mL) lekvar
Ground nuts for sprinkle
Powdered sugar for glaze

Combine flour, baking powder, salt, and sugar in bowl; cut in shortening. Blend in egg yolks, sour cream (or milk), and vanilla. Divide dough into 3 balls. Roll first ball to fit large cookie sheet 12x17 inches (30x43 cm). Spread apricot filling. Roll next ball of dough and place over top of apricot. Spread lekvar evenly across; cover with rolled out remaining ball of dough. Bake in preheated 350°F (180°C) oven for 30-45 minutes or until brown. Spread with a thin powdered sugar icing and sprinkle with nuts. These freeze very well.

Mrs. Joseph F. Kopachko
Smock, Pennsylvania   U.S.A.

CHEESECAKE SQUARES
Tvarožníky

2 packages crescent rolls
¾ cup (1¾ dL) sugar
2 packages (8 ounces each) (2-225 g) cream cheese
1 teaspoon (5 mL) vanilla
1 teaspoon (5 mL) lemon juice
Cinnamon sugar

Preheat oven to 350°F (180°C). Take a jelly roll pan, 9x13 inch (23x33 cm), and press one package of crescent rolls evenly across pan. With blender, mix softened cream cheese, sugar, vanilla, lemon juice. Once blended, place cheese mixture on top of dough in baking pan.
Finally, press second package of crescent rolls across cheese mixture. Sprinkle top with cinnamon sugar. Bake for 25-35 minutes.

Irene Las
Joliet, Illinois   U.S.A.

CHOCOLATE GLAZED CREAM PASTRY
Murín v košeli

Dough:
- 4 egg yolks
- 4 egg whites
- 2¾ cups (30 dkg) powdered sugar
- 1½ cups (20 dkg) coarse (gruel type) flour
- 1 teaspoon (5 mL) (½ Prašok do pečiva) baking powder
- 1 tablespoon (15 mL) hot water
- ½ cup (10 dkg) nuts, ground

Cream:
- 1 cup (2 dL) milk
- 1 tablespoon (1 dkg) coarse flour
- 5 egg yolks, beaten
- 2 sticks (20 dkg) butter
- 1 cup (20 dkg) sugar

Meringue:
- 5 egg whites, beaten stiff
- 1¼ cups (25 dkg) sugar

Chocolate for glaze

Dough: Beat egg yolks with sugar. Mix flour and baking powder, and add to egg mixture. Add hot water and nuts. Fold in stiffly beaten egg whites. Spread dough on greased and floured baking pan and bake in preheated oven 350°F (180°C) until golden brown. Let cool.

Cream: Beat egg yolks, add milk and flour. Cook until thickened, stirring constantly to avoid lumps. Cool. In a separate bowl, cream butter and sugar and add to cream mixture.

Meringue: In a double boiler (over boiling water) beat egg whites until stiff; add sugar and continue beating over heat until meringue consistency.

Spread cream mixture over cooled dough. Top with meringue. Drizzle with chocolate glaze or melted chocolate bits.

Marta Kováčiková
Zvolenská Slatina, Slovakia

DELICIOUS CHOCOLATE PASTRY
Jemné čokoládové rezy

Dough:
- 1/2 pound (225 g) butter
- 5 egg yolks
- 1/2 lemon rind
- 1 tablespoon (15 mL) vanilla
- 4 squares chocolate, melted
- 1/8 teaspoon (.6 mL) cinnamon
- 1/8 teaspoon (.6 mL) ground cloves
- 1 whiskey glass rum
- 1 1/2 cups (3 1/2 dL) powdered sugar
- 1 1/2 cups (3 1/2 dL) ground nuts
- 4 heaping tablespoons (45 g) flour
- 5 egg whites, beaten stiff

Raspberry jam

Rum Glaze:
- 1 cup (15 dkg) powdered sugar
- 3-4 drops red food coloring
- 1/2 bottle rum extract
- Boiling water

Dough: Cream butter, add egg yolks one at a time and beat well. Add melted chocolate. Mix spices, sugar and flour and add to creamed mixture. Add rum, lemon rind, and vanilla. Add ground nuts and lastly, fold in stiffly beaten egg whites. Pour into greased and floured oblong cake pan and bake at 350°F (180°C) until sides lift away from pan. Let cool. Slice baked dough lengthwise into two parts. For filling, spread raspberry jam across bottom layer. Place top layer over jam and top with a rum glaze.

Glaze: Mix all ingredients. Add just enough hot water to make a thick glaze. Spread over top of dough. Cut into squares and serve.

Ellen Gregus
Palisades, New York   U.S.A.

CREAM SQUARES
Nanukové kocky

Dough:
1/2 cup (10 dkg) butter
2 3/4 cups (30 dkg) powdered sugar
2 eggs
1/2 cup (10 dkg) chopped nuts
1 3/4 cups (25 dkg) cake flour
1/2 teaspoon (2.5 mL) baking soda
2 tablespoons (2 dkg) cocoa
1 cup + 2 tablespoons (270 mL) milk

Cream:
2 cups (1/2 L) milk
2 1/2 tablespoons (37 mL) cake flour
2 1/2 tablespoons (37 mL) plain flour
1/2 pound (25 dkg) butter
2 cups + 2 tablespoons (25 dkg) powdered sugar
1 egg yolk

Glaze: (Poleva)
1 square (1 varová čokoláda) chocolate
1/3 cup (8 dkg) oleo

Dough: Combine butter, powdered sugar, and eggs, and mix for 15 minutes. Sift flour, baking soda, and cocoa. Add flour and milk to butter mixture. Mix well. Roll out dough and pat into greased baking sheet. Bake in moderate oven 350°F (180°C) until lightly golden. Spread cream across completely cooled koláč.

Cream: Mix flour and milk and cook until thickened (thick kaša) mixing constantly. Add butter, powdered sugar, and egg yolk. Mix well, remove from heat and let cool. Spread over cooled koláč dough. Drizzle with glaze topping. Cut dessert pastry into squares.

Glaze: Melt chocolate and oleo. While lukewarm, drizzle over cream.

This recipe is from a relative in Bratislava

Mary Wendt
Sharon, Pennsylvania U.S.A.

DOUBLE-DECKER PASTRY
Prekladané rezy

5 cups (700 g) flour
1 cup (200 g) sugar
4 teaspoons (20 mL) baking powder
2 teaspoons (10 mL) baking soda
1/2 pound (225 g) butter
2 tablespoons (30 mL) shortening
4 egg yolks
1/2 pint (1/4 L) sour cream
1 teaspoon (5 mL) vanilla
Pinch of salt
2 1/2 cups (6 dL) ground walnuts
1/2 cup (100 g) sugar
1 cup or 1/2 pint (1/4 L) jam or lekvar

Sift together flour, sugar, baking powder, baking soda and salt. Add shortening and butter; add egg yolks, sour cream and vanilla. Divide dough into 4 portions.

Roll out first layer as for pie; place in bottom of a 10 inch (25 cm) spring form pan; spread 2/3 of nut and sugar mixture on first layer.

Roll out second layer; place over nuts, spread this layer with jam or lekvar.

Roll out third layer and sprinkle remaining 1/3 of the nut and sugar mixture over jam.

Roll out fourth layer; cut into strips; place on top to form lattice crust. Bake for 35 minutes at 350°F (180°C).

Sandra Sarosy Duve
Colorado Springs, Colorado
U.S.A.

FLAKY SQUARES
Chumáčiky

1 pound (450 g) leaf lard, ground
3 cups (420 g) flour
1 teaspoon (5 mL) salt
¼ cup (50 g) sugar
1 cake (21 g) yeast
½ cup (1 dL) warm milk
2 whole eggs
1½ cups (3½ dL) warm milk
2 tablespoons (30 mL) vinegar
1 egg yolk, beaten, for brushing
Powdered sugar for sprinkling

Nut or lekvar filling

Set aside ½ cup (1 dL) lard. Dissolve yeast in ½ cup (1 dL) warm milk. Mix dry ingredients with remaining lard and mix well. Add 1½ cups (3½ dL) milk, vinegar and eggs; work into a soft dough.

Roll out and spread with reserved ½ cup (1 dL) lard. Fold over four times and chill.

Roll out and fold over, repeating this process three times.

Roll out; cut into squares; fill each square with nut or lekvar filling. Chill in pans and brush with beaten egg yolk. Bake at 375°F (190°C) for 25 minutes or until golden. Cool. Sprinkle generously with powdered sugar.

Polly Torma
Trenton, New Jersey   U.S.A.

LAYERED FRUIT PASTRY
Ovocné zákusky (v závare)

- 1 cup (200 g) butter, softened
- 1 package ($^1/_4$ ounce) (7 g) dry yeast
- 2 teaspoons (10 mL) sugar
- $^1/_2$ cup (1 dL) milk, lukewarm
- 6 egg yolks, beaten
- 3 cups (420 g) flour
- 2 cups ($^1/_2$ L) fruit preserves (any flavor)
- 1 pound (450 g) nuts, chopped or ground
- 6 egg whites
- $^3/_4$ cup (150 g) sugar (for meringue)
- 1 teaspoon (5 mL) vanilla (for meringue)

Combine yeast, sugar, and warm milk, stir and set aside to dissolve. In the meantime, beat egg yolks, add softened butter and cream well. Add yeast mixture. Mix in flour to form soft dough. Divide dough into 3 parts. Roll out the first ball of dough to fit cake pan 9x13 inches (23x33 cm). Spread 1 cup ($^1/_4$ L) of preserves and sprinkle a third of the nuts across top. Roll out second ball of dough and place over filling. Spread the second cup ($^1/_4$ L) of preserves and sprinkle half of remaining nuts (reserve the last portion of nuts for meringue topping). Roll out third ball of dough and cover filled layers. Seal edges by pressing dough along the edges of pan. Set aside in warm place and let rise for 1 hour. Bake in preheated oven 350°F (180°C) for 25 minutes or until golden brown. Remove from oven. Beat egg whites until stiff, add sugar and vanilla. Continue beating until meringue stands in stiff peaks. Pile and spread across top of pastry, sprinkle remaining nuts. Return to oven and bake 15 minutes, or until meringue is golden brown. Do not over brown. Cool, cut into small squares.

Mrs. Joseph F. Kopachko
Smock, Pennsylvania   U.S.A.

LEKVAR LATTICE KOLACH
Mrežovník

Dough:
3½ cups (500 g) farina flour
¼ pound (1 smetol) margarine
1 teaspoon (1 prášok do pečiva) baking powder
1 teaspoon (½ vrecúška vanilkového cukru) vanilla
½ cup (100 g) sugar, refined, crystal
2 egg yolks
1 cup (2 dL) milk

Filling and Dusting:
¾ cup (150 g) lekvar
Powdered sugar
Vanilla sugar
Flour and fat for greasing and coating
1 egg yolk for brushing

In a bowl, crumble margarine (or smetol) into flour and work as for pie crust. Add baking powder and sugar. Mix well. Add egg yolks, milk, vanilla, working dough well. Divide dough into 3 parts. Set aside one part for top lattice strips. Combine the other two and work into a koláč dough. On a floured board, roll out to fit a large, greased and floured rectangular baking pan. Spread lekvar evenly across dough. From the dough set aside for the lattice top, divide into small pieces. Roll each piece into a long noodle strip. Place strips (šulánce) in lattice design across lekvar. Brush with egg yolk. Bake in preheated moderate oven 350°F (180°C) until golden and done.

Note: Old Slovak recipes do not specify exact baking time.
Combine powdered sugar and vanilla sugar, sprinkle koláč when cooled.

Very good with coffee or tea for dessert or as a snack.

PhDr. Zora Mintalová
Slovenské Národné Múzeum
Martin, Slovakia

PINEAPPLE SQUARES (PRUNE OR APRICOT)
Rezy - ananásové (lekvárové, marhuľové)

3 cups (420 g) sifted flour
2 teaspoons (10 mL) sugar
1 teaspoon (5 mL) baking powder
¼ pound (115 g) butter or margarine
¼ pound (115 g) shortening
6 teaspoons (30 mL) milk
4 egg yolks
1 teaspoon (5 mL) vanilla

Filling:
1½ pounds (675 g) pineapple jam, lekvar or apricot butter

Topping:
4 egg whites
1 cup (¼ L) powdered sugar
½ pound (225 g) chopped nuts

Dough: Mix flour, sugar, baking powder, shortening, and butter or margarine as for pie crust dough. Add milk, egg yolks and vanilla. Mix together thoroughly. Pat into a baking pan 11x18 inches (28x46 cm). Spread filling on top. Bake for 45 minutes at 350°F (180°C).

Topping: Beat egg whites stiff, add sugar. Spread on top of baked/filled pastry and sprinkle with chopped nuts. Brown to a delicate golden color. Cut into squares while still warm.

Kathy Ruszczyk Malone
Colorado Springs, Colorado
U.S.A.

RAISIN AND WALNUT PASTRY
Orechový zákusok s hrozienkami - košický

1½ cups (3½ dL) dark seedless raisins, chopped
1 cup (¼ L) water
1 tablespoon (15 mL) butter
2¾ teaspoons (13.75 mL) cornstarch
1 tablespoon (15 mL) water
⅔ cup (1½ dL) chopped walnuts
1 teaspoon (5 mL) grated fresh lemon peel
2 teaspoons (10 mL) lemon juice
½ teaspoon (2.5 mL) vanilla
1 package (17¼ ounces) (483 g) frozen puff pastry

In a medium sized saucepan, bring raisins, water and butter to a boil. Mix cornstarch and 1 tablespoon (15 mL) water; add to saucepan and cook, stirring constantly until thick. Remove from heat and stir in walnuts, lemon peel, juice and vanilla. Cool completely.

Thaw puff pastry for 20 minutes and unfold. On a lightly floured surface roll to a 9x15 inch (23x38 cm) rectangle, then cut into 3 inch (7.5 cm) squares. Put about 2 teaspoons (10 mL) filling in the center of each square, moisten corners of pastry with water and bring together above filling to make a four cornered pocket. Press together firmly to seal. Repeat with remaining pastry and filling. Put pockets on a cookie sheet and bake in a preheated 300°F (150°C) oven for 12-15 minutes or until puffed and golden. Serve warm or at room temperature.

Makes 30 pastries.

Ilonka Martinka-Torres
Castro Valley, California
U.S.A.

RHUBARB - COTTAGE CHEESE SQUARES
Rebarborový koláč s tvarohom

Dough:
- 4⅓ cups (610 g) flour
- ½ pound + 2 tablespoons (250 g) margarine or butter
- 1¾ cups (200 g) powdered sugar
- 2 egg yolks
- 1½ teaspoons (7.5 mL) baking powder
- 1 cup (¼ L) milk
- 1 tablespoon (15 mL) cocoa

Filling:
- 2½ cups (500 g) cottage cheese
- 2 eggs, separated
- 1 package vanilla sugar or 1 teaspoon (5 mL) vanilla extract
- Powdered sugar to taste
- 2½ cups (500 g) rhubarb
- 1 teaspoon (5 mL) cinnamon
- Lemon rind
- 1 egg yolk for brushing

Mix dry ingredients (flour, powdered sugar, baking powder and cocoa). Crumble butter into dry mixture (as for pie). Add egg yolks and milk. Knead dough on board. Divide into half, rolling each piece to fit size of baking pan. Place one piece of dough on greased baking pan and spread filling. Prepare rhubarb by peeling off outer layer and cut into small pieces. Mix rhubarb with cinnamon and sugar, and spread over cottage cheese filling. Cover with other half (rolled out) dough, pressing down with palm of hand. Brush top with beaten egg yolk and bake in preheated moderate oven, 350°F (180°C), until lightly golden. When cooled, cut into squares and dust lightly with powdered sugar before serving.

Filling: Put cottage cheese through sieve. Add vanilla sugar (or vanilla extract) and powdered sugar (sweeten to taste), 2 beaten egg yolks, lemon rind, and 2 stiffly beaten egg whites.

Anna Škovierová
Očova, Slovakia

WALNUT-JAM SQUARES
Orechové marhuľové štvorčeky

1 envelope (7 g) dry yeast
½ cup (1 dL) lukewarm milk
½ pound (225 g) unsalted butter
2½ cups (350 g) flour
3 tablespoons (45 mL) sugar
4 egg yolks at room temperature, beaten
1 teaspoon (5 mL) vanilla

Filling:
1 cup (¼ L) apricot jam
1 cup (¼ L) finely grated walnuts
¾ cup (1¾ dL) sugar
Rind of 1 lemon
2 tablespoons (30 mL) real rum or 1 teaspoon (5 mL) rum extract

In a 2 cup (½ L) measuring cup, dissolve yeast in warm milk. Set aside for about 10 minutes. In a large mixing bowl combine butter and flour using a pastry blender, two knives, or food processor. Stir together yeast mixture, egg yolks and vanilla and add to flour mixture. Mix well, then knead until smooth. Divide into three equal balls of dough. Roll each portion into a 9x13 inch (23x33 cm) rectangle. Prepare filling by combining all ingredients in a bowl. Divide into three parts. Place one dough portion into a greased 9x13 inch (23x33 cm) baking pan. Spread with one third of the filling. Place second rolled out dough on top of filling. Top with second third of filling. Lastly, place third rolled out dough over filling and top with rest of filling. Let rise in a warm place for about 1 hour, then bake in a 350°F (180°C) oven for 25-30 minutes. Cut into squares.

Irene Revtak
Toronto, Ontario, Canada

PASTRY SHELL
Cesto na paj

3 cups (420 g) all-purpose flour
1¹/₂ cups (300 g) shortening or lard
1 teaspoon (5 mL) salt
1 large egg
1 teaspoon (5 mL) white vinegar
5 tablespoons (75 mL) whole milk

With pastry blender or two forks, combine flour, shortening and salt until mixture resembles coarse meal. In small bowl, mix egg, vinegar and milk; add to flour mixture, mixing only until dough holds together in a ball. Refrigerate for 1 hour. Roll out on floured waxed paper or pastry cloth. Turn onto lightly-greased pie plate. Trim to a 1-inch (2¹/₂ cm) overhang and flute edges. Freezes well.

To bake: Prick all over with fork. Bake at 400°F (205°C) for 11 minutes or until lightly golden brown.

2 10-inch (25 cm) deep-dish pie shells.

Sandra Sarosy Duve
Co-editor
Colorado Springs, Colorado U.S.A.

PECAN PIE
Pikanový paj

¹/₂ cup (100 g) sugar
¹/₄ cup (¹/₂ dL) butter or oleo
1 cup (¹/₄ L) dark corn syrup
¹/₄ teaspoon (1.25 mL) salt
3 eggs
1 cup (1/4 L) pecans
9-inch (22.5 cm) unbaked pie shell

Cream sugar and butter. Add syrup and salt and beat well. Beat in eggs, one at a time. Add pecans. Pour into pie shell and bake at 350°F (180°C) for 45-55 minutes or until crust is light brown.

Mary Kay Ritchie
Garland, Texas   U.S.A.

CONCORD GRAPE PIE
Hroznový paj

4½ cups (1¼ L) purple grapes, washed
2 tablespoons (20 mL) flour
1 cup (200 g) sugar
1 tablespoon (15 mL) lemon juice
1 tablespoon (15 mL) grated orange peel
¼ teaspoon (1.25 mL) salt
Single crust for 9 inch (22.5 cm) pie

Squeeze grape centers into pan, reserving skins in a bowl. Bring pulp to boil over medium high heat; simmer for 5 minutes. Strain seeds from pulp and discard seeds. Add pulp to skins along with flour, sugar, lemon juice, orange peel and salt. Line pie pan with dough, crimping edges. Pour filling into crust. Bake in a 425°F (225°C) oven for 10 minutes; reduce to 400°F (210°C) and bake for 20 minutes or until filling is set.

Marge Koscak
Parma, Ohio   U.S.A.

BABA'S DREAM LIME PIE
Starej mamy snívaný citronový paj

4 large eggs, separated
1 can (12 fluid ounces) (354 mL) sweetened condensed milk
⅓ cup (¾ dL) lime juice or lime juice concentrate
1 graham cracker crust pie shell or any 9 inch (22.5 cm) baked pie shell of your choice

Beat 4 egg yolks and 1 egg white together until thick. Add milk and continue beating. Add lime juice and beat until thick. In a separate bowl, beat 3 egg whites until stiff peaks form. Fold beaten egg whites into milk/egg mixture. Pour into pie crust. Bake about 15 minutes in preheated oven 300°F (150°C) or until mixture in shell is set. Keep watch over baking period as top will brown quickly.

Edna Valašek Bresnie
Peoria, Arizona   U.S.A.

PRUNE PIE
Slivkový koláč

1³/₄ cups (25 dkg) flour
1¹/₄ cups (3 dL) powdered sugar
¹/₄ pound (120 g) butter
1 egg
Pinch of salt
Rind of one lemon
1 teaspoon (5 mL) vanilla
Bread crumbs

Filling:
¹/₂-1 pound (225-450 g) plums, pitted (approximately)
Cinnamon
Sugar

Topping:
Slivered almonds
Powdered sugar for sprinkling

Grease and flour a baking dish similar to a large pie plate, set aside. In a bowl, combine flour, sugar, butter, egg, salt, lemon rind and vanilla. Work into a smooth dough. Set aside and let dough rest for ¹/₂ hour. Meanwhile, wash and pit plums, drain well. Cut plums into slivers and place in a pan. Sprinkle with sugar and cinnamon. Fry or parch for about 5 minutes. On a floured board, roll out dough and with the rolling pin place dough into greased/floured pan. Pat a layer of bread crumbs on top of dough. Prick dough with a fork. Add parched plums and bake in preheated oven 350°F (180°C) for about 20 minutes. Before completion of baking (about 5-10 minutes) add slivered almonds and powdered sugar; return to oven and complete baking process for 5-10 minutes longer.

Courtesy of Viera Repková
Trenčín, Slovakia

Submitted by:
Dr. Edward Tuleya
Middletown, Pennsylvania
U.S.A.

APPLE STRUDEL
Štrudľa jablková

Dough:
2 cups (280 g) flour
½ pound (225 g) oleo
2 tablespoons (30 mL) vinegar
3 egg yolks
¼ cup (½ dL) water

Filling:
5 or 6 apples, sliced
¾ cup (1¾ dL) bread crumbs
¾ cup (1¾ dL) ground nuts
1 cup (¼ L) sugar
Cinnamon
Raisins (optional)
Oleo, melted

Mix flour and oleo as for pie dough. Add vinegar, egg yolks and water. Work into smooth dough. Chill 3 hours or overnight. Divide into three parts. Roll out dough as thin as you can (just like wax paper). Over ¾ of the dough, sprinkle ¼ cup (½ dL) dry bread crumbs. Sprinkle ¼ cup (½ dL) ground nuts. Sprinkle with ⅓ cup (¾ dL) sugar. Sprinkle cinnamon. Add as many raisins as desired. Add sliced apples; more sugar, if desired. Sprinkle with melted oleo. Roll up like a jelly roll. Place on cookie sheet. Brush with oleo. Repeat procedure for remaining two parts of dough.

Bake in preheated oven 375°F (190°C) for 45 minutes or until light brown.

Makes 3 strudels.

Mary Kronen
Rossford, Ohio U.S.A.

APPLE STRUDEL CRACKLING DOUGH
Jablkový závin z oškvarkového cesta

Dough:
- 1½ cups (215 g) flour
- ¼ teaspoon (1.25 mL) baking powder
- ½ cup (56 g) powdered sugar
- ⅛ teaspoon (.6 mL) cinnamon
- ½ cup (125 mL) cracklings, "oškvarky", finely ground
- 1 egg, slightly beaten
- 3 tablespoons (45 mL) sour cream
- 1 egg for brushing dough
- Powdered sugar for dusting

Filling:
- 1 pound (3 cups) (450 g) apples, pared and thinly sliced
- ½ cup (56 g) powdered sugar
- 1 small package vanilla sugar or 1 teaspoon (5 mL) vanilla extract
- ¼ cup (40 g) chopped walnuts
- ¼ cup (40 g) raisins
- ½ teaspoon (2.5 mL) cinnamon
- 1 tablespoon (15 mL) butter, melted
- ⅛ cup (25 mL) bread crumbs

Sift together flour, baking powder, powdered sugar and cinnamon. Grind oškvarky into a fine texture. Combine flour mixture, oškvarky, egg, and sour cream; work dough into a medium consistency (not too thin and not too heavy dough). On a floured board, roll out dough into rectangle ¼ inch (5 mm) thick, 9-10 inches (24 cm) wide and 14 inches (35 cm) long. Dust center of rolled dough with fine bread crumbs. Slice pared apples thinly and spread lengthwise, across center of dough. Add raisins and nuts over apples, sprinkle powdered sugar, vanilla sugar, cinnamon, and melted butter evenly across apples. (If using vanilla extract, add to melted butter). Flip one side (the length) over apples and brush with beaten egg. Bring the other side over, likewise, and brush top with egg. Place on greased baking sheet and bake in moderate oven 350°F (180°C) until lightly browned. To serve, slice ½ inch (1 cm) thick slices and dust with powdered sugar.

Martina Kovačiková
Zvolenská Slatina, Slovakia

POPPYSEED STRUDEL-YEAST DOUGH
Kysnutý makový závin

Dough:
1³/₄ cups (250 g) (polohrubej) flour
1/2 ounce (15 g) yeast
1/2 teaspoon (2.5 mL) salt
2 tablespoons (30 g) sugar
1 egg yolk, beaten
Milk

Filling:
6 ounces (180 g) poppyseed
1 cup (150 g) powdered sugar
1/2 cup (1 dL) water

Butter or margarine, brushing

Dough: In a larger bowl crumble yeast into flour, add sugar and salt and mix. Add egg and enough milk to make a medium, not sticky dough. Work dough well. Cover with cloth and set in warm place to double in bulk.

On a floured board, roll dough out to 3/8 inch (1 cm) thick. Spread cooled filling and roll up. Carefully place on greased baking sheet. Brush with melted margarine or butter and let rise. Before placing in oven, prick strudel with fork across top of roll. Bake in preheated moderate oven 350°F (180°C) until light golden brown. When cooled, slice into serving portions.

Filling: In a saucepan, mix sugar and water, bring to a boil. Add ground poppyseed, reduce heat and simmer until mixture thickens. Cool before spreading on strudel dough.

Served as a dessert or a party snack.

PhDr. Zora Mintalová
Slovenské Národné Múzeum
Martin, Slovakia

MAMA'S APPLE/ POPPYSEED STRUDEL
Mamičkina jablková/maková štrudľa

1 egg, slightly beaten
1 teaspoon (5 mL) vinegar
Lukewarm water
¼ teaspoon (1.25 mL) salt
1 tablespoon (15 mL) sugar
¾ cup (105 g) sifted all-purpose flour
2 tablespoons (30 mL) butter, melted
4 tablespoons (60 mL) vegetable oil
Confectioners' sugar for sprinkling

Filling:
3 cups (¾ L) shredded cooking apples
¾ cup (150 g) sugar
¼ teaspoon (1.25 mL) nutmeg
1 teaspoon (5 mL) cinnamon
¼ cup (½ dL) poppyseed
½ cup (1 dL) bread crumbs
½ cup (1 dL) butter, melted
Raisins (optional)

Break egg into measuring cup, add vinegar and enough lukewarm water to make ⅓ cup; mix well. Into this egg mixture add the salt, 1 tablespoon (15 mL) butter, 1 tablespoon (15 mL) sugar. Add the flour; mix to form a soft dough. On a board or pastry cloth sprinkled with flour, knead the dough lightly with fingertips until flour is absorbed. (Add just a minimum amount of flour if dough is too sticky.) Brush with 1 teaspoon (5 mL) oil. Cover with warm bowl. Let stand 2-4 hours.

Pat dough into flat circle and roll into a 12 inch (30 cm) circle. Brush top with remaining oil. Place on floured cloth spread on table. Using the back of hand, stretch dough from middle, until it is as thin as tissue paper. Spread filling over dough to within 1 inch (2½ cm) of edge. Roll like jelly roll; seal edge. Place in a semi-circle on cookie sheet, cut edge down. Brush top with remaining butter. Bake in preheated 400°F (210°C) oven for 20-25 minutes. Cool, sprinkle with confectioners' sugar.

(Continued on next page)

MAMA'S APPLE / POPPYSEED STRUDEL
Mamičkina jablková/maková štrudľa (Continued)

Filling: Mom would spread the tissue thin dough with melted butter, then sprinkle bread crumbs over the dough. Mix sugar, cinnamon, nutmeg and poppyseed and sprinkle over dough. For variation, grated apples may be spread over all the dough or they can just be placed along side of one edge. This makes a flaky, layered type of strudel with the apples only in the center. **Hint:** After the rolled strudel is placed on a cookie sheet, cut with a sharp knife to score into individual pieces. Do not cut completely through strudel roll. Cut completely through strudel only after baking. Sprinkle with powdered sugar before serving.

In memory of my mother,
Dorothy Sarvaš Zvara

Anne Zvara Sarosy
Slovak World Congress
Women's Committee
Chairperson
Campbell, Ohio   U.S.A.

MIMI'S MOTHER'S DATE BARS
Datľové tyčinky (Matky Mimi)

¹/₂ cup (1 dL) shortening
1 cup (200 g) sugar
³/₄ teaspoon (3.75 mL) salt
¹/₈ teaspoon (.6 mL) nutmeg
¹/₈ teaspoon (.6 mL) cinnamon
2 eggs
1 cup (140 g) flour, sifted
¹/₄ teaspoon (1.25 mL) baking soda
¹/₂ cup (1 dL) pecans, coarsley chopped
2 cups (400 g) dates, chopped
Powdered sugar

Pour ¹/₃ cup (³/₄ dL) boiling water over dates and let stand until cool. Place shortening, sugar, salt, spices and eggs in a large mixing bowl and mix well. Add chopped dates and water and blend thoroughly, Sift together flour and soda; add flour and pecans to above mixture. Mix well. Spread evenly into a greased 9x9x2 inch (23x23x5 cm) pan. Bake at 350°F (180°C) for 40-50 minutes. Cool in pan and cut into bars. Roll in powdered sugar. Makes 24. Can be frozen.

Mimi Danihels
Woodland Hills, California   U.S.A.

NUT STRUDEL
Krehký orechový závin

Dough:
- 4 1/2 cups (600 g) flour (polohrubej)
- 1 cup + 2 tablespoons (250 g) margarine
- 1/3 cup (50 g) powdered sugar
- 1 ounce (30 g) yeast
- 2 eggs
- 1 cup (2 dL) milk, lukewarm
- 2 tablespoons (20 g) powdered sugar
- Salt

Filling:
- 1 cup (200 g) nuts, ground
- 1 cup (200 g) granulated sugar
- 1/2 cup (1 dL) water
- 1 lemon rind
- 1/2 teaspoon (2.5 mL) cinnamon

Dough: Crumble yeast into lukewarm milk, add sugar and let stand until dissolved. Mix flour and margarine as for pie. Add salt and egg. Work in yeast mixture until smooth, not sticky. Add very little additional flour, if necessary. (European flour is of heavier texture). Cover and let rise until doubled in bulk. On a well-floured board, roll out dough to 1/4 inch (1/2 cm) thickness, spread with filling, roll up and place on greased baking sheet. Brush with beaten egg and let rise. Brush again with beaten egg, bake in preheated oven 350°F (180°C) until golden brown, about 35-45 minutes. Sprinkle with powdered sugar.

Filling: Cook sugar in water, add nuts, mixing well. Add lemon rind and cinnamon. Cool mixture before spreading on dough. **Note:** Strudel can be prepared with poppyseed or cottage cheese filling.

Ľudmila Šandorfi
St. Catherine's, Ontario, Canada

QUICK APPLE ROLL
Rýchly jablčný závin

Dough:
3 cups (420 g) flour
½ cup (125 mL) sugar
1 cup (250 mL) butter or margarine
2 egg yolks
2 egg whites, beaten stiff
4 tablespoons (60 mL) milk
2 teaspoons (10 mL) lemon juice
½ teaspoon (2.5 mL) salt

Filling:
Bread crumbs
Ground nuts
Butter or margarine, melted
Apples, peeled, and thinly sliced
Lemon Juice
Sugar
Cinnamon
Raisins
Lemon rind

Dough: Mix flour, sugar, and salt. Add butter and mix as for pie crust. Add egg yolks, milk and lemon juice. Mix dough thoroughly and divide into 2 balls.

Filling: Mix bread crumbs, nuts, and melted butter. Spread over rolled out dough. Place sliced apples in bowl and sprinkle with butter and lemon juice. Combine sugar, cinnamon, raisins, and lemon rind and mix with apples. Spread filling evenly lengthwise across center of rolled out dough. Cover filling with one side of dough. Spread egg white over top of folded dough. Flap over the other side of dough and spread top and edges completely over the whole strudel. Bake at 400°F (210°C) for 30 minutes or until lightly golden brown.

Ľudmila Šandorfi
St. Catherine's, Ontario, Canada

DOBOS TORTE
Doboš torta

Torte:
12 egg yolks
12 tablespoons (1 3/4 dL) sugar
12 egg whites
6 heaping tablespoons (60 g heaping) flour

1½ dozen lady fingers

Chocolate filling:
½ pound (225 g) sweet butter
1 cup (¼ L) powdered sugar
2 eggs
½ pound (225 g) German sweet chocolate
½ pint (¼ L) whipping cream

White filling:
½ pound (225 g) sweet butter
1 cup (¼ L) powdered sugar
1 teaspoon (5 mL) vanilla
2 eggs
½ pint (¼ L) whipping cream

Torte: Beat egg yolks with sugar until creamy. Beat egg whites until stiff, do not underbeat. Combine egg mixtures. (Hold lady fingers until later.) Bake in 4 round layer pans at 350°F (180°C) for 20-30 minutes or until cake center tests done.

Chocolate filling: Mix butter and sugar together. Slightly beat eggs and mix into sugar and butter. Melt chocolate in saucepan and stir in above mixture. Beat whipping cream until stiff; then add to above mixture; mix well.

White filling: Mix butter, sugar and vanilla together. Slightly beat eggs and mix into sugar and butter. Beat whipping cream until stiff then add to above mixture; mix well.

Assembling torte and fillings:
Cool torte layers. Start with one layer and halves of lady fingers - place lady fingers vertically, side by side around spring pan. Alternate fillings between layers. Chill thoroughly over night.

Joan Jurishica
Milwaukee, Wisconsin U.S.A.

EUROPEAN TORTE
Európska torta

Torte:
8 eggs, separated
³/₄ cup plus 2 tablespoons (1³/₄ dL plus 30 mL) granulated sugar
1¹/₂ cups (3¹/₂ dL) walnuts
2 tablespoons (30 mL) bread crumbs
1¹/₂ tablespoons (22.5 mL) coffee
1¹/₂ tablespoons (22.5 mL) rum

Frosting:
1 cup (¹/₄ L) heavy cream, well chilled
1 tablespoon (15 mL) confectioners' sugar
1 tablespoon (15 mL) instant coffee

Preheat oven to 350°F (180°C). Line bottoms of 3 buttered 9 inch (23 cm) round cake pans with rounds of wax paper. Butter paper and dust with flour. In a bowl with an electric mixer, beat yolks with ³/₄ cup (1³/₄ dL) granulated sugar until mixture is doubled in volume and forms a ribbon when beaters are lifted, about 5 minutes. In a food processor, pulse walnuts with the remaining 2 tablespoons (30 mL) of granulated sugar until it is ground fine. Then add egg yolk mixture to walnut mixture with the bread crumbs, coffee, and rum. Stir mixture.

In another bowl with clean beaters, beat the whites until they form stiff peaks. Whisk a large spoonful of whites into yolk/nut mixture and fold in remaining whites gently. Divide batter into pans and bake 20-25 minutes. Cool layers.

Frosting: Stir together 3 tablespoons (45 mL) of cream and 1 tablespoon (15 mL) instant coffee until coffee is dissolved. Add remaining cream and confectioners' sugar. Beat with mixer until thick. Fill and frost torte with coffee frosting.

Paul Ďuriš
Channahon, Illinois U.S.A.

FILBERT (HAZELNUT) TORTE
Liesková orechová torta

6 eggs, separated
¼ cup (½ dL) sugar
½ cup (1 dL) sugar (additional)
⅓ cup (¾ dL) dry bread crumbs
¼ cup (35 g) flour
1 cup (¼ L) ground filberts
2 cups (½ L) whipping cream
1 teaspoon (5 mL) vanilla
2-4 tablespoons (30-60 mL) sugar (additional)

In a large mixing bowl, with mixer at high speed, beat egg whites until soft peaks form. Beating at high speed, gradually sprinkle ¼ cup (½ dL) sugar, beating well after each addition. In a small bowl, with mixer at medium speed, beat egg yolks until thick and lemon colored, gradually beating in ½ cup (1 dL) sugar until well blended. Stir in bread crumbs, flour and ⅔ cup (1½ dL) of ground nuts; using wire whisk or rubber spatula, fold into beaten egg whites. Pour batter into a 10x3 inch (25x7.5 cm) spring form pan that has been greased. Spread evenly and bake in a preheated 325°F (160°C) oven for 40 minutes or until cake springs back when lightly touched. Invert cake on wire rack and let it cool completely. Cut cake horizontally into 2 layers. Whip cream at medium speed adding vanilla or other flavoring and 2-4 tablespoons (30-60 g) sugar. Spread ¼ of cream mixture on bottom layer of cake, top with second layer and frost sides. Using hands, gently press remaining ⅓ cup (¾ dL) of ground nuts onto cream coated sides. Use remaining cream to decorate top. A piping bag or parchment paper cone should be used to decorate this elegant cake.

Kathy Klas
Mississauga, Ontario, Canada

PUMPKIN TORTE
Tekvicová torta

2 cups (½ L) graham cracker crumbs
⅔ stick (90 mL) butter
5 tablespoons (80 mL) white sugar

8 ounces (225 g) cream cheese
½ cup (100 g) white sugar
2 eggs

1 envelope (¼ ounce) (7 g) unflavored gelatin
¼ cup (½ dL) cold water

3 egg yolks
½ cup (100 g) sugar
½ cup (1 dL) canned milk
1 teaspoon (5 mL) salt
1 teaspoon (5 mL) cinnamon
2 cups (½ L) pumpkin

3 egg whites
½ cup (100 g) sugar
Whipping cream
Chopped nuts

Crust: Melt butter, add crumbs and sugar and pat into 9x13 inch (23x33 cm) pan.

Filling: Cream the cream cheese, add sugar and eggs. Beat well and pour over crust. Bake 350°F (180°C) 15 minutes and cool.
Dissolve gelatin in cold water and set aside.
Beat egg yolks, add sugar, canned milk, salt, cinnamon and pumpkin; cook over medium heat. Stir constantly until thick (will bubble). Add dissolved gelatin into pumpkin mix and cool.
Beat egg whites until partially stiff. Add sugar gradually and continue beating until stiff. Fold into cooled pumpkin mix. Pour this mixture into graham cracker crust.
Refrigerate over night. Top with whipping cream, whipped, and chopped nuts.
Very good! Very rich! Enjoy!

Kay Sarosy
Seven Hills, Ohio U.S.A.

WALNUT TORTE
Orechová torta

⅞ cup (¾ cup plus 2 tablespoons) (125 g) flour, sifted
⅞ cup (175 g) sugar
½ teaspoon (5 mL) salt
1½ teaspoons (7.5 mL) baking powder

⅜ cup (¼ cup plus 2 tablespoons) (¾ dL) water
⅓ cup (¾ dL) vegetable oil
5 large egg yolks, unbeaten
½ teaspoon (2.5 mL) vanilla or 1 teaspoon (5 mL) lemon juice
1 cup (200 g) walnuts, ground

5 large egg whites
¼ teaspoon (1.25 mL) cream of tartar
¼ cup (50 g) sugar

Nut filling:
½ cup (100 g) chopped nuts
½ cup (100 g) bread crumbs
1 cup (¼ L) milk
1 tablespoon (15 mL) sugar
1 teaspoon (5 mL) butter
1 teaspoon (5 mL) vanilla
Powdered sugar for dusting
½ cup (1 dL) whipping cream, whipped
18 walnut meat halves

Put flour, sugar, salt and baking powder in a bowl; make a well in the above mixture and add the following: water, oil, 5 unbeaten egg yolks, vanilla or lemon juice, and 1 cup ground walnuts. Beat with a spoon until smooth. Whip egg whites with cream of tartar, gradually add sugar and beat until they form very stiff peaks. They should be much stiffer than for angel food cake or meringue. Don't underbeat. Pour egg yolk mixture gradually over whipped egg whites; gently fold with a wooden spoon or spatula. Bake in a greased and floured tube pan for 55 minutes at 325°F (165°C) and 10 minutes at 350°F (180°C) or until torte tests done, or in 3 greased and floured round cake pans for 25 minutes or until torte tests done. For tube pan, immediately turn pan upside down and cool. For round pans, remove layers to a wire rack to cool.

Filling: Mix nuts, sugar, milk, butter, and bread crumbs in a saucepan. Cook until thick. Cool. Add 1 teaspoon vanilla. Blend well.

Assembling torte: Horizontally slice tube pan torte into 6 layers, or each round layer in half for a total of 6 thin layers. Alternate torte layer with filling using all layers and ending with torte layer on top. Sprinkle top with powdered sugar. Put whipped cream in a decorating bag and pipe 18 dollops around cake top edge. Place walnut meat half in each mound of whipped cream.
Serves 18.

Sandra Sarosy Duve
Colorado Springs, Colorado, U.S.A.

FLUFFY EGG WHITE FROSTING
L'ahučká bielková poleva

2 cups (½ L) powdered sugar
10 tablespoons (150 mL) water
½ teaspoon (2.5 mL) cream of tartar
Pinch of salt
1 teaspoon (5 mL) vanilla or lemon extract
2 egg whites, beaten stiff

In a pan, combine powdered sugar, water, cream of tartar, and pinch of salt. Heat to boiling point for 1 minute. Remove immediately from heat.
Pour over egg whites to which vanilla or lemon extract has been added. Beat with electric mixer for 7 minutes or until stiff.
This frosting is ideal for Lamb Cake or angel food cake.

Martha Mistina Kona
Slovak World Congress
Heritage and Culture Commission, Chairperson
Wilmette, Illinois U.S.A.

VANILLA SUGAR
Vanilkový cukor

Place 1 pound (450 g) sugar into canister with an air tight lid and push 2 vanilla beans (6 g) way down in. Cover and let stand at least 1 week before using. If you want a supply of vanilla sugar on hand, replenish sugar as needed and add a fresh vanilla bean every 6 months. Use vanilla sugar wherever vanilla extract is called for. Allow 1 tablespoon (15 mL) vanilla sugar for each ¼ teaspoon (1.25 mL) vanilla extract. and decrease total quantity of sugar in recipes accordingly. For example: In a recipe that calls for 2 cups (400 g) sugar and 1 teaspoon (5 mL) vanilla, you would use 1¾ cups (350 g) sugar and 4 tablespoons (60 mL) vanilla sugar.
Note: Vanilla bean is imported from Madagascar and is 3 grams in weight.

- Editor

TRADITIONAL SLOVAK GINGERBREAD
Tradičné Slovenské Dumbierníky (medovníky)

7½ cups (1050 g) rye flour
1 pound (450 g) powdered sugar
1¾ cups (360 g) honey
6 whole eggs, medium size, beaten with fork
3 teaspoons (15 mL) baking soda
4 tablespoons (60 mL) of the following mixture of spices:
4 teaspoons (20 mL) cinnamon (škorica)
3 teaspoons (15 mL) anise (aníz)
2 teaspoons (10 mL) fennel (fenikel')
1 teaspoon (5 mL) coriander (koriander)
¾ teaspoon (3.75 mL) cardamon (kardamon)
½ teaspoon (2.5 mL) clove (klinčeky)
⅛ teaspoon (.625 mL) star anise (badian)
⅛ teaspoon (.635 mL) ginger (ďumbier)
⅛ teaspoon (.625 mL) pimento (nové korenie)
⅛ teaspoon (.625 mL) nutmeg (muškátový orech)
⅛ teaspoon (.625 mL) mace (muškátový kvet)
⅛ teaspoon (.625 mL) vanilla
1 lemon rind, finely grated and dried

CHOCOLATE ICING:
¾ cup (100 g) powdered sugar
½ cup (100 g) butter
3 tablespoons (30 g) cocoa
3 tablespoons (45 mL) cold water
1 tablespoon (10 mL) corn starch

Note: Use exact measurement for consistency of dough. Use medium-sized eggs, larger or smaller eggs will make dough either thicker or thinner.

Dough: Measure out all spices, sift and place in container with an air-tight lid. Measure out flour, powdered sugar and baking soda, and sift with spice mixture. Add lemon rind. Make an opening in center of dry mixture, pour in honey and beaten eggs. Work dough well.

(Continued)

The dough will be sticky, therefore, flour the sides of container. With a scraper form into one heap, or pile; flour once more, and in the container (clay-type bowl) cover tightly with a heavy lid to avoid the top from becoming dry during the process of maturation. Dough has to season not less than 4 days or up to several months. The honey has outstanding properties of conservation and will not spread any bacteria or any biological changes, not even in a warmer room temperature.

Upon maturation, remove dough from container and on a well-floured board, knead until dough becomes of rigid, smooth consistency. Roll out to required thickness - for larger forms roll to 1/8 - 3/16 inch (3 - 4 mm), for smaller forms 1/16 inch (1.5 mm). Using a cookie cutter, cut out gingerbread cookies and place on cooled cookie sheet that has been coated with bee wax. (To coat cookie sheet: use bee wax intended for coating, place into linen cloth and rub cloth over a sufficiently hot cookie sheet; continue to apply until evenly coated). Bake gingerbread about 10 minutes in preheated moderately hot oven 400°F (200°C). After baking, remove hot gingerbread with spatula and place on flat surface and let cool.

Icing gingerbread: To attain a shiny, darker surface, brush gingerbread with beaten egg, use a pastry brush, before baking; for more gloss, brush immediately after baking, when removing out of oven, while still hot and still on cookie sheet. The gingerbread, to be iced with either white or chocolate icing, should not be brushed with egg since icing will not adhere to cookie.

White Icing: Beat egg white slightly, add sifted powdered sugar and lemon juice. Mix until mixture thickens. Choose the amount of these ingredients in proportion, so as icing after mixing, will be smooth and shiny, not too thick or too thin, allowing only somewhat of a slow drip down side of form. Apply icing with a brush. Decorate or trim with walnuts, almonds, hazelnuts, coriander and raisins. Let dry about 24 hours.

Chocolate Icing: Cream butter, add powdered sugar and cocoa, mixing until light and foamy. Add cornstarch and water, mixing well again. Place mixture in double boiler and over boiling water continue mixing until glaze thickens. Keeping glaze continuously over hot water, take a brush and drizzle gingerbread, working above double boiler. Let dry 3-4 days, and only then trim with white icing.

(Continued)

However, decorating with nuts, almonds, hazelnuts, raisins and pistachios can be placed immediately upon hot drizzle.

This correct technological process or method is a guarantee of the durableness of the icing.

Gingerbread Decorations: When glaze, or icing is completely dry, the final and intricate decorating or touches are done with a parchment paper bag which has been folded into a cone shape. Cut the tip on an angle and to desired diameter of opening. Fill cone with white icing and decorate top of gingerbread.

Gingerbreads baked according to this recipe are excellent in taste and smell. They are to be sure, very hygroscopic. In a rather dry atmosphere, they will dry and harden, however, by placing them in a relatively average air moisture of about 60% relative humidity, they will soften; the topping is likewise preserved.

Slovak gingerbreads are original and native to Slovakia, and are an uncommon and an unusual compliment to the holiday table.

Elena Ulrichová
ul. J. C. Hronského 12, 831 02
Bratislava, Slovak Republic

About the author:
Elena Ulrichová is an authority on the art of Slovak gingerbread. She has been gracious in sharing her compiled history of gingerbread baking in Slovakia, this traditional pastry recipe, and the technological process, which is today a component of Slovak folk art. She is completing her book, "Gingerbread Bakery in Slovakia," which characterizes the life of gingerbread masters, development of trades and guilds and the genesis of gingerbread bakery up to the present. The book will contain original recipes, aesthetic forming of gingerbread dough and the works of the authoress.

- Editor

GINGERBREAD BAKERY IN SLOVAKIA

It is known from history that the gingerbread bakery flourished in Slovakia in olden days. The ancient books of archives of royal cities, Levoča, Banská Bystrica and Bardejov, contain references to this craft and to the taxes of gingerbread bakers as early as the 14th century.

At the beginning, the production of gingerbread cakes belonged to the bakery trade but later it separated from this trade because of its specific properties. The master gingerbread bakers started to associate and create guilds. The first gingerbread bakery guild was founded in 1619 in Bratislava. As a matter of fact, it was the first guild of this trade in the territory of Hungary. It associated the masters of the whole Slovakia and Transdanubia. Gradually, the guilds were established in other cities and towns, such as Trnava (1697), Košice (1738), and others. These craftsmen had their symbol - the guild sign or they used the sign and impress with a picture of God Mother with Child.

Because honey, the basic ingredient of the gingerbread production, was bought together with honeycombs, which were used in the production of candles, the gingerbread masters were also chandlers - producing candles, torches, and other wax products. The respective guild thus comprised both trades.

At that time, the appetizing gingerbread cakes were scarce articles especially in villages where people did not know other sweet delicacies besides traditional cakes from leavened dough. The master gingerbread bakers peddled them at fairs in district towns or offered them to pilgrims in sacred pilgrimage places.

The use of wooden moulds was characteristic of the production of gingerbread cakes in the 17th century. The gingerbread bakers themselves made them mainly of pear tree wood or obtained them from wood carvers. The motifs were different and every master tried to possess the most beautiful ones. The most frequent shapes were hearts, horses, hussars, cottages and dolls. Many moulds used at this time have been preserved and may be seen in our ethnographic museums, castles, and mansions. The gingerbread dough of tough consistence was crammed into these moulds. It obtained the necessary form and decoration. Then it was carefully taken from the mould and baked. Magic power was attributed to some moulds, e.g., to the mould "Seven Children for a Penny". This gingerbread cake, bought at a fair, served as a votive gift to childless women desiring children. Gingerbread cakes of round shape carved out in the center, the so-called pagle, were an exquisite delicacy. The gingerbread traders stuck them on wooden sabres and offered them to their customers.

The gingerbread bakery flourished in Slovakia in the second half of the 19th century. In this period of time the number of gingerbread bakery guilds and workshops considerably increased. At the beginning of the 20th century this trade started to decline. Manufactured products of lower quality, but less expensive, appeared on the markets and gradually suppressed the traditional kind of production. The dough used for gingerbread was of different composition and its consistency was no longer suitable to the way of production involving cramming into molds. The plate molds made by tinsmiths came into use. The dough was rolled to a thinner layer by using a roller and different figures were cut from this layer by using dough cutters of different forms. These figures were put on a plate coated with bee wax and baked. This method of making gingerbread cakes is employed up to now.

The surface of gingerbread cakes was decorated either with an original folk-motif typical of individual parts of our country, or represented events symbolizing Christmas, Easter and other feasts. This decoration was frequently motivated by traditional occasion and seasons of the year as well. The gingerbread cakes were also given to carol singers whose song and Bethlehem plays became an inseparable component of Christmas in our villages.

The tradition of gingerbread cookery, of this time-honoured craft, is still alive in our country. The production and decoration of gingerbread cakes has been preserved thanks to folk artisans. They decorate the gingerbread with original folk motifs originating from immediate sources of Slovak national culture or from their own fantasy. Although wooden moulds are no longer used, they are available in special shops with different popular craftsmanship products as well as pieces of gingerbread obtained from uncommon forms serving as decoration. They are quite expensive and regarded as artistic products. The Slovak gingerbread is a characteristic pastry. It is an adornment of the dining table and is also used as a decoration on the Christmas tree or for Easter in the Old Church Slavonic - "lesola", which greatly embodies the festive atmosphere in cottages and foothills villages.

Elena Ulrichová
ul. J. C. Hronského 12, 831 02 Bratislava
Slovak Republic

HOLIDAY TRADITIONS

Preserving traditions of a country embraces celebration of principal holy days such as Easter and Christmas. Food, which enhances every festivity, plays a significant role in these celebrations. These customs as related to us by our ancestors are still practiced by Slovaks who wish to perpetuate our Slovak culture.

In Slovakia, as in many predominantly Roman Catholic countries, fish play a natural part in traditional feasting, particularly during the Christmas Eve meal of fasting and on Christmas Day. On Christmas Day the principal dish of stuffed baked carp in a rich sauce is served in Slovakia and other mid-European districts where the lake-fish was especially available.

The Christmas Eve Village or meal of fasting began with the distribution and sharing of the Christmas oplatky among the assembled family. Oplátky were served with honey. The Christmas wafer signified the importance of the celebration and was believed to strengthen the family's togetherness and harmony with the church which distributed the blessed oplátky decorated with religious symbols. Sharing a part of this wafer with those assembled was a symbol of wishing each other peace and good will.

At Easter, baskets of food were brought to the church to be blessed. Foods included eggs, lamb or a symbolic lamb in the form of cake or butter, ham, sausage, bread, horseradish, salt, wine and other foods. The eating of the blessed food took place after attendance at the Easter Mass.

Christmas and Easter customs are described in the ensuing literature. The cookbook contains recipes for the foods featured on the menus. Enjoy! **Note:** The following holiday traditions and menus are typical in some, not all regions throughout Slovakia - holiday customs may vary even from village to village.   -Editor

                                      Sister M. Mercedes Voytko
                                      Director
                                      Jankola Library
                                      Danville, Pennsylvania   U.S.A.

VIANOČNÉ ZVYKY

Na Slovensku Vianoce patria k najkrajším sviatkom. Sú to sviatky rodiny, kedy každý sa snaží ich prežiť v kruhu svojich najbližších. Domácnosti sa už 2 týždne pred Božím narodením upratujú. 3-4 dní pred vilijou sa začínajú chystať tradičné vianočné jedlá. Oplátky sa pečú na fare, kde si ich každý môže kúpiť.

Kde majú malé deti, stromček sa pripravuje tajne. Obyčajne staršie deti pomáhajú s dekoráciou. Najčastejšie sa kupuje živý stromček. Iní používajú umelé stromčeky, na ktoré vešajú rôzne sladkosti a vianočné svetlá, gule a iné ornamenty. Pod stromček sa dáva Betlehem.

Týždeň pred Vianocami sa hromadne spovedá. Ľudia prijímajú sväté prijímanie a tak sa duchovne pripravujú na Božie narodenie. Počas adventu sa netancuje, nespieva a nepočúva sa veľmi ani radio ani televízia.

Na štedrý deň o 6:00 hodine večer sa všetci zídu pri stromčeku, pod ktorým si každý nájde svoj darček. Potom všetci zasadnú k slávnostne prestretému stolu a po modlitbe, ktorú obyčajne odrieka otec rodiny, zavinšuje všetkým požehnané Vianoce. Potom podáva každému oplátku s medom. Tak už matka rodiny prinesie jedlá v tomto poradí: kapustníky, podávané s cesnakom, šošovicovú polievku, s pripomienkou, aby každý mal dosť peňazí v nastávajúcom roku, hrachovú polievku, kyslú kapustu so zemiakmi, aby každý v nastávajúcom roku bol zdravý. Potom idú bobaľky s makom, juška s hubami a vyprážaná ryba, zvyčajne kapor. Na koniec sa podávajú koláče a zákusky-orechovníky, makovníky, tvarohovníky a jablkovníky a rozličné druhy ovocia / jablká, hrušky, orechy, banány, pomaranče, hrozno a mandarínky/.

Počas štedrej večere nikto neodchádza od stola. Po večeri všetci spievajú koledy: Tichá noc, svätá noc, Búvaj dieťa krásne, Do hory, do lesa, Čas radosti a podobne.

Pred polnocou všetci idú do kostola na polnočnú sv. omšu. Počas nej všetci radostne spievajú. Ďakujú Bohu, za narodenie syna, Ježiša. Nasledujúci deň sa rodiny navzájom navštevujú. Na 26. decembra sa oslavuje sviatok sv. Štefana, prvého mučeníka cirkvi. Rodina sa schádza k spoločnému jedlu.

CHRISTMAS EVE - ŠTEDRÝ VEČER

Origin: Slovaks everywhere celebrate Christmas with traditional, unchanging customs. The most anticipated day in the year, and of all Christmas holidays, is Christmas Eve or Štedrý Večer and the Vilija Supper.

The very word "vilija" comes from the Latin word vigilare, to watch, and is known as the day before a feast day, or the day before Jesus' birth. The day itself had much significance many centuries before His birth. Since it followed the longest night and the shortest day, it was considered the last day of the year, and the mystical symbolism associated with it was closely tied to the solar system.

Our Slovak ancestors were of peasantry stock - shepherds on the hillsides, laborers in the fields. Christ's humble birth appealed to them; for Christ the King of all creation could have chosen the most splendid castle, instead He chose to be born in a stable bedded upon straw in a manger. This elevated the status of our Slovak ancestors, giving them a feeling of worth.

Preparation: The moment the first star appeared in the evening of the 24th day of December, the entire family gathered at the table set with specially prepared foods and the father and mother came to the table with a lighted candle carrying holy water and honey. Either parent would then take a little honey to make a small sign of the cross on the foreheads of each one present at the table. This custom was a reminder of the sweetness and love of Christ, the Redeemer. The Christmas candle represented Christ, the Light of the World.

The food prepared for the Vilija Supper is so special there is no other like it throughout the year. It is based primarily on the elements of nature that produced home grown foods in Slovakia.

From the forest came the mushrooms, the nuts, honey and wild berries; from the fields came the grain and cereals; the orchards yielded the fruits, and from the gardens came the stored vegetables. In some villages it was customary to spread the tablecloth over clean straw, in other villages straw was laid upon the floor. This was a reminder that the Holy Child was laid upon straw.

Oplátky: The most significant moment of the entire Vilija Supper is the breaking and sharing of oplátky, Christmas wafers, the blessed bread symbolizing the Body of Christ at Communion.

The following prayer led by the head of the family is appropriate for sharing this family spiritual communion:

God's People were hungry in the desert, God sent them manna to eat.
Response: We thank you, Lord!

God's People were in danger and sin. The prophet said: "Out of Bethlehem shall come a Savior."
Response: We thank you, Lord!

God's People heard great news, they found Jesus lying in a manger.
Response: We thank you, Lord!

God's People pray: Give us this day our daily bread; Jesus says: not on bread alone do you live, but from the mouth of God.
Response: We thank you, Lord!

Heavenly Father, your Son's birth gladdens us. We take this bread (†) to remind ourselves that it is Christ's word that guides us, and Christ's Body that nourishes us, as we find our way to You, our God. Amen.

Enacting the rite of the oplátky, the father and mother face each other and holding each an oplátka would break and share a part of the other's. After expressions of love and warm wishes for one another, they would then break and share the oplátky with each one present, wishing all good health, happiness and a long, untroubled life.

Menu: First on the menu is the mushroom soup, most common is the soup of sauerkraut brine and dried mushrooms. The second course is fish prepared in a variety of ways, baked or breaded carp being the most popular, and served with peas and potatoes.

The most outstanding and traditional of all foods are the opekance, some call it bobaľky or pupačky, similar to an oyster cracker, but made of yeast-leavened dough. After baking, the opekance are steamed in milk and coated with a poppyseed mixture prepared with butter and honey. The roundness of each bobaľka signifies the world; the poppyseed, the people; the honey, the goodness in life and the sweetening or easing of daily toil.

One of the main desserts is the koláč, a standard Slovakian delicacy, served along with fruits, an apple being most common, nuts, raisins, dates and figs. Some Slovaks may include a cheese cake or a poppyseed cake, and a holiday drink, a brandy made of honey, spices and alcohol.

During the supper every member cracks open a nut and cuts an apple into halves. Each hopes for a sound nut and apple, free of interior decay, in hopes of a good health in the new year.

Jasličkári: According to Slovak tradition, on Christmas Day the Jasličkári, or Bethlehemci (Bethlehem Strollers) toured the village enacting a sacred drama in each home. With simplicity of expression and performance, this religious folklore has become one of the most significant contributions to Slovak dramatic art.

A small group of young men would perform the play in the fashion of a puppet show, carrying the manger called Bethlehem, which was constructed of artistically carved figures. Today these figures have become valuable museum pieces. The character "Angel" had the privilege of carrying the Bethlehem scene. The other four characters were Bacha, Stakho, Fedor and Kubo. The dramatization is in song, dance and verse. Each brings gifts to the Christ Child, presenting Him with foods of apples, grapes, honey, a sausage and some cheese, except Kubo who comes with empty hands, but offers the Baby Jesus his sandals which were lent to him by Bacha. The play closes with an appropriate song or verse of thanks by the entire troupe.

Slovak vinš: A staroslovenský "vinš" is an old traditional custom of greetings - an expression of joy and happiness passed on from one Christmas season to another, from one generation to another.

Various vinše, greetings, were adapted to the many villages throughout Slovakia, each differed somewhat in embracing a special "vinš" for that specific region. The following example brings greetings of the season of Christ's birth; a wish for happiness and good health; gratitude for the year passed and hope for prosperity, peace and good health in the year to come. Wishes are extended for a good life here and may the crown of angels be yours with the blessings of heaven. All praise and glory to our Lord, Jesus Christ.

>
> Vinšujem Vám vinšujem!
> na to Božie Narodenie:
> na šťastie, i na zdravie,
> ten starý rok prežiť,
> nového sa dožiť -
> hojnejšeho, pokojnejšeho,
> od Boha lásku,
> od ľudí priasku!
>
> Vinšujem Vám vinšujem!
> v tom časnom živote,
> a potom, po všetkej tej
> časnej dobrote:
> Slávu nebeskú,
> korunu anjelskú.

Pochvalený buď Pán Ježiš Kristus!

Note: The above is a representation of one of many customs throughout Slovakia.

Editor
Anne Zvara Sarosy

TRADITIONAL SLOVAK CHRISTMAS EVE MENU

Tradičné jedlá - Štedrý Večer

Oblátky/oplátky - Christmas Wafer/host
Honey - Garlic
Mushroom Sauerkraut Soup*
Opekance/bobaľky - Poppyseed Covered Buns*
Fish - Baked or Breaded Carp*
Potatoes
Peas
Holubky - Mushroom Stuffed Cabbage Rolls*
Pirohy - Filled Dumplings*
Fruit Compote or Baked Christmas Apples*
Fresh Fruit, Nuts
Medovníky - Christmas Cookies*
Koláč - Nut, Poppyseed, Layered Rolls*
Wine

All * recipes appear in this cook book.

TRADITIONAL SLOVAK EASTER FOODS

Tradičné Slovenské Veľkonočné Jedlá

* * * * * * * *

One of the most venerable traditions of Slovak culture is the blessing of the Easter baskets filled with foods that have a special significance and rich religious symbolism. On Holy Saturday, small portions of the prepared foods are placed into a wicker basket, which is covered with a special hand crocheted or embroidered cloth most often designed with a cross and the words, "Christ is Risen," and brought to the church to be blessed.

The foods for Easter Day include: Easter Bread - páska, symbolic of Christ who is our True Bread; eggs - kraslice or pisanky, hand decorated hard boiled eggs, New Life, a sign of His hope and Resurrection; Easter cheese - syrek, a custard-type cheese formed into a ball indicative of the moderation that Christians should have in all things; ham - šunka, the main dish exemplifies the great joy and abundance of Easter, a freedom from the old law forbidding certain meats, and a celebration of the end of penance, abstinence and fasting throughout the Lenten season. Sausage - klobásy, smoked pork links, serves as a reminder of the chains of death which were broken by the Resurrection; beet horseradish - chren, represents the bitterness of Christ's suffering, the thorns placed upon His head; butter - maslo, shaped into a lamb form is a reminder that Jesus is the Lamb of God. Wine - víno, is the drink of the Passover meal, the Last Supper and symbolic of the Blood of Life; salt - soľ, is a reminder of the need to flavor our interactions with each other; Easter lamb cake - Veľkonočná torta, and nut and poppyseed rolls - koláč, makovníky, symbolize the gladness of Easter Day and sweetness and love of the Lord. It was customary to abstain from sweets and all rich foods during the forty days of Lent.

A specially decorated Easter candle may also be placed in the Easter food basket and then used on the table as a centerpiece to remind us that Christ is the Light of the world and the center of our lives.

Easter Bread - Páska*
Hand decorated eggs - Kraslice - Pisanky*
Easter cheese - Syrek*
Ham - Šunka   Lamb - Jahňacina*
Sausage - Klobásy   Easter Meat Loaf - Sekanina*
Beet Horseradish - Chren*
Salt - Soľ   Butter - Maslo
Wine - Víno
Lamb Cake - Veľkonočná Torta*
Poppyseed Rolls - Koláč - Makovníky*

All * recipes appear in this cookbook.

VEĽKONOČNÉ ZVYKY

Počas pôstu každú nedeľu poobede sú v kostoloch rozjímavé kázne, na ktoré ľudia prichádzajú z celého okolia. Každú stredu a piatok je krížová cesta. Počas pôstu nie sú svatby, ľudia netancujú a vyhýbajú sa hlučným zábavám. Na Popolnú Stredu ľudia dostávajú popol na čelo. Na Veľký Piatok je prísny pôst.

Na Bielu Sobotu poobede sa svätia v kostole špecialne pripravené jedlá, ktoré sa prinesú do kostola v košíkoch. Obyčajne celá rodina príde na tento obrad. Sú v nich šunka, klobása, slanina, syrek-pripravený z vajec a mlieka, / maľované vajcia / kraslice, / páska, cvikla, jablká, maslo a soľ. Vajcia sa farbia deň predtým. V niektorých oblastiach vyfuknuté vajcia sa umelecký zdobia farbami a voskom.

Na Bielu Sobotu sa ľudia zúčastňujú na procesii s prevelebnou sviatosťou oltárnou a sochou vzkrieseného Krista. Všetci zo srdca spievajú: Pán Ježiš Kristus vstal z mŕtvych, Aleluja.

Vo Veľkonočnú Nedeľu, celá rodina, všetci počas raňajok jedia jedlo posvätené deň predtým / na Bielu Sobotu /.

Vo Veľkonočný Pondelok chlapci a muži idú do rôznych domov, kde majú dievčatá a olievajú ich vodou a voňavkou, ktorú lejú na ich hlavy. V niektorých oblastiach mládenci používajú na šibanie korbáče/ prút upletený z vetvičiek vŕby /. Na druhý deň v útorok robia to isté dievčatá chlapcom. Pri odchode obdržia kraslicu, maľované vajce alebo nejaké sladkosti. Malí chlapci dostanú peniaze. Dievčatá olievajú chlapcov vodou a voňavkou. Každý je šťastný a radostný.

Sister M. Mercedes Voytko
Director
Jankola Library
Danville, Pennsylvania U.S.A.

DECORATED EASTER EGGS

Kraslice - Pisanky

* * * * * * *

Eggs are an ancient heathen fertility symbol, easily associated with spring. The spring festivals of ancient Egypt, Persia and Greece all had brightly colored eggs associated with various rituals. Legend had it that the world was produced by the hatching of a huge world-egg. In Christian times, this took on a religious interpretation as a symbol of the rock tomb out of which Christ emerged to the new life of His resurrection.

From early times, the faithful painted Easter eggs in bright colors, had them blessed, and both ate them and gave them to friends as Easter gifts. They were especially appropriate since eggs were among the foods forbidden during Lent. Eggs were either stained in vegetable dyes or painted with striking designs and elaborate decorations.

To cook the eggs: Place the eggs in a single layer in a pan and cover with cold tap water. Set the pan, uncovered, over high heat and bring the water to simmering (when the bubbles just begin to rise to the surface). Simmer, do not boil, for 15-18 minutes. Drain immediately and cover with cold water to stop the eggs from cooking longer and to prevent the darkening of the yolk.

Egg dyes: Vegetable and plant dyes were used by our grandmothers and great-grandmothers. Today commercial edible dyes or food coloring and vinegar produce easy to use vivid colors. Wrapping eggs in onion skins before simmering results in a marbleized egg. Wrap a dry onion skin, preferably red, yellow or purple, around each fresh egg. Place the egg in a square of material such as a piece of an old sheet, handkerchief or cheese cloth and fasten with string or a twist tie. Hard cook the egg as usual. Color from the onion skins will transfer to the egg shells. You can add a little vinegar to the water to help set the color. Run cold water over the finished eggs and unwrap. No two eggs will look alike.

For plant dyes you can also use: carrot tops for yellow green and green; orange peel or marigold petals for yellow and gold; grapes for violet; beet juice for pink. Place each plant material in a separate pot and cover with water. Boil until the color has been extracted from the plant material. Add a pinch of salt to set the color. Be sure that you allow sufficient time to properly cook the eggs in addition to dyeing them. If you intend to keep your eggs for a number of years, boil them in the plant dye until they are the shade desired. Then remove them and continue to boil them in clean hot water until their total cooking time equals at least two hours.

No matter what method you use to dye eggs, remember that hard cooked eggs should not be kept at room temperature longer than two hours if you plan to eat them. They will keep for about a week if refrigerated.

Slovak Pisanky - Kraslice: For decorative and heirloom Easter eggs you may wish to make your own kraslice - pisanky. These beautiful eggs are intricate, a folk art and full of symbolism. Pisanky - kraslice are made by drawing beeswax designs on an egg with a stylus. The wax seals the areas underneath, leaving figures that will appear white or any other color on the completed Easter egg.

Eggs may be blown clean of the yolk and white or used unblown. To blow an egg do the following: Carefully make a hole in both the top and bottom of the raw egg with a large needle or hat pin. With the needle or some other long, thin object, pierce the yolk and gently shake the egg to loosen the contents and mix the white with the yolk. Hold the egg over a bowl and gently blow into the top hole until the contents of the egg have emptied out of the bottom hole. Once the shell is completely empty, blow in a mouthful of water, shake to rinse, and blow out. To make sure the insides of the eggs are completely dry, bake the eggshells in a 200°F (75°C) oven for 10-15 minutes. To dye a blown eggshell, hold it under the surface of the dye bath until the shell is completely filled with dye and will no longer float to the top of the dye container. Handle the blown eggs carefully. They are very fragile.

Contrary to common belief, an unblown egg may be decorated and kept for a long period of time if the following storage directions are followed. Keep the newly decorated egg away from strong heat such as direct sunlight. If displayed, the egg should be in a place that has good air circulation. If stored, place egg in a cardboard, not plastic, carton. Eventually the contents of the egg will evaporate and turn to dust. In the meantime, do handle with extreme care.

Materials - procedures: To make your pisanky - kraslice, you will need the following materials: fresh, raw eggs, at room temperature, or blown eggs; a pencil; wide rubber band; a stylus; a candle; beeswax or paraffin; egg or vegetable dyes prepared according to directions; a soft clean cloth; and shellac, varnish or clear acrylic spray.

1. Pencil lines are used as guide lines for the basic design. By using a rubber band around the egg, it will help you draw straight lines on the egg. Be sure not to erase the pencil lines because they will blotch on the egg. The pencil lines will not show on the completed egg. If you do not have a stylus you can easily make your own. Use a pencil-sized dowel, a small piece of copper foil or thin brass and some fine copper wire. Copper heats best and conducts the heat well. Cut a piece from the foil and roll it into a small cone, leaving a tiny hole in the tip. Next, bend the tabs down at right angles to the foil cone and attach to the dowel by wrapping with the fine copper wire. Enlarge the hole by rubbing the tip across fine sandpaper.
2. The head of the stylus is heated in the candle flame then dipped into beeswax. The melted beeswax or paraffin is scooped into the funnel of the stylus.
3. The stylus, which is held at right angles with the egg to allow the wax to flow evenly, is then used to write over the pencil lines.
4. White lines will appear on the finished egg where the wax lines were drawn because the wax seals the color under it.
5. The egg is then placed into the next color dye, usually yellow. Always begin with the lightest color of your design scheme and work towards the darkest.
6. All the lines of the design that are to be yellow, or your lightest first color, are drawn on the egg with the stylus.
7. Alternate sketching the designs and dipping the egg into the green, orange and red dyes.
8. The completed design is then dipped for a final coat of color into a black dye, although colors such as dark red, purple or royal blue can also be used.

9. The egg is then held to the side of the candle flame to melt the wax. Tissues or the soft cloth are used to wipe away the melted wax, a small portion at a time, revealing the colorful design underneath.
10. A coat of varnish, which adds protection and luster, is then applied to the egg.

If you wish to simplify the method, cover the parts of the egg you do not want dyed and draw your designs with a crayon. Continue waxing and dyeing in the same sequence as with the stylus. Remove wax and finish in the same way.

The most important thing to remember is to keep geometric balance with the design. The use of color and creativity will result in beautiful egg ornaments to last for a lifetime.

Colors: Colors are very symbolic. White symbolizes purity and virtue. Black represents the darkest time before dawn. Red signifies happiness in life, hope and passion, as well as bravery, devotion and nobility. Yellow represents wisdom and a successful harvest, the moon and the stars. Purple is associated with royalty and green with innocence, spring, freshness and the rebirth of nature. A combination of white and black signifies a protection from evil.

Symbols: Some symbols that are most frequently used are: the sun, portrayed as a circle, a flower or a spiral. Stars represent success; the cross symbolizes Christ's great gift to mankind, His crucifixion and resurrection; wheat signifies the bread of life and work of the peasant; a line encircling the egg without a beginning or an end represents eternal life. Triangles represent the Trinity and the netting also reminds us that Christ was the fisher of men; a bird represents fertility and the fulfillment of wishes; the fish represents Christ from the Greek acrostic for "Jesus Christ Son of God Savior;" prosperity and wealth are symbolized by animals, while the bee stands for both hard work and prosperity.

Sandra Sarosy Duve
Slovak World Congress
Vice-President, U.S.A.-West
Cookbook Co-editor
Colorado Springs, Colorado U.S.A.

THE SLOVAK REPUBLIC IN FACTS

LAND

Area: 48,995 sq.km. (18,917 sq.mi.)
Land use: (1990, everything in hectares) 2,448,000 of agricultural land: 1,509,000 arable, 808,000 meadows and pastures
Natural resources: mercury, iron ore, copper, lead, zinc, limestone
Agriculture: accounts approximately 11% of GNP, largely self-sufficent in food production: food crops - grains, potatoes, sugar beets livestock - pigs, cattle, poultry, sheep

PEOPLE

Population: 5,356,207, December 31, 1994. Women: 2,736,000
Density: 109 sq. km.
Distribution: 38.2% urban, 61.8% rural
Annual population growth rate: .3% (1990)
Ethnic groups: 86% Slovaks, 11% Hungarians, 2% Romany (Gypsy), 1% other
Religions: 60.4% Roman Catholic, 6.2% Lutheran, 3.4% Greek Catholic, 1.6% Reformed, 0.7% Orthodox, 10% no affiliation, 17.7% others
Languages: 89% Slovakian, 10% Hungarian, 1% other
Official language: Slovak
Major cities: (June 30, 1995) Bratislava (capital - 451,616 pop.), Košice (239,927), Banská Bystrica (88,390), Nitra (87,127), Prešov (92,013), Trenčín (57,921), Trnava (73,012), Žilina (86,373), Zvolen (44,380)

SLOVAKS IN SLOVAKIA AND OUTSIDE THEIR NATIVE COUNTRY

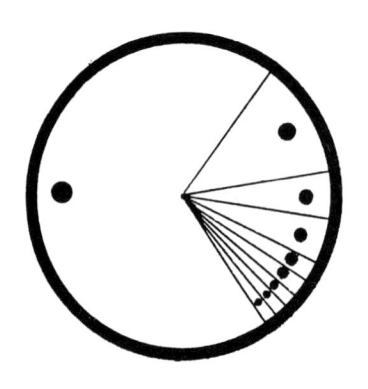

- Slovakia
- United States of America
- Bohemia and Moravia
- Hungary
- Canada
- Yugoslavia
- Romania
- Australia
- France, Switzerland, West Germany, Austria, and others.

METRICS

Ounces	Pounds	Grams	Kilograms
1 oz.		30 g.	
2 oz.		60 g.	
3 oz.		85 g.	
4 oz.	¼ lb.	115 g.	
5 oz.		140 g.	
6 oz.		180 g.	
8 oz.	½ lb.	225 g.	
9 oz.		250 g.	¼ kg.
10 oz.		285 g.	
12 oz.	¾ lb.	340 g.	
14 oz.		400 g.	
16 oz.	1 lb.	450 g.	
18 oz.	1 ⅛ lb.	500 g.	½ kg.
20 oz.	1 ¼ lb.	560 g.	
24 oz.	1 ½ lb.	675 g.	
28 oz.	1 ¾ lb.	800 g.	
32 oz.	2 lb.	900 g.	
	2 ¼ lb.	1,000 g.	1 kg.
	2 ½ lb.	1,125 g.	1 ¼ kg.
	3 lb.	1,350 g.	1 ⅓ kg.
	3 ½ lb.	1,500 g.	1 ½ kg.
	4 lb.	1,800 g.	1 ¾ kg.
	4 ½ lb.		2 kg.
	5 lb.		2 ¼ kg.
	5 ½ lb.		2 ½ kg.
	6 lb.		2 ¾ kg.
	7 lb.		3 ¼ kg.
	8 lb.		3 ½ kg.
	9 lb.		4 kg.
	10 lb.		4 ½ kg.
	12 lb.		5 ½ kg.
	14 lb.		6 ¼ kg.
	15 lb.		6 ¾ kg.
	16 lb.		7 ¼ kg.
	18 lb.		8 kg.
	20 lb.		9 kg.
	25 lb.		11 ¼ kg.
	50 lb.		22 ½ kg.

METRICS

CONVERSION OF LIQUID MEASURES

Spoons, Cups, Pints, Quarts	Ounces	Deciliters and Liters
2 Tbs.	1 oz.	¼ dL
¼ c. *(or 4 Tbs.)*	2 oz.	½ dL
⅓ c.	2 ⅔ oz.	¾ dL
½ c.	4 oz.	1 dL
⅔ c.	5 ⅓ oz.	1 ½ dL
¾ c.	6 oz.	1 ¾ dL
1 c.	8 oz.	¼ L
1 ¼ c.	10 oz.	3 dL
1 ⅓ c.	10 ⅔ oz.	3 ¼ dL
1 ½ c.	12 oz.	3 ½ dL
1 ⅔ c.	13 ⅓ oz.	3 ¾ dL
1 ¾ c.	14 oz.	4 dL
2 c. *(or 1 pt.)*	16 oz.	½ dL
2 ½ c.	20 oz.	6 dL
3 c.	24 oz.	¾ L
3 ½ c.	28 oz.	⅘ L *(or 8 dL)*
4 c. *(or 1 qt.)*	32 oz.	1 L
5 c.	40 oz.	1 ¼ L
6 c. *(or 1 ½ qt.)*	48 oz.	1 ½ L
8 c. *(or 2 qt.)*	64 oz.	2 L
10 c. *(or 2 ½ qt.)*	80 oz.	2 ½ L
12 c. *(or 3 qt.)*	96 oz.	2 ¾ L
4 qt.	128 oz.	3 ¾ L
5 qt.		4 ¾ L
6 qt.		5 ¾ L
8 qt.		7 ½ L

CONTENTS OF STANDARD CANS

8 oz. can	=	1 cup	No. 2	=	2 ½ cups
Picnic	=	1 ¼	No. 2 ½	=	3 ½ cups
No. 300	=	1 ¾	No. 3	=	4 cups
No. 1 tall	=	2 cups	No. 5	=	7 ¼ cups
No. 303	=	2 cups	No. 10	=	13 cups

METRICS

CONVERSION OF TEMPERATURES

Fahrenheit°	Celsius°	Fahrenheit°	Celsius°
60°F	15°C	205°F	96°C
72°F	22°C	212°F	100°C
85°F	29°C	225°F	110°C
100°F	38°C	250°F *Slow Oven*	120°C
110°F	43°C	275°F *Slow Oven*	135°C
115°F	46°C	300°F *Slow Oven*	150°C
135°F	57°C	325°F *Moderate*	165°C
140°F	60°C	350°F *Moderate*	180°C
150°F	66°C	375°F *Mod. Quick*	190°C
160°F	71°C	400°F *Mod. Hot*	205°C
165°F	74°C	425°F *Hot*	220°C
170°F	77°C	450°F *Hot*	230°C
180°F	82°C	475°F *Extremely*	245°C
190°F	88°C	500°F *Hot*	260°C
200°F *Warm Oven*	95°C		

CONVERSION OF LINEAR MEASUREMENTS

Inches	Centimeters	Inches	Centimeters
1/16 in.	1/4 cm.	5 in.	13 cm.
1/8 in.	1/2 cm.	6 in.	15 cm.
1/4 in.	3/4 cm.	7 in.	18 cm.
1/8 in.	1 cm.	8 in.	20 cm.
1/2 in.	1 1/2 cm.	9 in.	23 cm.
3/4 in.	2 cm.	10 in.	25 cm.
1 in.	2 1/2 cm.	12 in. *(1 ft.)*	30 cm.
1 1/2 in.	4 cm.	14 in.	35 cm.
2 in.	5 cm.	15 in.	38 1/2 cm.
2 1/2 in.	6 1/2 cm.	16 in.	40 cm.
3 in.	8 cm.	18 in.	45 cm.
3 1/2 in.	9 cm.	20 in.	50 cm.
4 in.	10 cm.	24 in. *(2 ft.)*	60 cm.

INDEX

APPETIZERS - *PREDJEDLÁ*

Cheese
Cheese Ball-Guľa, *19*
Cheese Log-Guľa, *19*
Sheep Cheese Appetizers, *25*
Meat and Poultry
Beef Tongue, *18*
Best Venison or Beef Jerky, *18*
Cocktail Meatballs-Fašírky, *20*
Creamed Chicken Livers, *21*
Jellied Pigs' Feet-Uspenina, *22*
Jellied Pigs' Feet-Kočenina, *22*
Liver Paté, *23*
Liver Paté, *23*
Meatballs-Fašírky, *24*
Meat Ball Creole-Gule, *25*
Seafood
Pickled Fish, *27*
Shrimp Mold, *28*
Vegetable
Marinated Mushrooms, *24*
Mushroom Phyllo Tarts, *26*
White Bean Dip, *29*
Beverages
Dad's Wassail, *30*
Hot Whiskey-Hriate, *30*

- B -

Baba *See Pastas-Baba*
Bábovka *See Pastas-Baba, Pastries-Cakes*
Beluš *See Pastas-Baba*
Bobáľky *See Breads*
Bochník *See Main Dishes-Pork*

BREADS - *CHLEBY*
(includes yeast and quick breads)
Slovak Basic Dough, *149*
Braided Bread, *150*
Cheese Rolls, *151*
Christmas Buns, *152*
Christmas Dumpling-Bobáľky, *153*
Christmas Eve Poppyseed Buns-Opekance, *154*
Crackling Biscuits, *157*
Easter Bread-Páska, *158*
Filled Crescents-Kiffles, *157*
Fran's Favorite Rolls, *159*
Slovak Rye Bread, *160*
Koláč
Christmas Holiday Layered Kolach, *162-163*
Filled Rolls-Koláče, *164*
Koláč, *170*
Cottage Cheese Squares, *155*
Margie's Cottage Cheese Rolls, *156*
Nut Rolls, *165*
Prune Filled Rolls, *166*
Slovak Nut Rolls, *167*
Slovak Nut-Poppyseed Rolls, *168*
Slovak Poppyseed Roll, *171-172*
Slovak Poppyseed Rolls-Makovníky, *169-170*
Sweet Bread with Cheese Filling, *173*
Two Hour Nut Roll, *172*
Walnut/Poppyseed Rolls, *174*
Water-Risen Crescents-Kifle, *161*
Quick Breads
Apple, Raisin, Nut Bread, *175*
Apricot Nut Bread, *176*
No Knead Raisin Bread, *178*
Poppyseed Banana Bread, *177*
Zucchini Bread, *179*
Miscellaneous
Substitution for Cake Flour, *179*
To Knead Dough, *177*

Bryndza
Crouton Soup with Sheep Cheese-Demikát, *64*

Sheep Cheese Appetizers, *25*
Sheep Cheese Dill Soup, *64*
Sheep Cheese Dumplings, *231*
Sheep Cheese Flat Cakes-Pizza, *192*

Buchty *See Pastas-Baba,*
Pastas-Dumplings
Burašky *See Pastas-Baba*

- C -

Cestovina *See Pastas*
Cheregies *See Pastries-Doughnuts*
Chren *See Salads-Horseradish*
Crackling(s) - *Oškvarky*
See Meats- Miscellaneous
(How to Render Lard)
Apple Strudel Crackling Dough, *309*
Crackling Biscuits, *157*
Crackling Cake-Trokšar, *185*
Scraped Dough Dumplings
with Sauerkraut, *210*

- D -

Demikát *See Soups, Bryndza*
Divina *See Main Dishes-Wild Meats*

- F -

Fanky *See Pastries-Doughnuts*
Fašírky *See Appetizers, Main Dishes-*
Beef, Pork, Wild Meats

- G -

Gingerbread
Gingerbread Bakery in Slovakia, *324*
Traditional Slovak Gingerbread-
Medovníky, *321-323*
Granadírmarš *See Pastas- Noodles*
Gruľovníky *See Pastas-Potato*
Pancakes
Guľa(e) *See Appetizers, Pastas-Fruit*
Dumplings

- H -

HOLIDAY CUISINE and
TRADITIONS
Christmas Eve - *Štedrý Večer*
Desserts
Baked Christmas Apples, *287*
Christmas Holiday Layered
Kolach *162-163*
Christmas Honey Cookies, *270*
Christmas Stars, *270*
Mom's Christmas Cookies, *271*
Slovak Nut Rolls, *167*
Slovak Poppyseed Rolls, *169-170*
Stewed Dried Fruit Compote
for Christmas Eve, *287*
Traditional Slovak Gingerbread, *321*
Entrées
Breaded Carp, *102*
Christmas Eve Carp in Tomato
Sauce, *102*
Christmas Buns, *152*
Christmas Eve Poppyseed Buns, *154*
Christmas Dumplings, *153*
Mushroom Cabbage Rolls
Casserole, *134*
Mushroom Stuffed Cabbage, *43*
Pirohy-*See Pastas*
White Bread Cake-Beluš, *196*
Soups
Buttered Mushroom Soup, *69*
Mushroom Cream Soup, *70*
Sour Mushroom-Barley Soup, *71*
Baba's Cream of Potato Soup, *74*
Miscellaneous
Christmas Eve-Štedrý Večer, *328*
Gingerbread Bakery in Slovakia, *324*
Holiday Traditions, *326*
Traditional Slovak Christmas Eve
Menu, *332*
Vianočné Zvyky, *327*
Easter - Veľká Noc
Baked Lamb, *107*
Beet Horseradish-Chren, *32*
Easter Bread-Páska, *158*

Easter Cheese-Syrek, *100*
Easter Meat Loaf-Sekanina(ica), *109*
Our Traditional Holiday
   Lamb Cake, *252*
Roast Leg of Lamb, *107*
Slovak Nut Rolls, *167*
Slovak Poppyseed Rolls, *169-170*
White Bread Cake-Beluš, *196*
Miscellaneous
Decorated Easter Eggs-Kraslice-
   Pisanky, *334, 336-339*
Holiday Traditions, *326*
Traditional Slovak Easter Foods, *333*
Veľkonočné Zvyky, *335*

Halušky *See Main Dishes,*
   Pastas-Dumplings
Haruľa *See Pastas-Baba*
Holubky *See Main Dishes, Appetizers*
Hrianky *See Main Dishes-Pork*
Hurka *See Main Dishes-Sausage*

- K -

Kapustníky *See Pastas-Baba*
Kifle(s) *See Breads, Pastries*
Klobásy *See Main Dishes-Sausage*
Knedle *See Pastas-Fruit Dumplings,*
   Pastas-Pirohy
Kočenina *See Appetizers*
Koláč *See Breads, Pastries*
Krapne *See Pastries-Doughnuts*
Kraslice *See Holiday Cuisine and*
   Traditions-Easter-Miscellaneous

- L -

Langoše *See Pastas-Baba*
Lekvár
Anne's Crepes, *199*
Apricot and Lekvár Squares, *293*
Christmas Holiday Layered
   Kolach, *162-163*
Crepes, *202*
Double-Decker Pastry, *297*
Dumplings, *205*
Filled Crescents, *157*
Gypsy Cookies, *274*
Lekvár Lattice Kolach, *300*
Lekvár-Filled Steamed Cakes, *186*
Lekvár, Nut or Apricot Cookies, *277*
Mixed Noodle Casserole, *223*
Mom's Christmas Cookies, *271*
Pineapple Squares-Prune or
   Apricot, *301*
Pirohy, *229*
Prune Filled Rolls, *166*
Rum Bars, *281*
Slovak Pancakes, *203*
Sour Cream Crescents, *283*
Steamed Dumplings-Buchty, *218*
Water-Risen Crescents, *161*
White Noodles, *226*
Lokša *See Pastas-Potato Pancakes*

- M -

MAIN DISHES - *HLAVNÉ JEDLÁ*
Beef
Beef Skillet Fiesta, *83*
Cabbage Beef Casserole, *84*
Calf Liver, *143*
Dough Covered Meat Balls-
   Fašírky, *108*
Meat Loaf with Cheese Filling, *110*
Sauerbraten-Sviečkova, *85-86*
Slovakian Barbecue Roast, *87*
Steak Louise, *86*
Chicken and Poultry
Breaded Baked Chicken Legs
   or Pork Chops, *88*
Broccoli Cheese-Rice
   with Chicken, *88*
Chicken Casserole, *89*
Chicken Livers and Gizzards *144*
Chicken Paprika, *90*
Chicken Paprika, *91*
Chicken Paprika, *92*
Chicken Paprika, *93*
Chicken and Rice, *94*

Chicken Souffle, *93*
Cream of Chicken Paprika, *95*
Dough Covered Meat Balls, *108*
Kona Glazed Fruited Chicken, *96*
No Peek Chicken, *97*
Roast Chicken, *97*
Roast Chicken, *98*
Sour Cream Chicken Bake, *99*
Roast Duck, *99*
Stuffed Turkey, *136*
Eggs and Cheese
Easter Cheese-Syrek, *100*
Easter Cheese- Syrek, *100*
Sunday Brunch Egg Casserole, *101*
Slovak Quiche, *101*
Fish
Breaded Carp, *102*
Christmas Eve Carp in
  Tomato Sauce, *102*
Fried Fish in Beer Batter, *103*
Goulash
Beef Goulash, *103*
Peasant Beef Goulash, *104*
Best Beef Stew Ever!, *105*
Beef Stroganoff, *106*
Mom's Sauerkraut Goulash, *106*
Lamb
Baked Lamb-Easter, *107*
Roast Leg of Lamb, *107*
Pork
Beggar's Porridge, *111*
Dough Covered Meat Balls-
  Fašírky, *108*
Easter Meat Loaf-Sekanica, *109*
Easter Meat Loaf-Sekanina, *109*
Ham-Hrianky, *112*
Ham and Bacon-Home
  Curing, *113*
Fried Hamburgers, *113*
Meat Loaf with Cheese
  Filling-Bochník, *110*
Governor George V. Voinovich's
  Pork Chops with Apples, *114*
Grandma's Slovak Pork Chops, *108*
Pork Roast with Sauerkraut
  and Dumplings, *115*

Mincemeat Country-Style Ribs, *116*
Sausage
Frankfurters with Sauerkraut, *117*
Pork Sausage-Hurka, *118*
Sausage-Klobása, *119*
Sauerkraut-Homemade Sausage, *117*
Sauerkraut and Sausage, *120*
Senator Mike DeWine's Favorite
  Sausage, Gravy and Biscuits, *121*
Slovak Klobásy and Sauerkraut
  Cooked with Beer, *123*
Slovak Potato Sausage, *122*
Slovak Sausage, *123*
A Slovak Texan's Kielbasa,
  Cabbage, Potato Supper, *124*
Bread Stuffing with Sausage, *125*
Stuffed Cabbage and Peppers
Betty's Stuffed Cabbage-
  Holubky, *126*
Dorothy's Stuffed Cabbage, *127*
Mushroom Cabbage Rolls
  Casserole, *134*
Stuffed Cabbage, *128*
Stuffed Cabbage, *129*
Stuffed Cabbage, *130*
Stuffed Cabbage, *131*
Stuffed Cabbage, *132*
Stuffed Cabbage, *133*
Stuffed Cabbage Rolls, *134*
Creamed Stuffed Peppers, *135*
Veal
Calf Liver, *143*
Easter Meat Loaf-Sekanica, *109*
Easter Meat Loaf-Sekanina, *109*
Veal and Caraway Seed
  Goulash, *137*
Veal Paprika Stew and
  Dumplings with Eggs, *138*
Slovak Veal Rolls, *139*
Wild Meats - *Divina*
Hunter's Stew, *140*
Rabbit in White Wine Sauce, *141*
Wild Game, *142*
Wild Meat Hamburgers-Fašírky, *143*

Miscellaneous Meats
Headcheese, *144*
Kidneys with Rice, *145*
Miscellaneous
Lard-How to Render, *146*
Stuffing, *145*
Dill Gravy-Omáčka, *147*
Paprika Gravy-Omáčka, *147*
Dumplings for Meat Dishes-
   Basic Recipe, *147*

Makovníky See *Breads-Koláč*
Medovníky See *Pastries-Cookies, Gingerbread*

- N -

Nákyp See *Pastries-Desserts, Salads*
Nalečníky See *Pastas-Baba, Pastas-Potato Pancakes*
Nalešníki See *Pastas-Baba, Pastas-Potato Pancakes*

- O -

Omáčka See *Soups-Miscellaneous, Main Dishes-Miscellaneous*
Opekance See *Breads*
Oplátky See *Pastries-Cookies, Holiday Cuisine and Traditions-Christmas Eve*
Oškvarky - *Crackling(s)*
   See *Meats- Miscellaneous, (Lard-How to Render)*
   Apple Strudel Crackling Dough, *309*
   Crackling Cake-Trokšar, *185*
   Scraped Dough Dumplings with Sauerkraut, *210*

- P -

Pagáč See *Pastas-Baba*
Palacinky See *Pastas-Crepes*

Páska See *Breads, Holiday Cuisine and Traditions-Easter*

PASTAS - *CESTOVINA*
Baba
   Baked Potato Pancake
      Casserole-Bábovka, *181*
   Cabbage Cake-Kapustníky, *183*
   Cabbage Cakes-Kapustníky, *182*
   Cabbage Filled Patty-Pagáč, *184*
   Crackling Cake-Trokšar, *185*
   Fried Hot Cakes-Langoše, *181*
   Lekvár-Filled Steamed Cakes-
      Buchty, *186*
   Garlic Potato Cake, *187*
   Potato Cake-Stará Baba, *187*
   Potato Cake with Bacon-
      Haruľa, *188*
   Potato Cakes-Nálečniky, *188*
   Potato Cakes-Haruľa Baba, *238*
   Potato-Poppyseed Pie
      Wedges-Burašky, *189*
   Press Cake-Pagáč, *190*
   Romanian Potato Placinta, *191*
   Sheep Cheese Flat Cakes-Pizza, *192*
   Slovak Unsweetened Filled Cake-
      Pagáč, *193*
   Small Unsweetened Cakes, *194*
   Turkey "Longush" Meat Pie, *195*
   White Bread Cake for
      Christmas/Easter-Beluš, *196-198*
Crepes - *Palacinky*
   Anne's Crepes, *199*
   Broccoli Crepes with Ham/
      Bacon, *200*
   Cabbage Crepes, *200*
   Congressman James A. Traficant's
      Cottage Cheese Crepes, *201*
   Crepes, *202*
   Pancakes (So Light They Fly), *203*
   Slovak Pancakes, *203*
Dumplings - *Halušky*
   Cottage Cheese Dumpling Balls, *204*
   Dumplings, *205*
   Dumplings, *205*

- 348 -

Dumplings Tossed with
  Sauerkraut, *211*
Liver Dumplings, *206*
Noodle Dumplings, *206*
Potato Dumplings, *207*
Potato Dumplings, *208*
Potato Dumplings with Cottage
  Cheese, *209*
Scraped Dough Dumplings with
  Sauerkraut-Strapačky, *210*
Slovak Dumplings, *211*
Slovak Sauerkraut with Potato
  Dumplings, *212*
Smoked Meatball Dumplings, *213*
Torn Dough Dumplings with
  Milk-Trhance, *219*
Dumplings - Fruit, *Knedle*
Apple Dumplings-Knedle, *213*
Apricot Dumplings, *214*
Cherry-Potato Dumplings, *214*
Fresh Fruit Dumplings, *215*
Peach Dumplings, *216*
Plum Dumplings-Gule, *216*
Plum Dumplings, *217*
Steamed Dumplings-Buchty, *218*
Lasagna
Wilmette Lasagna, *220*
Noodles
Cabbage and Noodles, *225*
Cottage Cheese Noodles-
  Šúľance, *221*
Fried Noodles-Čir, *222*
Mixed Noodle Casserole, *223*
Potato and Noodle Flakes
  Casserole-Granadímarš, *224*
Poured Dough Noodles, *225*
Sauerkraut and Noodles, *226*
Slovak Egg Noodles, *222*
White Noodles, *226*
Pirohy
Cousin Rita's Baked Dumplings-
  Pirohy, *227*
Dumplings-Knedle, *228*
Pirohy, *229*
Potato and Cheese Dumplings, *230*

Sheep Cheese Dumplings, *231*
Potato Pancakes
Mashed Potato Pancakes, *235*
Potato Pancakes-Palacinky, *232*
Potato Pancakes-Nalesníky, *232*
Potato Pancakes, Baked, *233*
Potato Pancakes with
  Applesauce, *233*
Potato Pancakes with
  Bratislava Butter Sauce-
  Lokša, *234*
Potato Pancakes with
  Sauerkraut Filling-Lokša, *235*
Potato Patties-Grulovníky, *236*
Potato Thin Pancakes-Lokša, *237*
Slovak Potato Pancakes, *238*

**PASTRIES, DESSERTS, FRUITS -
*PEČIVO, ZÁKUSKY, KOMPOT***
  Cakes - *Bábovka, Torta*
  Apple Cake, *240*
  Apple Prune Cake-Bábovka, *240*
  Raw Apple Cake-Bábovka, *241*
  Old Fashioned Applesauce
    Cake-Bábovka, *242*
  Banana Split Cake-Torta, *243*
  Black Russian Kahlua Cake, *244*
  Blueberry Cake, *245*
  Carrot Walnut Cake-Bábovka, *246*
  Ann's Cheesecake, *247*
  Cheese Cake, *248*
  Cherry Cheese Cake, *249*
  Cinnamon Coffee Cake, *250*
  Cinnamon-Raisin Coffee Cake, *251*
  Mom's Chocolate Cake, *251*
  Earthquake Cake, *252*
  Our Traditional Holiday
    Lamb Cake, *252*
  Lattus Cake-Bábovka, *253*
  Lindy's Tropical Delight, *254*
  Lunch Box Cake, *255*
  Excellent Bundt Nut Cake, *255*
  Cheese and Poppyseed Cake, *256*
  Lemon Poppyseed Pound, *257*
  Poppyseed Cake-Bábovka, *258*

Poppyseed Cake-Makovník, *258*
Poppyseed Cake-Bábovka, *259*
Pound Cake-Bábovka, *260*
Mom's Sour Cream Cake, *260*
Sour Cream Cake, *259*
Sour Cream Coffee Cake, *261*
Sour Cream Pound Cake, *262*
Zucchini Cake, *263*
Zucchini Chocolate Cake, *263*
Cookies
Almond Wafers-Oplátky, *264*
Mardi Gras Angel Wings, *265*
Oven Baked Angel Wings, *266*
Anise Horns, *267*
Barbara Bush's Oatmeal Lace Cookies, *267*
Bear Claws, *268*
Bratislava Bars, *268*
Butter Cookies, *269*
Butter Wedges, *269*
Christmas Honey Cookies-Medovníky, *270*
Christmas Stars, *270*
Mom's Christmas Cookies, *271*
No Bake Chocolate, *272*
Devil Eyes Cocoa Balls, *272*
Cream Cheese Crescents, *273*
Date Sticks, *273*
Fig Rolls, *274*
Gypsy Cookies, *274*
Honey Cakes-Medovníky, *275*
Lorry's Grandmother's Jam Cookies, *276*
Lekvar, Nut or Apricot, *277*
Deluxe Lemon Bars, *278*
Pecan Fingers, *275*
Marble Pizzelles-Krapne, *279*
Mimi's Mother's Date Bars, *312*
Raisin Bars, *279*
Raisin Puff Cookies, *280*
Rum Bars, *281*
Secret Kisses, *282*
Slovak Spritz-Šišky, *282*
Slovakian Bars, *281*
Slovakian Cookies, *278*

Sour Cream Crescents-Kifle, *283*
Ma Polakovic's Sugar Cookies, *283*
Vanilla Horns, *284*
Walnut Crescents, *284*
Desserts
Apple Cream Parfait, *285*
Apple Dumpling Pudding-Nákyp, *285*
Apple Pudding, *286*
Baked Christmas Apples, *287*
Breaded Crepes with Apple Filling, *288*
Plum Pudding-Nákyp, *289*
Rice Pudding-Nákyp, *289*
Stewed Dried Fruit Compote for Christmas Eve, *287*
Doughnuts - *Fanky*
Doughnuts, *290*
Doughnuts, *290*
Doughnuts, *291*
Doughnuts, *291*
Fried Doughnut Strips-Cheregies-Krapne, *264*
Pastries
Apple Squares, *292*
Apricot and Lekvar Squares, *293*
Chocolate Glazed Cream Pastry, *294*
Delicious Chocolate Pastry, *295*
Cheesecake Squares, *293*
Cream Squares, *296*
Double-Decker Pastry, *297*
Flaky Squares, *298*
Layered Fruit Pastry, *299*
Lekvár Lattice Kolach, *300*
Pineapple Squares-Prune or Apricot, *301*
Raisin and Walnut Pastry, *302*
Rhubarb-Cottage Cheese Squares, *303*
Walnut-Jam Squares, *304*
Pies
Concord Grape Pie, *306*
Baba's Dream Lime Pie, *306*
Pecan Pie, *305*

Prune Pie, *307*
Pastry Shell, *305*
Strudel
Apple Strudel-Závin, *308*
Apple Strudel-Crackling Dough, *309*
Poppyseed Strudel-Yeast Dough, *310*
Mama's Apple-Poppyseed, *311-312*
Nut Strudel, *313*
Quick Apple Roll-Závin, *314*
Tortes - *Torta*
Dobos Torte, *315*
European Torte, *316*
Filbert-Hazelnut Torte, *317*
Pumpkin Torte, *318*
Walnut Torte, *319*
Miscellaneous
Fluffy Egg White Frosting, *320*
Vanilla Sugar, *320*

Pirohy *See Pastas-Pirohy*
Pisanky *See Holiday Cuisine and Traditions-Easter*

- S -

SALADS - *ŠALÁT*
Beet Horseradish-Chren, *32*
Broccoli and Cauliflower, *32*
Cole Slaw, *33*
Corn Salad, *33*
Lindy's Vegetarian Salad, *38*
Mandarin Spinach Salad, *37*
Sauerkraut Side Dish, *37*
Mixed Endive Salad, *34*
Octopus Salad, *35*
Pacific Slovak Shrimp Salad, *36*
Saffroned Rice, *36*
Slovak Potato Salad, *35*
Sour Creamed Cucumbers, *34*
Honey Mustard Dressing, *39*
Escalloped Pineapple-Nákyp, *39*

Sekanina(ica) *See Main Dishes-Pork, Holiday Cuisine and Traditions-Easter*
Šišky *See Pastries-Cookies*
SOUPS - *POLIEVKY*
Barley
Barley Soup, *53*
Bean
Bean and Vegetable Soup, *53*
Bean Soup-Romanian Style, *54*
Green Bean Soup with Buttermilk, *55*
Slovak Sour Lima Bean or Potato Soup, *56*
U.S. Senate's Favorite Bean, *57*
Young Green Bean Soup, *55*
Beef
Beef Bouillon with Baked Beef Dumplings, *58*
Beef Soup, *60*
Beef Soup with Liver Dumplings, *59*
Cabbage
Cabbage Soup, *61*
Ham Bone-Cabbage Soup, *60*
Sauerkraut, Lentil, Mushroom, *77*
Sauerkraut Soup with Sausage, Mushrooms and Prunes, *78*
Tossed Cabbage and Potato, *62*
Caraway
Caraway Soup, *63*
Slovak Caraway Soup, *63*
Cheese and Egg
Crouton Soup with Sheep Cheese-Demikát, *64*
Sour Egg Soup, *67*
Sheep Cheese Dill Soup, *64*
Chicken
Chicken Soup, *65*
Chicken Soup, *65*
Dill
Dill-Buttermilk Soup, *66*
Dilled Potato Soup, *75*
Dill Soup, *66*

Fish
Fish Chowder, *67*
Mushroom
Buttered Mushroom Soup, *69*
Mushroom-Barley Soup, *69*
Sour Mushroom Barley Soup, *71*
Mushroom Cream Soup, *70*
Mutton
Mutton Goulash Soup, *72*
Mutton Pea Soup, *72*
Potato
Baba's Cream of Potato, *74*
Potato Soup, *75*
Pumpkin
Slovak Pumpkin Soup, *76*
Ribs
Orava Soup, *73*
Tomato
Cream of Tomato Soup, *62*
Vegetable
Barley-Beet Soup, *52*
Red Beet Soup, *57*
Endive Soup, *61*
Lentil Soup with Prunes, *70*
Mom's Lettuce Soup-Omáčka, *68*
Camp Onion Soup, *73*
Slovak Spinach Soup, *76*
Creamy Vegetable Soup, *79*
Vegetable Soup, *79*
Miscellaneous
Basic White Sauce-Omáčka, *80*
Roux Soup, *80*
Thickening Soup-Roux-Zápražka, Zátrepka, Zhustenina, *81*

Štedrý Večer *See Holiday Cuisine and Traditions-Christmas Eve*
Strapačky *See Pastas-Dumplings*
Šúľance *See Pastas-Noodles*
Sviečková *See Main Dishes-Beef*
Syrek *See Main Dishes-Eggs and Cheese, Holiday Cuisine and Traditions-Easter*

- T -

Torta *See Pastries*
Trhance *See Pastas-Dumplings*
Trokšar *See Pastas-Baba*

- U -

Uspenina *See Appetizers- Meat and Poultry*

- V -

Vanilkový Cukor *See Pastries-Miscellaneous*

VEGETABLES - *ZELENINY*
Best Baked Beans, *41*
Green Beans, *42*
Red Cabbage, *43*
Zesty Carrots, *44*
Quick and Easy Corn Pudding, *44*
Baked Eggplant, *45*
Cooked Lettuce, *45*
Cauliflower and Mushroom Casserole-Nákyp, *42*
Mushroom Stuffed Cabbage, *43*
Ham and Mushroom Stuffed Peppers, *46*
Baked Cheese Potatoes, *46*
Potato Croquettes, *47*
Sauerkraut, *48*
Sauerkraut and Onions, *49*
Green Tomatoes, *49*
Green Tomato Relish, *50*
Betty's Tomato Sauce-Omáčka, *50*
Vegetable Casserole, *47*

- Z -

Zápražka *See Soups-Roux*
Zátrepka *See Soups-Roux*
Zavin *See Pastries-Strudel*
Zhustenina *See Soups-Roux*

ORDER FORM

SLOVAK WORLD CONGRESS COOKBOOK
"A Culinary Collection of our Slovak Heritage"
183 Struthers-Liberty Road
Campbell, Ohio 44405-1965 U.S.A.

I wish to order _____ copies of the **"Slovak World Congress Cookbook"** at $16.00 (USd), per copy, plus postage/handling.

(Please Print)

NAME: _____

ADDRESS: _____

CITY: _____ STATE: _____ ZIP: _____

COUNTRY: _____ PHONE: _____

<u>MAKE CHECK OR MONEY ORDER PAYABLE TO **SWC COOKBOOK.**</u>

Enclosed please find payment for: _____ Cookbook(s)
@ $16.00 (USd) per copy $ _____

POSTAGE/HANDLING

U.S.: $3.00 (USd) per first book.
Add $1.50 for each additional book.
(No Limit to quantity of order)   _____

Canada/Europe/Other: Surface of $5.00 (USd) per book.
Add $2.50 (USd) for each additional book.
(Canadian Postal regulations - Limit of 2 books per order)
(Europe/Other Postal regulations - Limit of 5 books per order)   _____

TOTAL: $ _____

Thank you for helping to preserve our Slovak heritage!